The Foggy Ruins Of Time
A Memoir

Aubrey Malone

chimpmunkapublishing
the mental health publisher

All rights reserved, no part of this publication may be reproduced by any means, electronic, mechanical photocopying, documentary, film or in any other format without prior written permission of the publisher.

>Published by
>Chipmunkapublishing

http://www.chipmunkapublishing.com

Copyright © Aubrey Malone 2013

Edited by Clare Younger

ISBN   978-1-84991-976-0

Cover picture: Raheen House in Roscommon, where my mother grew up.

Chipmunkapublishing gratefully acknowledge the support of Arts Council England.

Contents

1. Escape
2. Norfolk
3. Transitions
4. Expanding Frontiers
5. America
6. Tales Out of School
7. Wanderlust
8. Embattled
9. Orphans
10. Auto-Pilot
11. Between Two Stools
12. Into Book Writing
13. Elvis and Other Headaches
14. Division Four
15. Return
16. Sedentary
17. Family Fortunes
18. Where We Are Now

Escape

It's a night in the spring of long ago and I'm lying in bed waiting for sleep to come. The lights of the cinema glint from across the street. In the town hall I hear the sound of a band playing out of tune at the local hop. There are voices raised every now and again as people pass the door, the sounds of laughter and tears, violence and camaraderie. The cacophony blends into the music like a counterpoint, rising to a crescendo and then drifting away again until the street is as quiet as a tomb.

It's the time of the night when phone numbers are taken, when hopes are raised and lies embellished to hide the embarrassment of commitments made in the heat of the moment. I listen to the words of an Everly Brothers song coming through the window like some long-forgotten memory. They're singing about weekend passes, about ebony eyes, about a woman who died on Flight 1203. My eyes water with sadness for someone I never knew and never will know.

I look at the posters of Elvis Presley on my wall. Outside is the cold grey light of the moon. The wind is blowing softly, the rain making a sound like the crushing of plastic on the roof of the garage next door.

Now and again I hear the siren of an ambulance puncturing the night and I wonder if it's for my father. I think the same if I hear a police car or even a bottle breaking outside. He's drinking again after a long time being off it. I thought he'd grown out of his dependency but I also know this is the way it goes, the feverish abstention followed by the equally feverish indulgences. He has to do everything by extremes, sweating the poison out of his system and then loading it back in again just when you thought he was going to be your father again and not this stranger who falls in the door after midnight, abusing everybody within earshot.

It must be the middle of the night when the call comes. Even before my mother picks up the receiver I know who it's going to be. It's always the same call at the same time, with the same message from a hotel manager to ask if we could arrange to have him picked up because he's causing a disturbance.

'Yes,' my mother says in a strained voice, 'I'll send someone now. I'm sorry. It won't happen again.' But she knows it will, as I do, again and again and again as long as he has life in his body.

I drift in and out of sleep. The next thing I'm aware of is a taxi-man depositing him at the door, being over-polite to my mother as he leads him into the hall. 'Thank you, you can go now,' she's saying. Afterwards I hear my father coming to life, raising his voice to her about some slight he feels he's suffered at her hands, real or imaginary.

She says it's anger at himself that makes him do this, anger and frustration that life hasn't worked out for him as he would have liked it to. He's always contrite afterwards as if it was someone else who said the cruel words so everyone forgives him. My mother calls it a sickness, a sickness that makes people lose control of their lives.

I come down the stairs and wipe the tiredness from my eyes. In the kitchen my mother is smoking a cigarette, her one vice in life. My father looks up at me from his chair. He's wearing his Trinity College jacket and the same trousers he wears seven days a week, fifty-two weeks a year, having two sets of each for when they need to be cleaned. He calls me over to him and I sit on his lap. He gives me a wet kiss that I wipe away. The smell of drink coming from him is so strong it takes my breath away when I inhale.

He starts to get into good form now, telling me about what was going on in the pub before the row started, that everything was fine until the subject of Charles Stewart Parnell came up. I'm as bored by this as I am by every reason he gives for a row. I know it will be a different one next week, a different one on any of these wild nights that we always know will sooner or later come to blows. It's got to the stage now where the people he drinks with are afraid to go to the toilet for fear of being badmouthed in their absence.

My mother motions to me from behind his back to humour him. She knows he'll fall asleep in a few minutes and she doesn't want to take him on. I listen to what he says without replying. After a few minutes his voice starts to weaken and his eyes become heavy. Then he puts his head back and starts to snore.

As my mother takes his jacket off she hears the clink of a bottle. She searches his pockets and finds a naggin of whiskey in one of them. She puts it in the cupboard. Tomorrow she'll go down to Geraghty's to get the money back and buy some groceries with it. She knows she's safe doing this because my father never remembers. He'll wake up tomorrow and forget about the taxi-man and the disturbance and the bottle of whiskey and the argument about Parnell and all the other things that happened on a night that passed like any other one for him. The important thing is that there weren't any other solicitors there to embarrass him about what he did because he moved from the hotel he was in with them to Tony Crane's bar.

The following morning my mother knocks on the door. There's a cold sun slanting through the window of my bedroom making the dust dance. I don't know what day it is for a moment and then the realisation dawns. I've only had a few hours sleep and I don't want to go to school but I know she'll make me. If it was my father he wouldn't because he never wanted to go to school either at my age so he understands what it feels like. But he's still asleep so I know I have no choice. To make it easier for myself I count down from twenty in my head, like the opposite of counting sheep. I tell myself when I reach three I'll get up. That way I have some preparation. So I go, 'Twenty, nineteen, eighteen,' and so on. But I always get up at about eight or nine.

My mother puts some porridge in front of me when I come down to the kitchen. She asks if I was upset last night and I lie that I wasn't. I have nightmares about nights like this sometimes but there's no point in telling her that. I know she loves him but she also sees him as her cross in life.

After breakfast I take my bicycle out of the garage and pack my school books. I didn't do my homework last night because of my father and I know there'll be trouble about that. But even when I've done it perfectly there's trouble with Jacko so maybe it makes no difference. We have him for two classes today, Geography from 9.30 to 10.15 and History from 10.15 to 11. That's why this is always my worst morning of the week..

I cycle down Arthur Street, then down by the Market Square and across the bridge to the college. When I get there it's 9.35 so I'm five minutes late for class. That means two slaps if I show myself. I decide to hide in the cloakroom instead until the first class is over. I crouch in the corner and smell the sweat and rubber from the coat-racks.

At 10.15 I hear the sound of voices emerging from corridors and make my way to the main building. Jacko spots me crossing the quadrangle. It's almost as if he's been waiting for me. He intercepts me half way across and leads me towards the classroom. 'We must have been playing snooker again last night,' he says, smiling faintly as he dusts down his soutane.

Jacko is from a small parish outside Crossmolina. He's had a set on me since the first day I entered the college. I'm not sure why but I think it's because I'm a townie. His best friends in the class are the farmers' sons, people like himself who used to milk cows before breakfast, who cycled six miles to Muredach's in the driving rain and never moaned. He thinks of me as one of the privileged ones, the solicitor's son with the double-barrelled name. It seems to be his ambition in life to bring me down to size.

When class begins I know he'll stand before me with that smile of derision on his face, wedging himself in between my desk and the one in front of me as he proceeds to pummel me with his fists whenever I get a history date wrong, or a geographical direction. It's the way it's been since he first set eyes on me and the way it will continue until I leave this college. But I've vowed he won't break me. Each time he hits me now it only deepens that resolve.

When we get into the classroom he asks me why I'm late. When I say I had to do a message he hits me in the shoulder. This is his favourite stroke, like the jab of a boxer. 'That's a lie,' he says. 'You were in the Hibs, weren't you?' There's no point denying it because I know he has spies everywhere. I nod my head and he smiles.

It turns out he saw me himself. 'I was coming from Connolly Street and I saw you inside. You were dancing around to some music.' I vaguely remember one of the other players showing me a record he'd bought in Byron's. 'You'd be better off concentrating on the Ten Commandments instead of the Top Ten,' he taunts, referring to the programme that documents the latest hits. He believes it isn't only snooker that's the sign of a misspent youth but music as well. These are the two main no-nos. Especially for me, a quiet boy from the Dillon-Malone household with two brothers already in the priests. I know I'm expected to become one too because the college is almost like a recruitment centre in that respect, a breeding-ground for dog-collars.

'I suppose you went to the hop afterwards,' he accuses. 'No,' I say, 'I went home.' 'Don't answer me back!' he roars. I get a jab for each syllable.

When I say I wasn't answering him back I get another punch. He smiles now. 'So you'd prefer to be a snooker player than a historian when you grow up,' he says. I'm looking at the ground so he puts his hand under my chin and lifts it up. 'A snooker player,' he says again, 'A professional snooker player from Ballina, County Mayo. That would be a nice way to put us on the map, wouldn't it?' He looks round at the rest of the class for their reaction. There are some nervous laughs at the lame jibe.

But now the smile changes to a growl as he shows his teeth. 'Well I've got news for you, Malone, there'll be no snooker playing in this class until you get your notes down. Do you understand?' I say I do and then he repeats it. 'Do you understand?' I get more jabs for the syllables. 'Do. You. Un. Der. Stand?'

He goes away from me to the top of the room, a brief respite from what seems to be like an obsession on his part with cracking my spirit. He says the Morning Prayer and then he scribbles a map of Ireland on the blackboard and starts to talk about some battle that was fought long ago, one of those uprisings where there was a chance Ireland would get help from some foreign country before the connections broke down or the bad weather caused a ship to be crushed against the rocks after its arrival on Irish soil. We jot down notes as he talks. Now and then one of the other pupils asks me what was going on a few moments ago. I shrug my shoulders as if to say I don't know. I do but there's really no point talking about it because I know it won't stop it happening.

At 11 o'clock the bell rings and we go out to the handball alley. We slap the ball against the wall a few times but then it starts to rain, as it always does, and we're ushered into the Rec.

The Rec stands for Recreation Room but the only thing inside it is an old table tennis table that's falling apart. A better name for it would be The Wreck. Maybe this is where the name came from. We play push-penny on the table until the bell goes for the next class

Everyone asks me if Jacko hurt me. I say no. I don't mind him punching me. What I mind more are the insults. I got off light this morning. Sometimes he uses his cane as well. When he does that it's like a swordfighter removing his sword from his scabbard. It's made of bamboo. It makes a swish as he takes it out. The end has been cut with a knife to make it fan out. That's what he hits you with. If you pull your hand away you get two hits.

The next class is English. We call the teacher Tag because he's so small. Some of us are even bigger than him. That means he has to reach up to us when he's pulling our locks. Sometimes we jump up on the window-sill to get away from him. 'Come down, student,' he says in his high-pitched voice.

Tag was in my brother's class so he takes a special interest in me. I don't like this kind of attention. He doesn't have a set on me like Jacko but he's always asking me questions about my family in front of everyone else and that bothers me. Another thing that bothers me is the way he throws my copy down at me like a boomerang after he corrects my essays. He always asks the same question as he throws it: 'Did you write this yourself?' My father does most of my essays for me but I can't tell him that or he'd be up to the house like lightning.

My father has been doing my essays for me since the first day I went into Muredach's. Every time we get one he asks me for the name of it. When I tell him he lights up a cigarette and puffs on it as he starts to think. He walks up and down the kitchen with his hands behind his back, clicking his fingers without unclasping his hands to knock the ash from the cigarette onto the floor. Then he starts dictating what I'm to write and I take it down. There are always a lot of long words that I don't understand. He quotes from poets as well, people like Hilaire Belloc and Tennyson. Sometimes Tag reads my essays out to the class and I get embarrassed. As long as he doesn't ask me to explain them I'll probably continue getting away with it.

I cycle home when the last bell of the day rings out. The journey home is always easier because I don't have a knot in my stomach. I go up by the church and across the bridge to where my father's old office used to be. I go into Wellworths to buy *Victor*, a comic I read every week. I walk the bike up Garden Street past the Market Square. I stop at the Savoy to see what film is on next week. Usually we go to the Estoria because that's on our street but sometimes I go to matinees in the Savoy on Saturdays, especially if it's a cowboy film. The one that's on is called *The Sand Pebbles* with Steve McQueen. He's my mother's favourite actor. It doesn't look much good so I probably won't bother with it.

When I get to the house I see Audrey and Jacinta playing outside. They're my two sisters. They go to the Convent of Mercy. Every day when they come home they throw their books and copies all over the carpet in the sitting-room and spend the whole day doing their homework on the floor.

'Did you get *Bunty* for us?' they ask, almost in the one voice. They're disappointed to see I only have *Victor*. They read *Bunty* together every week, sitting side by side on two kitchen chairs as they turn the pages. Neither of them speaks as they do that. They just nod their head when they're finished the page so the other one knows they can turn it.

Tina has my dinner on the table as I go in the door. Tina is our girl, as my mother puts it. She came to the house when I was only a few days old. 'I need him out from under my feet,' my mother said. As well as taking care of us she helps my mother around the house. They often laugh together about things. One day Tina left a pair of my father's trousers into Loftus' to be cleaned. The next day my mother said to her, 'Did you get the trousers off Loftus?' That became a family joke.

Tina thinks I'm clever because I'm always reading. 'Are the brains still bursting out of your head?' she says as I sit down, 'One of these days we'll have to get a helmet to keep them in.' When I was a child she brought me down to Brennan's one day on the carrier of her bike. After I got off it I said to her, 'Where are we going to leave the bike when I go to university?' That became a family joke too.

Every day after dinner Tina cuts up a bar of Milk Tray and puts it into a sandwich for me. That's my favourite thing to eat. I don't know anyone else who likes chocolate sandwiches. After I finish them I read my *Biggles* book until it's time to go back to the college. I ask her where my mother is and she says, 'She's having a lie down.' I'm not surprised because of her being up half the night waiting for my father to come home.

She goes to bed a lot these days because she's always tired. We're all worried that something might be wrong with her. Sometimes she goes down to Dr Igoe for tests as well. We used to have a jingle we chanted when we were children: 'You go, I go, down to Dr Igoe.' He's a kindly man who never says much but you know you can trust him. He's given her pills lately to relax her, yellow ones that have just come on the market. The word Roche is written on them. She told me they're like miracle pills and that they've changed her life.

After I finish my dinner I go into my father's office. It doesn't really look like an office. There's a mahogany table in the middle of it with a white tablecloth on it. Sometimes we eat there when we have company but other times we take the cloth off to play table tennis.

There's a hole in the wall behind the table with a door on each side. We call it The Hatch. It connects the office to the kitchen. Tina puts cups of tea in there at all times of the day and gives a little knock to let my father know they're there. Then he goes and collects them. Up until a few years ago I was small enough to fit my whole body in The Hatch during games of Hide and Seek but now I'm too big so we just use it for the tea.

When we're not eating at the table or playing table tennis on it my father puts all his files on it. He used to have his office down on Bridge Street but it caught fire a few years ago so he moved back to the house. My mother didn't think this was a good idea because he used to like the walk down town in the mornings. He has less pride in his appearance now. Some days he doesn't even dress. He just puts his smoking jacket on over his pyjamas to do business.

Many of his clients are farmers. Some of them just want something signed so he's only with them a few minutes. As well as being a solicitor he's a Commissioner for Oaths. That means he can sign things other solicitors can't. He only gets a small amount of money for this service. He always brings a Bible with him when he's doing it. I never know what that's for.

My mother usually acts as his witness. He often says she knows so much about the law she could put a plate outside the door and set up shop. Sometimes I wonder if it will come to that because when he's drinking he can't see the clients so she has to cover for him. She also has to see them when they come to take their files away. That's been happening a lot lately because of his drinking. She tells him he should retire but he says he can't afford to. Then he goes on a binge and blows a month's earnings in a night.

I call down to Michael, my friend from across the street. I ask him if he'd like to go over to the Hibs for a game of snooker. He says he would. Michael is a class behind me in Muredachs. He has red hair and a dog called Jaffa. Sometimes we play football in the lane behind his house, at least if T.V. Lowther lets us. T.V. Lowther is a barber whose shop backs onto the lane. He's always giving out to us if we kick the ball against his door. Every Saturday he gives me a neck shave.for one and six.

Michael and myself walk up past my house. We look at what's on in the Estoria and then go over to O'Hora's for an ice cream. 'Going to the matinee, are we?' Mr O'Hora says, but we say no, that we're going for a game of snooker.

Sometimes if he's at the end of a carton he gives us half a cone each for a penny. The ice cream is always really hard after coming out of the fridge. He puts a little bit of strawberry in it for me. 'A strawberry for Aubrey,' he says, and gives a big laugh. It's his one joke.

We walk up by the font and sit there for a minute eating our ice-cream. Paddy Bluett passes by and asks us for a lick. He's always doing that. No matter where you go, Paddy seems to turn up. Michael breaks off half his ice-cream for him and he prances off as happy as Larry. Janey O'Hora is across the street and she waves at us. 'How is your mother?' she says. I say 'Fine'. Janey used to work in my mother's house when she was growing up in Roscommon. It was called Raheen. It's a ruin now. She says she'll drop in later tonight to see her when she's on her way to bingo in the Town Hall.

We go down Bury Street past Tommy Burns' house. When we get to Bourke Carraig and Loftus, Michael says, 'Your father does business with them, doesn't he?' I nod my head. Vincent Troy works there. He's always asking my sister June to go out with him. He wears a hairpiece on his head.

As we head into the Hibs I feel a surge of excitement as if the day is only now beginning. The Hibs is short for The Hibernian Hall. It's a huge building off King Street. It has two full-size tables. Upstairs there's another room where people box. Michael and myself don't go up there. Sometimes when you're playing a shot the table shakes and you can see the sawdust coming down through the beams. You can also hear the thunk of punches. Sometimes the boxers come down for a game of snooker afterwards and you can smell the sweat off them.

Before you're allowed play you have to put a shilling in the meter. That gets you a half-hour of light on the table. Sometimes we just watch the other players. There's a man called George who's a genius at billiards. I don't like billiards because it's boring. It's played with just three balls, two white ones and a red. One of the white balls has a spot on it. That's the cue ball.

George puts it in the D, a semi-circle at the end of the table, and then he puts the red on the black spot at the other end. He nearly always gets the white to go in off the red in the top pocket. He can play this shot up to twenty times in a row without missing. I love the way he can get the white to arc like a banana on its way to the pocket.

He has no time for snooker. He regards as a children's game. He doesn't play billiards either when you think about it. He just wants to play this one shot all day. I could watch him at it forever. His expression never changes as he plays the shot.

George stops playing when the lights go out. Then he puts his cue into a case and hangs it up on the wall. He has a lock on it to stop people stealing it. That makes me think he must have paid a lot of money for it.

Before he goes out he throws me a stick of chalk. George always has better chalk than anyone else so I keep it. I take a penny out of my pocket and dig it into it to make a bowl effect. That makes the chalk stick better to the top of the cue so you don't miscue.

I put a shilling in the slot and twist it and the light bathes over the table. We get the triangle from under the table and put the fifteen reds in it and then put the six colours on their spots. Michael breaks off and scatters them all over the place.

I'm just getting ready to play my first shot when a group of football players come in. This is always happening to us. They're from the Stephenites Club. That's the local football team. They're talking about a game they just played, some refereeing decision that went wrong. A few of them unlock their cues from the racks and wipe them down with cloths.

One of them, a young man we call Ballina Town, asks me how much time is left in the meter. I've never asked him what his real name is. Everyone just calls him Ballina Town. When I tell him we've only started he reaches into a pocket and gives me a shilling. I tell him I don't want it, that I just want to play my game, but he just laughs.

Michael and myself watch The Stephenites playing for a few minutes. They don't have much interest in the game, jumping on each other's backs between shots and still talking about the football. I ask Michael if he'd like to come back later. He nods.

We get our coats and walk out into the cold. We walk back down Bury Street in the biting wind. We're disappointed at not getting our game but it happens so often we're hardly surprised now.

When we get to the font I ask Michael if he'd like to come into the house for a game of table tennis. He says he would.

Before we go into the house I suggest going down to Geraghtys for a bar of chocolate. Geraghtys is our local grocery shop. It has a bar in the back. It's one of the places my father drinks when he doesn't want to be seen by the other solicitors. We also buy most of our food there. We don't pay for it in cash because we have a book that we write all our orders into and my father tots them up at the end of every month and pays whatever he owes to Jimmy Geraghty. He has bad writing so it's often hard to see what he owes him. Sometimes I think he just makes up a figure out of his head.

I ask Jimmy for a macaroon bar for myself and a bar of Aero for Michael. It's all he ever eats. There are holes in the chocolate that make it look like the craters of the moon.

'It must be great not having to pay for anything,' Michael says as I give him the bar, but I tell him we have to at the end of the month.

When we get back to the house my father is in the kitchen. He's reading the paper. He looks tired. I wonder if he's forgotten about last night. Sometimes he does and sometimes he doesn't.

'I suppose you were in the snooker hall,' he says. I tell him I was but that I didn't get a game.

He doesn't like me going to the Hibs. He thinks I only meet the riff-raff of the town there. 'You'd be better off going to the Moy Club,' he says. I don't like the Moy Club. It's where all the snobs of the town go. There's only one table there as well so you spend most of your time just watching.

I ask him if Michael and myself can have a game of table tennis. He says we can if we tidy up after ourselves. That means taking all his files off the table and putting them on the shelves along the wall until we're finished and then putting them back again.

We go into the office and start putting the files away. The net is in a drawer and Michael gets that and starts screwing it onto the table. It's one of those tables that can be made into double the size when you take out the folding part so we do that. There's a crack in the wood where one of the folds is. When the ball hits that it bounces up into the air and leaves the other player an easy slam. We always laugh when that happens.

We play for about half an hour but then we get bored. Maybe we're still annoyed about being pushed off the snooker table. We unscrew the net and put it back in the drawer and then put my father's files back.

Before we go out I take a cigarette from my pocket that I got from Goofy Granahan earlier today. Goofy is doing his Leaving Cert next year. We shouldn't really call him that but his front teeth stick out so much it's hard not to. When he was giving it to me he said one cigarette can cause cancer. Maybe that's why he parted with it.

I don't like cigarettes but they make me feel grown up. I don't really know how to smoke them but I like trying. When I light it up I start to choke. Michael laughs. Then he has a puff. Michael is better than me at it. He can blow circles out of his mouth. He does a big one that goes up towards the ceiling but then we hear my father's footsteps outside and we wave our table tennis bats to get rid of it.

I look at the files on the table and I remember a night a few years ago when I saw it full of Christmas presents. It was a few days before Christmas Day and I was just about to go to bed. I heard a ring and thought there was someone at the door. I went downstairs to answer it but there was no one there. The ringing continued and after a minute I realised it was coming from the office so I went in. Inside the door I saw the table filled with dozens of presents. My brothers were standing beside them. They were playing with a train set. That was what made the ringing sound. There was a Scalextric set in the middle of the table. That's what I was getting for Christmas. 'Why did Santy come so early?' I asked them. They got all flustered when I said that and pushed me out of the room. Suddenly I realised the toys didn't come from Santy Claus at all. The next morning they told me they were from the International Stores. That was Benny Walkin's toy shop beside the Moy. So Benny Walkin was Santy Claus.

I go out to the kitchen and tell my father we're finished. He asks me if we put the files back and I say we did. He says he's sorry about last night and I tell him it's all right, that I don't mind. He promises he's not going to drink again, telling me he's going down to the church later for Confession. After that he says he'll take the pledge. I know he will but I know equally well that he'll be back on the drink next week or the week after. That will mean more apologies and more pledges and more nights with my mother waiting by the phone for a call from a hospital or Garda station to collect him.

The day has become darker as we walk back to the hall. Michael has heard my father apologising to me but he doesn't say anything and I don't either. One day Brian Mullis, a pupil from my class, accused my father of being a drunk and I hit him. That was the only time anyone ever said anything to me about his problem but I know the talk goes on. Maybe it's worse when people whisper about it behind your back.

The Hibs is quiet when we walk inside. The football players are all gone and so are the boxers. There are two players on the table but they've just started a game so it could be a long wait.

At the card table in the corner there are a few old men playing 110. They play this all the time without variation. It's like an extended form of 25. Every trick you get is worth five points and you try to work your way up to the final tally. If there's a group playing they try to band together against the man with the most tricks. Sometimes I join the game when I'm waiting for my turn on the snooker table but if my name is called I give somebody else my cards.

I go over to the blackboard beside the snooker table and put my initials on it. You have to do that to book your place in the queue. I don't want to lose out a second time.

I usually put AM, which stands for Aubrey Malone. My father always tells me to sign myself ADM because my full name is Aubrey Dillon-Malone but I don't bother with the Dillon. I think it sounds too flowery. You'd also be laughed out of the hall by the people who come in here if you used it.

'How is Audie Murphy?' says one of the old men, chewing on a matchstick. He has a problem pronouncing the word Aubrey so he's started comparing me to the famous cowboy actor.

I've always hated my name and I resent my father for saddling me with it. I've been told I'm called after Aubrey de Vere Bourke, the doctor who delivered me. It's also possible I'm called after the poet Aubrey de Vere because my father was reading his autobiography the day I was born. That was St. Patrick's Day so I really should have been called Patrick.

I'm now aged thirteen. At this point of their careers the world class snooker players are probably making their first centuries. I'm happy if I just get two or three balls in in a row. I'm not naturally talented but I get the odd good shot and that keeps me going.

Michael is more consistent. We play here most days until we get bored or until the Stephenites come in and take the table. If the hall is empty we might play for four or five hours. After sessions like that we tell ourselves we'll take a long break from the game but after a while the bug bites again and we return to the scene of the crime, doing everything in our power to whirl the white ball round on an imaginary string.

One day we're brilliant and the next we're cat. That means terrible. Someone told me it's short for 'catastrophic'. There's no in-between. It's like a lottery. The memory of that one good shot is the drug. It keeps you going through all the bad times when nothing is going in.

They call me The Fifteen Minute Player. I can play well for that amount of time but then I usually crumble. I don't know the reason for that. Maybe I just lose interest, knowing I can't improve on what I've done already. I often attempt mad pots. 'A cue must be handled with delicacy,' John Diamond likes to tell me, 'just like a woman.' (Then he proceeds to scatter balls around the table like a madman).

I'm also called The Olympic Player. That's because I spend so much time on the table. The 1966 Olympics are taking place in Mexico soon. Sometimes I'm asked when I plan to pack my bags for 'Mehico'. There's no snooker in the Olympics but that's beside the point.

The other players finish and Michael and myself go over to the table. Just as we do, the old man who calls me Audie Murphy gets up from the card table and stands in my way.

'Would you mind going to the other table, Audie?' he says, 'A few of us thought we might have a knock-up.' I know he's doing this to annoy me but I don't say anything. He knows the second table in the club is useless. There are rips on the cloth and when you hit the ball it keeps moving for an eternity. There's a joke that you could go to the café across the road for a cup of tea and have it drunk between the time you hit the ball and it stops moving.

'All right,' I say and he grins at me. We go over to the bad table and set up the reds. As Michael gets the triangle from under the table I look over at him lining up a shot. He's pretending to be interested but he can hardly hold the cue. I know he'll go back to his card game if I leave the hall. Somebody told me once that he had a grudge against my father. I don't really care.

We play for a few minutes but it's impossible because the cushions are so rubbery. 'This is ridiculous,' Michael says after a blue springs off a cushion and onto the top of another ball. I ask him if he wants to go. He says he does. The old man is listening to us and trying to conceal his delight.

We put our cues back on the racks as he spits on the floor. 'You're not off already, are you Audie?' he says, flushed with his little victory.

'Enjoy your game,' I reply as I get ready to face the other world outside.

Norfolk

The house we lived in was called Norfolk. My father named it after the Duke of Norfolk, the only man who didn't have to bow before the King of England. It was a large house with four rooms downstairs and four more upstairs. We always painted it yellow and black, my mother's riding colours.

There were nine in the family but there could have been thirteen. A pair of twins only lived a week and my mother also had a miscarriage and a stillborn child. The only time she ever got a holiday was when she was in hospital having babies.

Keith was the eldest. Clive arrived a year later. Afterwards came June and Ruth. June got her name because she was born on the last day of May. My father said, 'The last of May saw the first of June.' Ruth was a year younger but June was kept back at school so they could be in the same class. The same had been done with Keith and Clive.

It was also done with the next two children, Hugo and Basil, and the next two, Audrey and Jacinta. That made it two boys, two girls, two more boys, two more girls. I was the last to arrive.

I grew up mainly on my own and that gave me a stubborn independent streak. Most of the other people in the family were big talkers but I was quiet. My mother used to say, 'Aubrey only speaks when he has something to say.' I never understood what she meant by that. Why should people speak when they hadn't?

I was left-handed. My brothers and sisters tried to make me throw a ball with my right by pinning my left and behind my back but I always found a way to free it. At school it was more difficult. The nuns switched me to my right for writing without any room for argument. It was the way things were done at the time.

A funny story was told about an incident that happened when I was a child. My father kept all his important files in a safe. One day when I was about four I saw the key on the table and buried it in the yard for reasons best known to myself. When my father couldn't find it he flew into a rage. An emergency was declared: nobody was to leave the house until it was found. At a certain stage of the search the attention turned to me. I must have had a taste for drama because shortly afterwards I led the whole family out to the garden and began to dig for the key. After a few minutes I found it and there were celebrations all around. I was forgiven. Maybe I was even something of a hero.

I didn't like being the youngest of the family. My father said he kept the best wine for last but I saw it differently. I felt like the scrapings of the barrel. I missed out on seeing everyone else growing up and also on the crowded atmosphere around the house.

I never got to meet any of my grandparents. My grandfather on my father's side was called P.J. Malone. He was a self-made man, rising from humble origins to become a magistrate and a Poor Law Guardian. He had J.P. after his name, which stood for Justice of the Peace. I always thought that was strange because J.P. was P.J. back to front. It was as if his name was a circle.

He married three times, outliving his first two wives. His third one had the maiden name of Dillon. She wanted to be distinguished from the families of the other two so she insisted on keeping her name. That's why Dillon-Malone was on all our birth certificates.

My father asked me not to tell the story of my grandfather's multiple marriages to anyone. He thought it sounded better if we left the origin of our double-barrelled name up to people's imagination. Otherwise it seemed like we were trying to apologise for something. 'To explain is to excuse,' was the way he put it.

I could never understand his logic. He acted as if we were blue blood but we were far from it. We may have had breeding but we had no money so what good was it? Why should we pretend to be something we weren't? He didn't like it when I talked like that any more than he liked me hanging around with people from Lord Edward Street. (He called it Guntown). He was afraid they'd put bad ideas about him into my head. 'If you give the people in this town a stick they'll beat you with it,' he said.

He was one of the few Catholics to go to Trinity College in the 1920s. You had to get a dispensation from the Archbishop to go there then on account of it being a Protestant university. People joked that the church would look more kindly on you if you consorted with a prostitute rather than a Protestant.

My father spent his happiest years in Trinity. He had his own room there, Number 9. He was studying Law, at least in theory. In effect he spent most of his time partying with a friend of his called Mido Cooligan.

He was being bankrolled from Ballina. He spent whatever money was sent to him almost as soon as it arrived and then wrote home for more. Much of this came from his mother. He was the apple of her eye.

He failed his exams religiously every year, taking the news with an element of bravado. One term he managed to squeeze through a paper on Jurisprudence, afterwards apologising profusely to his friends. He was forgiven as long as it didn't become a habit. Graduation was the ultimate crime.

Stories of his carousing eventually reached Ballina. One summer when he came home on a term break his father said to him, 'If some of the stories I hear about you in Dublin are true I'd prefer to see your corpse come through the door rather than yourself.'

He tidied up his act when he met my mother. She was the daughter of a gentlemen farmer from Roscommon. They met on a boat trip organised by her sister Valerie. It was a windy day and the sea was rough. My father talked nonstop to her because he was nervous. He was afraid the boat was going to capsize. Every time the waves chopped he hurtled backwards, hugging the sides. My mother was highly amused. Afterwards he followed her all round Ireland proposing marriage to her. She finally got tired of saying no and gave in.

They got married on October 5th 1935. It was really an elopement, her mother not approving of the match. Afterwards my father concentrated on his studies for the first time in his life. They moved to Greystones in County Wicklow and he burned the midnight oil. 'I wasn't getting any smarter,' he said to me, 'and the exams weren't getting any easier.' When he qualified he felt like he'd climbed Mount Everest. By that time he could almost have been given an honorary degree for staying power. He was almost thirty by now. After he graduated he moved back to Ballina and set up a law practice there. The children followed afterwards like the steps of a stairs.

Keith and Clive left Ballina in 1955 when I was just two. Keith went to university that year and Clive entered the Jesuits. I have only vague memories of them. June and Ruth I remember better. Ruth was very meticulous. She had beautiful handwriting and kept her copies immaculately. She had a hobby of making bags from pieces of plastic stuck together with masking tape. She also liked cutting coupons out of magazines and entering competitions. One year she won a Raleigh bicycle.

June was more scatty. She hated school. One day a guard had to be called to the house to get her to go. My mother hated the idea of calling him but she felt she had to. If my father had had his way we'd all have been at home all day playing games.

Most of the family inherited my father's impracticality. None of us were handy around the house. When it came to fixing things we were all thumbs. Basil put his hand through a window once when he was trying to put putty on it and it broke. He had to be taken to hospital and suffered from numbness in his fingers for years afterwards. Hugo used to say, 'I don't know my own strength.' He could break something simply by holding it. 'Hanging a picture on a wall is a day's work for me,' he said. I envied people who could do things with their hands but my father said books were more important. He kept hundreds of paperback novels in a cabinet in the front room, most of them with orange covers.

My father carried himself around town like a lord even though we had no money. 'There are two kinds of men in the world,' he said to me once, 'The first walks down Bond Street as if he owns it. The second walks down Bond Street as if he doesn't care who owns it.' He never explained which type he was. Maybe he was a bit of both.

In time he became something of a dandy like his own father. Elegance was everything to him whether we had two pennies to rub together or not. He liked to quote the lines of W. F. Hargreaves: 'I'm Burlington Bertie, I rise at ten-thirty and saunter along like a toff. I walk down the Strand with my gloves in my hand, and then down again with them off.' His Strand was Garden Street but it might as well have been Buckingham Palace. He had the ability to imagine himself on an Olympian height even if he was only putting the bins out. (Though I never remember him doing that).

I often asked him which of his father's three wives would be his real wife in heaven. He couldn't answer that. He said there were some things about life we could never understand. We could only see 'through a glass darkly' until we died. Everything would be explained to us then. But in other moods he professed to believe in nothing. He told us all once, 'If God exists he must be evil because of all the horrors he's perpetrated.' Afterwards anytime he mentioned God he added, 'If there is a God'.

He hated the way religion changed after the Second Vatican Council. He wanted to get back to the Latin Mass. The idea of guitar players on an altar revolted him and so did the idea of priests facing the congregation. There was no mystery in that, he said, no mystique. 'Nuns are jumping the wildcat up and down the aisles today,' he complained. The church needed to get its authority back. It needed to get back to the era of 'Rome hath spoken'. These days it was even afraid to whisper because the Pope had lost all his authority. Politically speaking he felt a benign dictator worked best in a country. Otherwise everything was up for grabs.

There were four in my father's family. His sister Nellie lived closest to us on the Killala Road. She often called to have a chat with my mother. She was less interested in my father. 'We love each other from a distance,' she said. She always wore a fur coat and enough perfume to knock you flying if she passed too close to you. She'd ask you a few questions and then swing off to another room before you got a chance to answer them. She had 17 cats. She never married, the cats seeming to fulfil any need she might have had for company.

My mother was in Aunt Nellie's house the day John F. Kennedy was assassinated. A friend of hers rang her with the news. My mother was listening to the call in the next room. She didn't know what it was about. All she could hear was Aunt Nellie saying 'I don't believe it.' When she left the receiver down, my mother asked her what was wrong. By now she was nearly hysterical. Aunt Nellie said, 'President Kennedy has just been shot.' My mother let out a sigh of relief. 'Oh thank God,' she said, 'I thought something happened to one of the children.'

She didn't mean it the way it came out. We laughed about the story afterwards even though we shouldn't have. Everybody loved

John F. Kennedy. Most houses had a picture of him on their wall beside the Pope. I remember listening to the news of his death on the television. The newsreader was crying. They cut off the programme that was on to announce it. It was a programme with Peter Lawford in it. I always thought that was strange because someone told me he was related to him through marriage.

My father had another sister called Mary. She lived across the river. She was married to Eddie Murphy, one of the richest men in Ballina. He owned a flour mill and various other businesses. Aunt Mary was a saintly woman who spent a huge amount of time in the church. I often saw her doing the Stations with a devotional look in her eyes.

Sometimes I went down to Aunt Mary's house in Bunree to play a game of bagatelle. I wasn't sure of the rules of this but I enjoyed potting the balls in the holes that were in the middle of the table. They were surrounded by mushroom-like plastic objects you had to avoid knocking over. In later years her son Paddy installed a full-sized snooker table in a different room. I only played on that once. He insisted it was too big to fit in the door so he had to gelignite his roof and have it lowered down afterwards. I didn't know if he was being serious about this or not.

Aunt Mary got cancer when I was ten. We were all shocked. The disease had spread too far when it was discovered so an operation was ruled out. She started to lose weight almost immediately. She spent most of her time in bed, barely making a crease on the sheets. My father and mother went down to see her every night. When they came back they were always crying. She died very quickly but her husband couldn't face life without her. Within six months he was gone too, from heartbreak.

The fourth person in my father's family was his brother Louis. I don't remember ever meeting him. He became a doctor and moved to Birmingham when he qualified, marrying another doctor there. My father didn't get on with her. When Uncle Louis died, she didn't tell him about the death until it was too late to go to the funeral. There was time to get a plane but she knew he had a phobia of flying. The boat was useless in the circumstances. He never forgave her for that.

As well as flying my father also had a phobia about driving. He owned a car for a short time but wrote it off after crashing it into a wall. Afterwards he employed a taxi-man, Pat Hughes, to drive him anywhere he needed to go. Most of his trips were down the country whenever he had to get documents signed by farmers. Pat Hughes drove very slowly. There was a story that he once offered a lift to some people walking along the road and they refused because they were in a hurry.

Pat Hughes brought the family to the beach at Enniscrone when the weather was fine. This was a beach town eight miles from us. Going there was the highlight of our week. I willed the sun to come out so my father could leave his work aside and bring us. Usually he didn't need much persuasion.

There wasn't much to do in the town itself but the beach was huge. At the end of the long stretch of sand there was a sunken area filled with seashells that we called The Valley of Diamonds because when the sun shone on the seashells it made them resemble jewellery. My father didn't come to the Valley of Diamonds much with us. He preferred to sit on the sand and look out at the sea. He always wore his Trinity rig-outs on these occasions. He looked funny sitting on the sand in his monocle and pin-striped suit. (The monocle came about as a result of an allegedly defective eye but we suspected he wore it more for effect than anything else).

Apart from the trips to Enniscrone we didn't go out much. There was always too much happening in the house. Neither did many of the family have my father's sociable nature.

Basil came closest to him in that way. When he was at school he was always going up to the teachers to ask questions after class. The rest of us would usually run the other way if we saw a teacher or a priest. Basil was a bright spark and sailed through all his exams. He also invited a lot of people to the house. Visitors arrived at Norfolk at all hours. People used to say, 'There's always a light on in Malones.'

One of the family's closest friends was Gerry Courell. His father had been on the Mayo team that won the All-Ireland in 1950. He often called in on the way home from the Estoria and stayed half the night talking with Hugo and Basil about films. A good one was 'a classic' and a bad one an 'alp' or a 'capture'. Our friend Peter O'Hora was the projectionist. He often cut the films short if he wanted to get home for something. It was a Ballina form of censorship.

My cousin Ann O'Grady came to live with us in 1963. Ann was the same age as me but she was only my second cousin rather than my first one. Her mother Grace was the daughter of Valerie, my mother's sister. (She'd been in the boat with my parents the first day they met). Grace felt Ann would get a better education in Ballina. The school in Roscommon was tiny and the teacher spent most of his time asleep, waking up only to beat the pupils senseless.

Most years we went on holiday to the O'Grady's for the summer. They had a big house in the country and a farm with lots of land in the surrounding area. I remember saving the hay with them and the lovely smell it had when you had it stacked. On a tree in their garden we used to play a game called The Wild Cat's Trick. It involved hanging on a branch and twisting your legs in through your arms like an acrobat. They had a shop as well. It had a post office attached to it. Sometimes we'd be eating our dinner and a customer would come in looking for a stamp and we'd have to stop eating until they were served. A woman half a mile away had a television set and sometimes we cycled down to her house to watch it. It didn't matter what programme was on, It was just a thrill to see anything at all.

Having Ann in the house was like having an extra sister. She was more extrovert than me and brought me out of myself. We went everywhere together like twins. I remember skating with her on Convent Hill. The hill wound round a corner and was dangerous if you hit a bump on the path beside Gurks Molloy's house.

Ann liked taking chances like that. She had a wild streak that I admired. Sometimes we dropped trays out the bedroom window when people were passing by the door at Norfolk, scaring the daylights out of them as they crashed down behind them. Or we might throw water on their heads. Another thing I remember about her was that she never wore a coat when she went out no matter what the weather was like. My mother was always giving out to her about that.

She was bright academically. The nuns in the convent took a special interest in her and made her into an A-student. She won a scholarship to a school in Belmullet one year. As well as being at the top of her class she acted in plays there. I could never understand how someone could have that kind of confidence. She had a part in John B. Keane's *The Year of the Hiker* in her Leaving Cert year and got a write-up in the *Western People,* the Ballina paper. The priests in Muredach's held her up as a kind of example to me. Why couldn't I be like that?

After Ann left I was thrown back on my own resources. I got used to not being with people again. My father tapped into this tendency. He told me it was best not to socialise with the people around us.

The Corcorans lived next door to us but we didn't have much to do with them. We played handball up against their back wall which they didn't approve of. After a while they started leaving their windows open so the ball would go in. Whenever it did we never got it back. In the end we stopped asking for it.

A part of the wall below their window was just above our garage, a little arc-shaped area just a few inches wide. My father claimed it was our property and the Corcorans claimed it was theirs. When we painted it yellow they repainted it grey. This went on for years. It must have cost us both a fortune in paint..

Our neighbour on the other side was even stranger. His name was Gildy Ahern. He owned an orchard. Sometimes we sneaked in over his wall and stole his apples. My father told us not to do this but we didn't listen to him. All sorts of rumours went around Ballina about Gildy. I was told he killed his wife and buried her under the floorboards. His house was covered in ivy and the curtains were usually closed. One day he left them open and I looked in.

Everywhere was filthy. It looked like a haunted house to me. After that I quickened my step every time I passed his door. I imagined loads of dead people lying under the floorboards.

Around the corner there was a creamery where we got our milk from a man called Arthur Wills. Every few days I went up to him with a pail and he filled it. When he was finished, he always took up a little ladle and added in an extra bit 'for the cat.' I never knew what he meant by that.

Our cat was called Tabby. She was very old when I first remember her. Every so often she'd disappear and then come back a few weeks later. But then one year she didn't come back and nobody knew what happened to her, whether she'd been knocked down or not.

We also had a dog, Deezer. I don't know where the name came from. We bought him from a man on Lord Edward Street who almost starved him. He used to keep him tethered to a kennel. The rope was tied so tight around his neck that it bled. He would probably have died if we hadn't bought him. He was a cross-breed between a Pointer and a Setter and had a brown patch over one of his eyes. Whenever we went to Enniscrone he followed us all the way even if we shouted at him to go home. He was so hungry the day we bought him he jumped up on the table and ate six pork chops. We all had to go without dinner that day.

The dog we had before Deezer was knocked down by a car outside the school. I was too young to remember that. He was called Rover. I only knew him from photographs.

The school was just across the road from us. People used to joke that we didn't have to leave the house until we heard the bell. One night Hugo was supposed to have heard the bell in his sleep and dressed himself in the middle of the night.

There was a fire station on one side of the school and a place that made headstones on the other. Farther up the road was The Estoria, our local cinema. Most of the family practically grew up there. As soon as we were old enough to walk my father was bringing us to films. I had a red velvet cushion that the manager kept beside the projectionist's booth to prop me up to see the screen. His name was Paddy Mulligan. He was a client of my father and gave him loads of free passes every time he called to the house. When *The Dirty Dozen* came to town I had passes to go it every night. I didn't watch it in sequence, just different parts of it each night. Eventually I saw it all.

Any time Hugo saw a film he liked he got so excited he practically told us the whole story afterwards. If he was with Gerry Courell that meant you got to hear it twice. Hugo also loved drama. He used to put on little plays in the back garden. One year he did a version of *West Side Story*. We all got to play members of the street gangs, clicking our fingers as we tried to look cool with far too much Brylcreem in our hair.

Shane was our favourite film of all. Keith called it 'the mother and father of all cowboys.' I remember the poster of it on the stairs in the Estoria with Alan Ladd's buckskin. It was retained for a week and we went to it nearly every night, with or without passes. Eventually we almost knew the script off by heart.

We used to quote it to each other in the kitchen as we acted out the parts. 'Your kind of days are over, Ryker.' 'What do you mean my kind of days? What about yours, gunfighter?' On Hugo's 20th birthday in 1966 Jacinta came home with the *Evening Press*. The headline said 'Alan Ladd is dead'. It was a weird coincidence. He was supposed to have died of a combination of alcohol and pills but I heard later that it could have been suicide.

1966 was also the year the film *One Million Years B.C.* came to town. It had lots of monsters in it and a very beautiful woman called Raquel Welch. (Basil called her 'Rachel' Welch for some reason). In the poster she looked sexier than any women I'd ever seen in my life. She seemed to be wearing a bikini. I wondered how they could have had these a million years ago.

It was funny to see her wrestling dinosaurs looking like she'd just come out of a beauty parlour with her hair back-combed. Hugo said she also looked like she worked out. (That was something else they didn't have a million years ago: gyms). Hugo and Basil were more interested in Donna Cottrell, a beautiful girl who lived across the road. She was like a Madonna. Half of the men in the town seemed to be in love with Donna Cottrell but most of them were too tongue-tied to do anything about it. Raquel Welch came a poor second.

Another actress I loved watching was Veronica Lake. She was in a lot of films with Alan Ladd. A man I knew from Ardnaree had a riddle: 'What's a fisherman's Paradise? A night on Veronica Lake.'

When women appeared on the screen we usually went out to buy sweets but as we got older we got more interested in the kissing scenes. The priests in Muredach's warned us about the 'temptations of the flesh'. When they used that expression all I could see in my mind were big fat women even though I knew that wasn't what they meant.

I watched a lot of Elvis films too. I always wanted to have his locks. I used to wash my hair and then selotape it around my ears but the tape always came off. Hugo was able to imitate Elvis. He looked a bit like him, even moreso when he put the collar of his shirt up and went down on one knee to sing 'Don't Be Cruel.' One year Aunt Mary gave us a tape recorder and Hugo used to record himself singing Elvis songs on it.

Hugo and Basil left Muredach's the year I started in it. Everyone thought Basil was going to be a priest. (He had a big devotion to

Dominic Savio). He often talked about wanting to be one but after he did the Leaving Cert. he decided he wanted to go to university instead. One day he went cycling to Enniscrone with Hugo. On the way home he broke the news to him. He was afraid to tell my parents. Hugo said, 'Don't worry, I'm going to be one myself.' It was as if he was filling in for him. Shortly afterwards Hugo entered All Hallows seminary in Drumcondra.

All Hallows wasn't as strict as the Jesuit order Clive was in. Hugo got home often but we only got to see Clive one every seven years after he left Ireland to go to Zambia.

My mother would be excited for weeks before he came home. He always brought masks from Zambia with him. He told us stories about primitive tribes. He even learned to speak Tonga, one of the African languages. We loved the masks but if Aunt Nellie called up we had to take them out of the sitting-room. She hated anything like that. Even dolls terrified her.

People thought Clive was my mother's favourite child but she said she had no favourites, that she loved all of us in different ways. That was probably true but she was more emotional with Clive than with any of the rest of us. When his visits were over she couldn't even bring herself to say goodbye to him because she knew she'd break down. She always stayed in the back room as he collected his cases and made his way to the train station.

I did my Inter Cert in 1967. One day that year I was in Enniscrone with June and I fell off a wall when I was playing a game. Fluid swelled up on my knee so I had to be taken to hospital. I was told I'd have to have it lanced but the night before the operation the doctors changed their minds and said they were going to let it go down naturally. I studied for the exam with my leg in plaster.

I thought I'd do miserably in the exam but somehow I scraped through it. My father said he was disappointed in me. 'You've broken a family tradition,' he said. He gave me £5. 'It would have been double that if you failed,' he informed me.

He was drinking more than ever now and out most of the time. The bills were piling up and less money was coming in. What small fees he earned usually ended up in publicans' tills. There was talk of Eddie Murphy's son Paddy buying Norfolk and using the money to set us up in a house in Dublin. 'All I want is a room,' my father said, 'nothing else.' By now he'd left Ballina in his mind; there would be no more glory days defending beggars in the local courthouse.

One day shortly before we left the town I saw him deep in concentration and I asked him if he was working on a case. 'Yes,' he replied, 'a case of Scotch.' There was a time I might have laughed but not now. Sometimes I thought he drank as much as he did out of guilt over his father. He felt he failed him and maybe even contributed to his early death. (P.J. Malone died in his fifties while he was saying the Rosary). 'He made an empire for me and I destroyed it,' he used to say when he was feeling bad about frittering all his money away at Trinity. If he was drinking he'd bring his mother into it. 'She ruined me,' he said, 'I had her twisted round my little finger.'

By now my mother was the real head of the house rather than my father. She saw all the clients and covered for him when he was under the weather. Whenever I asked her what was going to happen she changed the subject.

She tried to act casual but I often heard her crying in her room. She was up with Dr Igoe a lot as well. One day I saw her grasping her chest as if she was in pain but she wouldn't talk about that either. When I asked her what was wrong, she just kept saying, 'Don't worry, everything will be fine,' as she drew on yet another cigarette.

Transitions

1969 was the year everything changed for me. Violence erupted in the North, giving the death knell to the hippie ideals of peace and love. In California a gang led by Charles Manson broke into a house where the actress Sharon Tate was living and brutally stabbed her to death along with a number of other residents.

At home everything seemed to be changing as well. Clive came home from Zambia and arranged for my father to go into St. Patrick's Hospital to be dried out. He wouldn't have agreed in the normal way but he was on a lot of tablets and didn't really know what was happening. Then Dr Igoe told us my mother had breast cancer and had to go to Dublin. He said it was in the early stages and there was every chance she'd make a complete recovery but she needed to go to St Luke's Hospital as soon as possible. She'd probably have to have a mastectomy. That was the first time I heard the word.

She kept delaying going because of my father. Some nights in bed she sweated so much the sheets were saturated. But she still kept postponing the operation. When she finally agreed to go she had to be carried out of the house in an ambulance.

There was no money in the family now so Audrey and Jacinta had to be taken out of school. Jacinta went to London to work in an office and Audrey started studying nursing in Surrey. I stayed in Norfolk with a friend of the family called Sean McDonnell. He'd been doing odd jobs for us for a few months now. Tina went to Roscommon to work for another solicitor.

Sean had more or less moved in to the house with us bit by bit over the years. His father was an auctioneer but they didn't get on. He'd been a wild child but he said that was only because nobody understood him. He felt he didn't get enough praise from his parents. He had a million ideas about how to get rich but was never able to stick with any of them. As soon as something started to look good he walked away from it.

Sometimes I helped him with his jobs around the house. He was a jack of all trades but he had an eccentric approach to everything. Some of his ideas were ingenious but others were completely off-the-wall. I felt he'd wind up either a millionaire or on Skid Row. There could be no other possibility.

When he wasn't busy I persuaded him to come to the Hibs with me. (By now Michael had traded in his snooker cue for a guitar). Most of the other players were amused by his approach to the game. He hit the balls so hard they often flew off the table. 'Why don't you hit them a bit easier?' I used to ask him. He always replied, 'I don't want to leave them for the other bastard.' (Presumably that was me).

1969 was also the year a man was put on the moon. I sat watching this on the television with Sean and couldn't really believe what I was seeing. I looked at the giant orb on the screen and then ran out into the street and looked at it in the sky. How could it be the same moon that a man was now walking on? We used to talk about the man in the moon as children. 'Can you believe there's one up there now?' I asked Sean. He said someone down the town told him that in the next century we'd all be taking day trips to the moon instead of going down to the beach at Enniscrone for our holidays.

The next few months had no pattern for me. I missed a lot of days at school but nobody seemed to care. I was even let off the hook by Jacko. It was as if I'd turned into a man suddenly by the sheer fact of living in a house without my parents. I spoke to them on the phone every now and then but only for short periods. My mother had her operation and it went well but she was in an out of hospital for tests. She also visited my father in Pat's. She kept asking me how I was but I didn't really have anything to say to her. After school each day I wandered in and out of the Hibs whenever I felt like it.

When the summer ended Sean told me I was being taken out of school. The house was being sold and we were moving to Dublin. This came as a shock to me. Nobody had told me anything about it up until then. I knew it made sense because most of the family were in Dublin anyway. What would be the point of two of us being on our own in this huge empty house?

The night before I left Ballina for good, Sean brought all our belongings down to the Town Hall and auctioned them off to the highest bidder. Everything went for a song. I watched possessions I treasured being sold for as little as £1 because we needed the quick money. It was almost like prostitution. All my father's paperbacks were lined up against a wall, all his Agatha Christies and Nevil Shutes and Arthur Conan Doyles and Hilaire Bellocs.

By the end of the night Sean was flogging them for as little as a shilling a copy. As I watched him pounding his gavel on a rostrum and speaking in a strange language he seemed like a different man to the one I knew. I wondered if he got his way of expressing himself from listening to his father at auctions. Before we left the hall I saw wads of notes sticking out of his pockets. I thought to myself: That accounts for thirty years of my father's life. I wanted to cry but I couldn't. I felt my past was dead.

I went to Dublin in August, bringing nothing with me but the clothes I had on my back. Before I left I put all my old toys and copybooks into boxes and left them out in the backyard for binmen to collect. Then I walked down the town in an attempt to imprint its details on my mind for all the years I'd be out of it, as a kind of hostage to fortune. I went down by the cinema, the church, the soccer pitch: all the benchmarks of my days that would be more precious to me now that I would only have them to think about now, not see anymore.

Why was I born last, I asked myself. Why couldn't I have been the eldest of the family and set up a legal practice here, or even sell nails in Woolworths for a living? I would even have accepted that. I couldn't understand why my life was changing when I was hardly old enough to know what change was. I walked to the train station with a knot in my stomach, the same knot I used to get going down to Muredach's each morning. It seemed crazy but I would even miss that old place now, like someone addicted to his own pain.

It started to rain as I got on the train and the dull sky suited my mood. I watched the landscape whizzing by, wondering what was in store for me. How would my mother's health be? Would my father get well? What school would I be going to?

The journey passed in a blur. Keith was supposed to meet me at Connolly Station but I got the arrival time wrong so he wasn't there. Crowds milled around me as I got off the train, more people than I'd ever seen in one place in my life. A tannoy was barking out departure times for the other trains.

I went out onto the street and walked up by the Liffey. It looked like coffee and smelt putrid. There were neon signs everywhere and people going in and out of shops with demented looks on their faces. When I got to O'Connell Bridge I turned left. I walked up by Eason's and the GPO to the stop for the 22A bus across the road from the Gresham Hotel. I had a piece of paper in my pocket with that number on it. Ruth had sent it to me from Dublin with a lot of other directions in her tall straight handwriting.

My stomach churned as the bus brought me to St. Peter's Church, rocking its way through Dorset Street and the North Circular Road. When I got off I asked a man if he knew where Cabra Park was. 'Just follow your nose,' he said. I went through a laneway with a stone pillar in the middle of it. When I came out the other end I found myself in an estate where all the houses looked the same.

I went up the door that said 66 and knocked. Ruth opened it with a big smile. She was dressed in a blue suit as if she'd just come from work. I'd only seen her in Dublin once before, at Keith and Clive's graduation. She gave me a hug and brought me in. I could hear Gene Pitney singing 'Lookin' Through the Eyes of Love' on the record player. Ruth turned it off.

Keith and Clive were at the table. Keith was eating a grapefruit he'd cut in half. The two of them got up and hugged me. There were cheese sandwiches on the table and a little wooden stand for holding letters. Keith showed me a postcard Basil sent from Eindhoven in Holland. He was over there with some engineers. 'June will be joining us soon,' he said. She was in a flat in Haddington Road but would be leaving when her lease expired.

Ruth bustled around the kitchen making tea. Clive told me he'd just been over to Battersea and had met Audrey and Jacinta there. They were both getting on great. He showed me a photograph of the three of them. After all the years of the family being too enclosed together in Norfolk it was as if we were suddenly being splintered to the four corners of the globe.

Clive asked me if I liked Dublin. I told him I didn't know yet, that it was hard to tell. My head was spinning. I asked him if this was our new home. 'No,' he said, 'this is just a flat. Sean is putting carpets and curtains into a place in Iona Villas in Glasnevin. That's where we'll be eventually but we're going into a house in Shandon Drive first while he gets it ready.'

When I asked about my mother and father he went quiet. My mother was still having tests but she was fine. She'd probably be home in a few days. My father was so heavily drugged there was no point in going to see him yet. He wasn't even going to be told my mother had had a mastectomy.

When I asked what school I was going to, Clive told me he had some good news for me. Due to his being a Jesuit he'd managed to get me accepted into Belvedere College for my last year. It was run by Jesuits and carried a lot of prestige. I told him I'd prefer to go to an ordinary school but he said that was short-sighted thinking, that Belvedere could open doors for me in the future. Keith and Ruth agreed with him. In the end I was won round. Maybe it didn't really matter what school I went to now because I'd know nobody there anyway.

The next day he brought me in to be vetted by the President, Fr McGowran. I had nothing to wear so Keith loaned me a white mackintosh coat he had. It was a few sizes too big for me. I was brought into a big room with a huge mahogany table in it. I was freezing sitting in Keith's flimsy coat. I thought of our own mahogany table and what might have happened to it. Who owned it now? How much had Sean McDonnell got for it at the auction? I doubted we'd have any use for it in Dublin as the rooms would probably be much smaller than the ones in Norfolk.

Fr McGowran came in and shook my hand. He started talking to Clive about me. Clive explained that school might be difficult for me seeing as I was breaking off from curriculum and starting off with a new one. Fr. McGowran said not to worry, that he understood perfectly. The meeting was over in no time. 'That went very well,' Clive said as we went back onto North Great Denmark Street but I didn't think so. It was the last place I wanted to be.

I started in Belvedere the following week. It was an unfriendly school and nobody bothered with me much. I sat in rooms with people who'd known each other since the cradle, people who had no interest in making friends with a stranger from the country. I wasn't interested in making friends with them either.

One of the priests asked me if I'd play rugby. I said no. That would have infuriated my father if he knew. Another one asked me if I'd join the tennis club but again I refused. The only person who addressed a personal comment to me was the English teacher. He said he'd been in Ballina once. 'Nice town,' he remarked. Under the circumstances this seemed like a huge gesture of goodwill to me. .

When I left the school that day Basil was waiting outside the gates for me. He'd just come back from Eindhoven. He was wearing a leather waistcoat and jeans. He had pointed shoes like they wore in the fifties. His girlfriend, Ann, was with him. She looked beautiful. She was studying Social Science at Earlsfort Terrace.

'How do you like the big smoke?' she asked me. I didn't know what to say so I just shrugged my shoulders. They brought me into the Garden of Remembrance for a walk and then we had coffee in Barry's Hotel. I couldn't finish the coffee because it made me sick. Basil was excited telling me about his trip. He used a lot of technical language that I didn't understand. When I told him about the rugby he was disgusted. 'You have to play it,' he said, 'I'll get you a book of the rules.' I told him the game did nothing for me, that I'd have preferred to be playing pushpenny in The Rec in Muredach's.

'Rugby is a great game,' he said, 'except when you get your head mistaken for the ball.' Ann pushed him in the ribs when he said that. He put on his anorak. 'Look at this,' he said, digging his hands into the pocket, 'If you get one of these you can wear it to Lansdowne. You can put your hands in the pockets and your elbows don't stick out so you won't hit the guy sitting next to you.' Landsdowne Road was where all the international rugby matches were held.

Before we left the hotel he told me he'd be going to America soon but that I could have his Honda 50. I couldn't believe it: my own motorcycle. 'You should bring it into Belvo,' he said. I knew I'd be too self-conscious for that but I was still delighted to have it. It was a long way from the crock I'd been cycling into Muredach's for the past four years.

Over the next few weeks I sat in classes feeling a million miles away from everything that was being said. There was pupil involvement in Belvedere unlike in Muredach's where you were just fed notes but I was too used to being a sheep to want this. I wasn't used to being asked for my opinions and didn't seem to have any as a result. (My father, I felt, would hardly be writing essays for me here.)

There was also a lot of insolence tolerated. One day a priest told the pupil sitting beside me that he didn't like him very much. 'The feeling is mutual, Father,' he replied. If somebody said something like that to a priest in Ballina it would have been the talk of the town.

He'd nearly have been in the *Western*. He'd also have a thick ear to show for his troubles. But here it was common practice.

My mother came home from hospital the next week. It was the longest time we'd been apart since I was born. She looked me up and down as if I was some kind of exhibit. 'I expected you to be skin and bone,' she said, 'Did Sean feed you at all?' We'd been living on junk food but I told her he cooked every day. She said I was a bad liar.

She looked very weak but the doctors had given her a good prognosis. 'You'll have to go off the cigarettes now,' I said. 'Don't remind me,' she said, 'I heard that piece of news already.' She used to give them up every Lent. When she went back on them again she'd throw up after the first one. She'd been smoking butts given to her by her brothers since she was five.

As I talked to her I felt strange. I'd never seen her outside her home environment before. She wasn't like my mother here, she was just like any other woman. She asked me how I was but I told her I wasn't the issue, that she'd have to start looking after herself now. She said she would but I doubted it.

She asked me how I was settling in to Belvedere and I said not too bad, that I was getting used to it. If we were in Ballina she'd have quizzed me more but we were all a bit shell-shocked now and unable to react normally. I felt unreal as we talked, as if the conversation was happening to someone else. It was like speaking under water, or through a glass wall. Everyone was buzzing around me getting meals and making arrangements to go out for the night but I just felt numb.

My father came out of Pat's the next day. He was emotional when he saw me and grabbed me in a tight bearhug. It was the same kind of emotion he had with drink but there was no smell of drink off him now. I thought it must have been the pills that were doing it. He looked sleepy and slurred his words. My mother looked as if she was about to cry but when he fell asleep she said, 'Isn't it great he's not missing the drink?'

We left Cabra Park the next week and moved into the house on Shandon Drive. People were coming and going all the time like in Norfolk but it was different because you knew no one when you walked out into the street.

June came over from Haddington Road one day and moved some of her things in. She was dressed in her tennis gear because she'd just finished a game with her friend Rose Woolf in Herbert Park. She had a novel in her hand written by a man called Robert Ruark, one of those blockbusters people usually brought on holiday with them. No sooner was she in the door than the phone rang. It was some man who wanted to take her out. She got flustered because she wasn't interested in him. 'I'm heading for the hills,' she said, 'Tell him I'm not

33

here.' These words would be repeated more than once to me in the following years as she staved off unwanted suitors.

June took Clive's room because he was back in Zambia now. Basil had gone to America to work in a company called General Electric. That left just Keith, Ruth and myself in the house apart from June and my parents. June was working in the Irish Permanent Building Society in O'Connell Street. 'Come in and see me anytime,' she said but I knew I'd be too shy to do that.

We moved to Iona Villas coming up to Christmas. It was a red-bricked semi-detached house on a hill in a cul-de-sac. There was a small hallway when you went in the door and a sitting-room and dining-room to the right. The kitchen was like an extension of the hall. It was a long room with an Aga cooker in the middle of it and a glasshouse off to the side.

When my father saw it first he couldn't believe everything was so small. He thought we owned the house next door as well. 'Is this all?' he said, throwing his hands in the air. After Norfolk it looked like a shack to him.

The walls were bare and the floors uncarpeted. Sean promised us that it wouldn't be long like that, that he'd have it like a new pin in no time.

He brought me upstairs and led me into a small room at the front of the house. 'This would be ideal for you,' he said. It had flowery yellow wallpaper. There was just room for the bed and a tallboy but I didn't mind that. I looked out the window. There was a shop across the street called The Hillside. All the houses had the same redbrick colour but they had different styles. The people next door had a palm tree in their garden that looked exotic to me. It reminded me of something I saw in the Estoria once in a film. I'd never seen one in Ballina in all my years there. At the end of the hill there was a roundabout with a lot of vegetation in the middle of it.

I went downstairs with Sean. Nobody seemed to know what to say so I didn't know how they were feeling. There was a bottle of champagne on the kitchen table so Sean opened that. It spilled all over the floor when he popped the cork. My mother said 'Oh Jesus Mary and Joseph' and cleaned it up with a cloth.

. He gave everyone a glass. 'Here's to the future,' he said, his adam's apple sticking out as he lowered a mouthful. His face was beaming. 'I put a fiver under one of the floorboards for luck,' he added. It was an old builders' superstition. My mother said if she found it she'd spend it and everyone laughed.

We spent the rest of the day unpacking whatever we brought with us into our rooms. I put up some posters of Elvis Presley in my one as well as a photo of Bob Dylan from the cover of 'Nashville Skyline'. He was holding a hat on his head in the photo. I got a scissors and cut off the top of the picture and tied a string to it. When you pulled the string it was as if he was tipping his hat to you. For the first time since I got to Dublin I felt this could be a home for us after all. I looked out the window again and the sky looked all blurry from the champagne.

I felt woozy all the next day at school and wasn't able to concentrate. When it was finished I walked to Shandon Drive instead of Iona Villas by mistake. A stranger opened the door and said, 'Who are you?' 'What do you mean who am I?' I replied, 'I live here. Who are you?' It was almost funny.

My head was in a jamjar for the next few weeks. I sat at the back of the classroom gazing into space, not even aware of being there as teachers snapped their fingers over my head and asked me questions I couldn't answer. Sometimes I felt they didn't care if I knew the answers or not and because of that I stopped caring myself. It was less strict than Muredach's but maybe I missed a part of that strictness.

I seemed to be in a daze most of the time. One day as I was crossing the street at Doyle's Corner a car screeched to a halt before me and the driver leapt out and started roaring at me for not looking where I was going.

Everyone thought I was pining for Ballina. Maybe they were right. No matter how miserable Muredach's was I still had friends there. That was impossible in Belvedere. I was intimidated by most of the students and in another way bored. There seemed to be no heart in the school. If it was to be of any benefit to me it was going to be purely for the sake of having it on my CV if I was looking for a job.

I was in a class called Rhetoric A. I never understood what this meant nor did I want to. After the first two periods each morning we all adjourned to the refectory for tea and apple pie. 'Could you fix me up with a tart?' was the catchphrase. Sometimes I felt I was in an English public school rather than an Irish one.

The pupils talked knowingly about religion and sex between classes. John Charles MacQuaid, the archbishop of Dublin at the time, was the butt of many of their jokes. They also talked about the problems in the North a lot. Everyone seemed to know the way out of these. Solutions were outlined in velvety tones by people who weren't yet old enough to vote. The History classes were more discussions than lectures. (Fortunately I'd given the subject up after the Inter Cert. so I didn't have to participate in these).

One night I was invited to go to a film with Bill Cunningham, another pupil in the class that I knew slightly. It was called *Satyricon* and was directed by Federico Fellini. I felt it was selected because of Fellini's reputation rather than anything particularly good about it. I didn't enjoy it and said as much to Bill when it was over. 'I don't know why not,' he said, 'I thought it was a classic.' On the way home he started talking about Albert Camus. He said 'Camus' in a way that made it rhyme with 'Seamus'. I took some small consolation in the fact that he got the pronunciation wrong.

In the middle of the year we were sent on a retreat to Milltown Park. Clive had been ordained there shortly before. Everyone sat around discussing Liberation Theology and Humanae Vitae. I didn't know Humanae Vitae from a hole in the ground. I was more accustomed to demented priests chasing me around Mayo classrooms with copies of the Penny Catechism in their hands. Towards the end of the week one of my classmates started ranting on about the destructive influence of Christianity during the Crusades. You would have got a thick ear for that in Muredach's as well.

There were debates every week in the main hall. Sometimes I went to these but they made about as much sense to me as Einstein's Theory of Relativity. Adrian Hardiman often presided at them. He was in the class ahead of me and President of the Student's Union. (He would later go on to become a High Court Judge). I was in awe of how he could develop an argument even if I didn't understand it. One night I met him in a bar and told him I was in the class behind him. He looked me up and down and said, 'So what?' For me those two words seemed to sum up my year in Belvedere. So what.

I confided a lot in Hugo at this time. He came out to the Villas every few weeks and we had chats about books and films. We didn't always have the same tastes but he had so many extravagant ideas it was always interesting talking to him. Or as was the case more often, listening. Apart from Keith he was the biggest talker in the family.

He was coming up to ordination now but he wasn't sure if he wanted to be a priest or not even after six years in the seminary. In the past year he told me he'd started writing articles in the college magazine which skated close to the wind theologically. Some of them he illustrated himself with graphic pictures. He showed me one drawing he did of Jesus on the cross that looked unusually stark. It was as if he was trying to goad the authorities into taking him on. I told him I was having problems in Belvedere as well. 'Maybe we should burn the two buildings down,' I joked.

One day I was playing a game of tennis with Hugo and Keith when Hugo said out of the blue, 'I'm leaving All Hallows.' I thought I was hearing things. Keith didn't believe him. 'The shit hit the fan during the week,' he said.

We went into the clubhouse and he told us what happened. After he'd become a deacon the previous summer he went to Georgia to work in a parish as a kind of preparation for his future. It was intensively conservative there and his progressive sermons didn't go down too well. Some of the priests also annoyed him with the vulgar personal habits they had. He saw racism there as well, and a crude celebration of wealth. When he got back to Dublin he continued writing contentious articles for the magazine but found himself being muzzled. After that there was no going back. He had a set-to with the Dean and walked out.

I asked my mother how she felt about him leaving. She said, 'I just want him to be happy.' He spent many nights explaining his decision to her. 'I didn't know who I was when I went in there,' he said. The seminary brought him out of himself by putting him into drama and public speaking but it also brought out his radical side.

One of the books that changed him was Albert Camus' *The Outsider*. He read it so much he practically knew it by heart. 'This is a book,' he said, 'about a man who's executed because he wouldn't cry at a funeral.' My mother could never understand what he meant by that. He read passages of it to her that meant even less. One of them was where Camus captured the atmosphere of a lazy Sunday by having a cat stroll across a street. He went on about this so much my mother said to me, 'I'll be dreaming about that cat yet.'

My father was more troubled about his decision to leave the priesthood. 'What's he going to do now?' he said, 'There's no money in the family if he wants to go to university. We haven't a rex.' Hugo didn't seem too bothered about where he'd go from here. He was just glad to be out of 'the madhouse'. He bought a guitar and started writing songs, accompanying himself on them with it almost every night.

A few of the other seminarians had left with him. This seemed to reassure him that he'd done the right thing. He also stayed friends with some who stayed on. One of them, Jim O'Mahony, came out to Iona Villas sometimes when we had get-togethers. One night he started showing a romantic interest in June. Hugo joked that she should stop wearing short dresses or she might endanger Jim's vocation. After Jim was ordained he became a right hand man to the bishop in Hawaii. I always felt June gave him a feeling for the exotic.

I used to love these nights where we all sat on the floor and sang songs into the small hours. Hugo and June in particular seemed to have inexhaustible repertoires. The seminarians sang different kinds of songs to the rest of us, songs with messages like 'You've Got a Friend' and 'Where Have All the Flowers Gone'. They were full of the excitement at their sudden life-change. It was as if they'd been released from prison into a new self-enlightenment. Everyone was talking about Simon & Garfunkel at the time. They also sang songs like 'Bridge Over Troubled Waters' and 'The Dangling Conversation'. It was as if they were anthems to their new identities.

Hugo started dating a lot of women now, as if to make up for the six years he'd lost in the seminary. He didn't seem to have any trouble getting them. He could talk about anything and was also very handsome. Basil used to say about himself and Clive, 'How come the two best-looking guys in the family went into the priesthood?'

He had all their names written on the wall, with phone numbers beside them in his illegible scrawl. I could never figure out how he was able to read them. Every few days one of them would be crossed off and another would take its place. He seemed to be going through them like a knife through butter. He had a book called *Women* that he dipped into. I think it was from the All Hallows library. It was as if this one book could unlock all their secrets. I'm sure it made more interesting reading than Hans Kung or Martin Heidegger.

One night as he was on his way out the door to Zhivago's discotheque I said to him, 'How did you last without female company for six years?' 'I didn't think about it,' he replied, 'It was just part of the deal.' I could never understand how anyone could make that kind of sacrifice.

When Hugo wasn't out carousing he was playing Bob Dylan songs on his guitar at ear-piercing levels at the dead of night. This used to drive Audrey crazy. She was working as a psychiatric nurse in Palmerstown now and had to be up at the crack of dawn for the long journey to the hospital.

'If you don't keep it down,' she'd say, 'I'll end up as one of my patients.' Hugo put his guitar aside and paced up and down the kitchen in his grey bellbottoms with his hands dug in his pockets. He had these big philosophical discussions with me about the meaning of life - or the last film he'd seen. He made toast at all hours, invariably burning it. He'd put it on the grill and then start singing Dylan again, usually one of his 85-verse songs, forgetting all about the toast until smoke started billowing out of the cooker. When Audrey wasn't listening to 'The Times They Are A-Changin'' at full blast she was listening to black toast being scraped at 3 a.m.

Keith had a few blow-ups with Hugo at this time. 'Why don't you get a job?' he'd say to him. Hugo would reply, 'There's time enough for that. I don't want to go from the frying pan into the fire.' Keith wasn't impressed when he went into long discussions about corruption in the church. 'You're dancing on the soutane,' he challenged, 'I don't mind you leaving the seminary but don't spoil religion for the rest of us, that's lousy.'

One night the pair of them got into an argument about plenary indulgences and Keith broke one of Hugo's guitar strings. Hugo retaliated by tearing up a religious relic Keith had in his missal. My mother came down from bed and tried to keep the peace. 'Not much has changed since you were all in short pants,' she said. She used to listen to us arguing about a penny for hours over a card game in Ballina. The next morning she'd find the penny under the table.

Hugo started a B.A. degree in U.C.D. in 1970. Keith got married that year as well. He was 33 now. 'The same age as Jesus when he was crucified,' he reminded us. Jacqueline, his wife, wasn't amused by the analogy.

He bought a house in Artane but there was a problem with the builders so he couldn't move in straight away. My mother said he could stay in the Villas with Jacqueline until it was sorted.

After coming back from his honeymoon himself and Jacqueline slept in the back bedroom. Hugo had to sleep there as well as there was no other room for him. It was hardly an ideal start to their marriage, especially when Hugo stumbled in the door in the middle of the night one time and fell over the pair of them with his guitar slung over his shoulder. (I think he was looking for someone to join him in a Dylan duet).

Hugo met Kathleen, the woman he would eventually marry, at a party the following year. We threw it for Jacinta for her 21st birthday. She'd been over and back to London repeatedly in the last few years but was now working in a cosmetics firm called Schwarzkopf in Glasnevin. Kathleen was a nurse from Westmeath who was from a family of nine like ours. She was practical by nature and an ideal partner for Hugo because he had his head in the clouds a lot of the time. I think he spent the whole party talking to her about Shakespeare. Maybe he was lucky to get a second date.

Jacinta went to America not long after the party. Ruth went to live there as well after marrying a tax consultant from New Jersey that she met at a function in the American Embassy. That meant three of the family were in America now. The rest of us were stay-at-home types, maybe too much so.

Even after Keith moved into the house in Artane he was over and back to the Villas like a boomerang. Jacqueline came with him sometimes but he was usually on his own. I had a friend called Dermot who was in the house off and on. One day he said to me as he watched Keith having a conversation with my mother, 'Is Keith not married?' I said he was but that he was visiting. Then he said, 'Was he not here last week as well, and the week before?' It was only when an outsider commented on something like this that I noticed it.

My father loved to see Keith coming over because he took him out of himself. They spent hours discussing everything from politics to racing form. Sometimes he almost missed the bus home, haring off down Hollybank Road like Ronnie Delaney to make the last 16A for Artane before half-eleven.

My father was often restless from having nothing to do all day. He didn't miss Ballina because he knew there was nothing there for him but he found it difficult to fill his time. Sometimes he wrote letters to the papers to give himself something to do but a lot of his old vivacity was slowly being drained from him. He still had the craving for drink but he was fighting it. It was easier to do that in Dublin because his old drinking acquaintances were 150 miles away in Mayo - or dead.

'They weren't bosom friends,' he'd say to me when he was in one of his cynical moods, 'just boozing ones.'

When he was in good form he used to bring me my breakfast in bed. The toast would be as black as the ace of spades and the tea was usually made from half-boiled water but I still loved these treats. I appreciated them all the more because anything in the kitchen was usually foreign to him. Shortly after he married my mother, the story went, she asked him to make her a cup of tea one day when she was sick in bed. After a few minutes he's supposed to have shouted up the stairs to her, 'The kettle is making a noise, Pat, now, what do I do next?' (My mother's first name was Patricia, which made it even more surprising that I wasn't called Patrick).

As I ate my breakfast he'd sit on the bed with his pyjamas at half-mast, giving out about something in the news or bursting out laughing at some story about his past. He spent half the night tearing articles out of newspapers, which drove my mother crazy. I don't know how she ever got a wink of sleep.

He didn't bother to dress most days. That was also his tendency in his last years in Ballina. My mother moved a bed downstairs for him and he stayed in it more often than not. He had a bell beside it that he rang when he wanted a cup of tea. If you ever went into the room he was either drinking tea or smoking. In later life he smoked a pipe more than cigarettes. He'd use nearly a full box of matches trying to light it. He threw all the spent matches into the fire but sometimes they weren't totally out and they set the mattress up in flames. He got so used to doing this he thought nothing of it. He often continued reading the paper as my mother tried to stamp them down.

He spent a lot of time phoning bookies with bets on horses. Sometimes he'd put a shilling on about twenty different nags. He hadn't a clue about anything to do with form, basing most of his choices on whether he liked the name of a particular horse or not. Other times he'd choose one simply because he'd been backing it all his life without success. 'I'd never forgive myself if it won now,' he'd joke.

He said if he got £6000 he'd be happy. He never explained why he chose that figure but he never changed it. Every now and again a cheque would come from America in a letter from Basil or Ruth or Jacinta. If there was no cheque enclosed they'd write 'M.T' on the envelope so he wouldn't get his hopes up. MT meant empty.

Basil's letters were usually photocopied and sent to every member of the family in separate envelopes. (He'd leave a line at the top blank so he could write in the name). He sent so many postcards home we wallpapered a whole wall with them once.

Jacinta's letters were equally frequent. My mother used to say that she didn't need to read them to know how she was, she just looked at the writing. If it was straight she was relaxed and if it was slanted or crooked that meant she was stressed.

Jacinta packed so much news into her letters you could hardly see the page. After she ran out of space she kept writing extra bits up and down the margins so you had to turn it sideways to read it and then maybe upside down. 'That's my exercise for the day,' my father would say after finishing one of them.

He still cracked a lot of jokes but I sensed a sadness in him despite them. I knew he pined for the past even though he dismissed it as so much idle folly. 'Memory is the only friend that grief can call its own', he'd say. Or 'Authority forgets a dying king.' He still had grand notions about himself, even if all he had was 'a room'. His heroes were people like Napoleon, Franco, Mussolini. He was also fascinated by Hitler and devoured books on him. He always admired Hitler's ability to work a crowd. He had indulged that streak in himself whenever he was in court. His strength as a solicitor had always been his court appearances. In these situations he could give full vent to his theatrical side. In Ballina they said he was so persuasive he could have got Judas off with a warning. And yet my mother usually had to give him a Valium on a day when he had a court appearance. Like most showmen he was shy at base.

As he closed in on seventy he started to think he'd die soon. He spoke of wanting to put God in the witness box and cross-examine him for the mess he'd landed us all in. Life seemed to be the one court-case he couldn't win. 'There are no damages payable by the Almighty,' he'd say, 'You can't sue the creator of the universe even if it's unsatisfactory to you. You can't subpoena him to come to court to defend Himself. He has too many alibis and all we have is circumstantial evidence.'

Some of his outpourings sounded like black comedy. 'No matter how bad you feel,' he'd say, 'don't worry because you'll be worse tomorrow.' Or: 'The only time I feel well is when I get bored of being bored.' It sounded like self-pity but his humour was always waiting to get out, barbed and all as it was.

'Happiness is a man called Joe,' was another one of his epigrams. ' In his sardonic fashion he accepted the fact that life was a tragedy, that we were all stuck in this vale of tears together to make of it what we would, either by sinking or swimming. Or, in his own case, drowning himself in a sea of whiskey and stale beer.

Expanding Frontiers

The main place I played snooker when I came to Dublin was a dingy club in O'Connell Street called the Cosmo. It was located in a basement. There wasn't even a sign for it on the street. You walked down a stone staircase and pounded on a door to get in.

It was the biggest hall I'd ever seen in my life. There were over a dozen tables and two huge one-armed bandits just inside the entrance. The first time I walked in, the smell of cigarette smoke and coffee was so strong it almost knocked me out. It was also very quiet, like a church. You could hear nothing but the pock of the balls or an expletive or hoarse laugh. The plaster was peeling off the walls and the tiles on the floor were cracked. It was a lived-in place, a bit like the Hibs but much more impersonal to me.

A little old man with a patch over one eye came up to me that first day and asked me what I wanted. I told him I was just looking around but he said that wasn't allowed so I asked for a table. When he brought the balls over to me I put the reds in a triangle in the middle of the table and started to hit them all over the place.

It was like coming off cold turkey for me, this simple action. It put me in mind of the Hibs. I wondered who would be there now, insulting one another over a missed pot or a faulty stance, doctoring the scoreboard or upping the ante after a best-of-five.

The Cosmo regarded itself as high class even though it was falling to bits. A sign on one of the tables read, 'This Hall is Reserved for Players Who Take the Game Seriously.' That would have been laughed at in the Hibs. There was no personal touch in the club but it still became a sanctuary for me in my early years in Dublin, a reminder of what I'd left behind me. I went in there many days after school and soaked myself in its atmosphere. There was something reassuring in the way the light shone on the rectangle of green, the quietness that blocked out everything outside. It seemed to act as a kind of stability for me, a home from home.

Sometimes between frames I asked the old man with the eye patch for a cup of coffee. As we sat together I looked at the pictures on the wall. Most of them were drawings of snooker players from the past that I didn't recognise but they gave the place a sense of history for me. I wondered how many hundreds of frames of snooker had been played here, how many hundreds of players had nurtured dreams of making the big time, people who might have been local legends on these tables but unknown outside a two-mile radius of them.

The better I got to know the other people in the club the more I began to play with them. Most of them were wily old warhorses who'd have sold their mothers down the river to win a point but they still had an attraction for me. They were like characters from a

Damon Runyon novel. Many of them were unemployed so they had a lot more time to practise. Some of them were taxi-drivers and played well past midnight, waiting for the discos to disgorge their revellers. Occasionally we'd get journalists in for a quick game between shifts in the nearby offices of the *Irish Times* or the *Independent*.

This was different for me than playing in Ballina. I liked the fact that nobody knew me personally. Because of that fact I started using a different name. I called myself Peter and began to take on a new identity almost immediately. It was as if the name freed me up to be more in tune with my real self. All the Victorian bullshit that went with being Aubrey de Vere Patrick Dillon-Malone evaporated and gave birth to a new creation who could tough it out with these hardchaws on their own terms.

As was the case with the Hibs, I started to get too fond of the Cosmo after a while. It was a dump but that was part of the charm. The fact that it stayed open all night meant it was somewhere you could retreat to like any other sun-hater, joining your fellow vampires underground.

Some of the players were on the fringes of crime. One day I came into the club after buying a pair of cowboy boots, a fad I was going through at the time. I was getting ready to start a game when one of the regulars told me there was a call for me on the phone in a pub nearby. I was on my way out when I thought: How could there be a call for me when nobody knew my real name? I turned back to see the man who'd given me the message taking up the boots in his hands. The irony was that lying about my name had been a benefit. 'I was going to put them behind the counter for you,' he reassured me.

We got a lot of down-and-outs in as well. Another night during a game I heard a noise from under the table, the sound of a man clearing his throat. It was after midnight so I was a bit confused. 'Don't worry,' the man I was playing with said to me, 'that's just Bob.' It turned out Bob was a homeless person who had nowhere else to sleep. A few minutes later I heard him snoring.

Fights often broke out with people who came in from the pubs after closing time. One night a man knocked over one of the one-armed bandits for no other reason than that he felt like doing so. The guards were called and he was led away. Normal service was resumed afterwards. All the man I was playing with said to me was, 'Whose shot is it?' As we resumed playing we could hear the police siren screeching through the night.

Sometimes I wandered out of the club at four in the morning and saw people outside the door that seemed to be making drug deals. There were some suspicious characters in the Hibs but nothing compared to here. It was like the flipside of life the stuffiness of

Belvedere. Somehow I doubted I'd run into any of my classmates there. They'd sooner have gone to Beirut.

The streets were usually empty as I walked home except for a few taxis prowling around the streets like gigantic spiders. I loved going down by Bachelor's Walk and looking at the neon sign for Donnelly's sausages. It had a man flipping the sausages from a pan. There was a separate bulb every few feet so it looked like the sausages were moving. Afterwards I walked up by Dorset Street and Whitworth Road and over by the iron bridge at Claude Hall before coming out at the church on Iona Road. Often when I got to the Villas it would be nearly dawn. Now and then I even met the milkman on his rounds.

My parents disapproved of me being out at such hours but by now I was breaking away from their shell. It was as if my emotions had been sucked out of me by leaving Ballina. Suddenly I didn't care what I did or didn't do. Sometimes I walked all the way into the club after midnight. The next day I'd sit slumped over my seat in Belvedere in a half-daze as I listened to forty well-heeled Dubliners discuss the perils of bourgeois society.

As we came towards the Leaving Cert I gave up snooker for a while and knuckled down to my work. I wasn't arriving into school with my eyes falling out of my head now and was able to give myself to the job in hand. I filled my mind with data and vomited it out in examination halls before forgetting it all immediately afterwards. I always seemed to have the ability to do that. It was like putting material into the disc of my brain and then erasing it just as suddenly. If I had to do the same exams a day later the answer-sheets would have been blank.

There was one part of the exam where we were guaranteed a question on the sociology of our time. I prepared a general essay and learned it off in English, Irish and French. I basically wrote the same essay three times, taking care to make minor adjustments so that the title of the essay appeared to be adhered to. I don't think anybody noticed as I ended up getting four Honours.

That was enough to get me into university but I didn't know what I wanted to do there. Ireland had just joined the Common Market and Keith felt accountancy would be a profitable career for me. He was an accountant himself in a firm in Finglas called Unidare but he hated it. He had an ulcer from the stress. It seemed like strange logic to me. 'Most people hate their jobs,' he reasoned, 'so you might as well pick one that pays you to be miserable.'

I applied to the Accountancy faculty without much conviction. I could have stuck a pin in any of the other ones on the noticeboard and felt as enthusiastic about it. With the exception of Medicine – I'd sooner have put lighted matches under my fingernails than that.

For the next year I got the Number 10 bus out to Belfield every day. (The question of where to park Tina's bike didn't arise). Basil described the campus as an architectural monstrosity but I didn't mind that. Its blandness relaxed me. He did his degree in Earlsfort Terrace where everything was more intimate and as a result thought moving the university out to the sticks was insane but that aspect of it didn't bother me. I just wanted to drift back into the woodwork like I'd done in Belvedere.

The only thing that made UCD different from Belvedere was the number of pretty girls in the class. Chauvinist that I was, I was surprised to learn that women could actually be good at subjects like Maths and Economics. Or maybe it was just that my four sisters hated anything mathematical and I was generalising from that.

One day during a lecture I was chatting to a friend when the lecturer stopped talking and looked up at me. 'Silence!' he said, rapping his desk with a cane. I gasped in shock. It was like being back in school.

I boycotted his lectures afterwards in protest. They were mostly useless to me anyway. I worked better from books in the library rather than taking down notes from some self-satisfied talking head.

The year dragged on interminably. I had no social life to speak of, my head swimming with figures. I buried my head in books heavier than the telephone directory and memorised whatever data I thought I needed. If the subject matter interested me it might have been bearable but it didn't. I would have preferred to be at the dentist. When I was informed I'd passed all my exams I greeted the news passively. I couldn't see myself carrying on with this mental torture for two more years, let alone for life.

I spent the summer working in an Irish pub in London. It was called The Blackstock Hotel but it was more like a tip. Hugo was supposed to go instead of me but he spent so much of the year partying he failed his exams and had to stay in Dublin for the repeats. He was set to go to London with a classmate of his, Chris. Chris heard about the job from a priest he knew and I fell into the empty slot.

Chris and myself shared a room in the hotel for the summer. I'd known him slightly in Dublin. He was fascinated by literature and was rarely without a book under his arm. He spent a lot of time talking about W.B. Yeats as he'd grown up in Gort, which was in the heart of Yeats country.

On our second night in the pub the head barman robbed the till and gave the manager two black eyes on his way out. He was well out of sight before the police arrived. We learned later that he was a fugitive from a psychiatric institution in Scotland.

The building we were working in was condemned. Some nights I thought I felt it shaking. Chris told me that was probably a result of my drinking. I'd never touched a drop of alcohol in Ireland before coming over but on my first night off in the pub I positioned myself on the other side of the counter and knocked back six glasses of bitter in record time. That set a trend. I spent all my days off afterwards outside the same counter, exchanging stories with the Irish emigrants who'd come over to work on the buildings because there was nothing at home. Now and then a barrel would need to be changed so I'd be called on to go down to the cellar and do that before resuming drinking duties.

I was earning the princely sum of £11 a week. That included my board and food. A pint of Smithwick's was 19p and Harp was 25p. For £1 you could get drunk and still have change for a Cornish pasty (which we also sold).

After the pub closed every night we gathered around the counter for some private drinking. The conversation usually turned to the Troubles in the North, about which I knew very little. The manager asked me for my views on internment but I didn't have any. I hardly knew what the word meant. One of the other barmen said he believed the whole population of Ulster, both Catholic and Protestant, should be put in a boat and shipped off to a desert island and left there. Everyone seemed to think this was a suggestion of remarkable genius so another round was called for to celebrate it.

The manager was gay. He had a reputation of coming on to his staff. 'If you drop a bar of soap in the shower,' Chris warned me, 'don't bend down to pick it up.' It was difficult to relax knowing he slept in a room two doors down from me. One of the regular customers, Keith, was also gay. He showed me a scar that ran across his stomach. It came from one of his boyfriends. He accused him of being unfaithful to him and lunged at him one night with a Stanley knife.

I asked Keith if he'd ever been attracted to a woman. 'I tried to make love to a bird once,' he said, 'but I ended up throwing up all over her.' That was the end of that conversation.

Work began at dawn and went on until the last customer was booted out. I reckoned we worked over sixty hours a week – for slave wages. You were also expected to serve Guinness slops, a health hazard. I refused to do that and earned the manager's wrath as a result. He had it in for me after that. 'How do you think I'm going to pay you if you don't do what I ask?' he said. Some nights I saw him watering the whiskey before he served it to customers who were too drunk to know the difference.

He accused me of being too conversant with the customers. 'Just get the lolly,' he said, 'there's no need to hear their life stories. While you're talking to one person, two or three have come and gone to another bar for want of service.' This was nonsense because there were always at least two other barmen on duty. He probably sensed my insecurity in what was my first job and was playing on that. I decided it was better not to confront him. We didn't talk unless it was something to do with the work. During my breaks I avoided him like the plague, spending most of my time with the other barmen.

Most of them were Irish or second generation Irish. Some were just off the boat like myself. These were the ones he recruited from the priest in Dublin that Chris knew.

Others wore the scars of broken lives. Many of them had drink problems. They had little love of the work, putting in the hours solely for the money. I watched them going up to their rooms on Fridays with their little brown paypackets in their hands, working out what had to be sent where. I hoped I'd never find myself in that position in life but I feared I would.

One man I became friendly with was running away from a bad marriage; another was in trouble with the law. Both of them sought solace in the haven of the pub like I did. This was where the real stories of our lives were unleashed, the din of juke-box music replaced by so many whispered confessions in the snug.

Some nights I lowered the better part of a bottle of whiskey listening to such confessions. I felt privileged at being chosen to witness such intimate revelations but the following day I always felt guilty if I heard too much. I tried to lose myself in chores to take my mind off them. In this way work, even boring work, became therapy.

The worst part of the day was the time before the first customers came in. We had to wash glasses until they were so clean you could read the newspaper through them. The manager was rarely satisfied with my efforts in this regard.

Another thing he didn't like was if he caught you reading when you were supposed to be working. Jacinta sent me a letter one day and he spotted me looking at it through a secret mirror he'd put at the end of the bar for such a purpose. He blew a cylinder head gasket at this, even threatening to sack me as a result.

Every Tuesday we had to get fish from a shop on the far end of Seven Sisters Road. Chris and myself always fought over who'd get to go. Both of us loved the idea of getting out of the pub for the half hour for a walk. Chris usually swung it. It was left to me to stay behind and open the 'pearly gates' for the first few stragglers.

Sometimes a beautiful woman would come in and we'd all rush to serve her. We weren't much good at keeping our attractions subtle. I found it easier to talk to English girls than Irish ones. They were less shy and weren't put out by my own shyness. Maybe I was an antidote to the cocky cockneys they were more used to talking to. They seemed to enjoy my accent but after a conversation it was difficult to know what to do next. It was hard to date anyone when you were living in. Where would you bring them? The manager didn't like any of his staff venturing into the West End because he felt we'd be bleary-eyed the next morning at work.

One night when I went to a disco I came home to find myself locked out. It was only after about twenty minutes of rapping on the door I managed to attract the attention of one of the other barmen.

He threw a key down to me from his room but when I got inside the manager was there waiting for me. He didn't say anything but I felt as if I'd committed a crime.

I didn't go dancing for a long time after that. It was made clear to me that I was employed as little more than Paddy slave labour. We were also meant to live like monks in our spare time.

As punishment I was marshalled even more closely in the following days. Faults were picked with how I filled a pint. The glasses I washed were held up to the light and examined meticulously for blemishes. As the summer went on I could see why my predecessor gave the manager two black eyes. I was often tempted to blacken them again.

One night soon afterwards I saw the film *Love Story* in one of the local cinemas and promptly fell head over heels in love with Ali MacGraw. I even fell in love with her name in the film: Jennifer Cavaleri. The fact that she died in it made it more emotional still. As soon as Ryan O'Neal said, 'What can you say about a 25-year-old girl who died' I was gone. When I came out of the cinema I was walking into walls. I must have seen the film about five times altogether. Or not seen it five times. I decided the woman I was going to marry had to have long hair parted in the middle.

Hugo flew over to London at the end of August. He had done his Psychology repeats and was anxious to have some fun. He said he was envious of me having had the summer in London but I told him he didn't miss much, that you'd have more excitement in a nunnery. After closing time we stayed at the bar and knocked back pints and shorts. He talked a lot about Freud, about how he was as relevant today as ever. One of the other barmen said, 'Wasn't that lad the sex maniac?'

When the results of the exam were due Hugo sent a postcard to Keith with a question mark on it. That was his way if asking if he'd got it. Keith sent one back with an exclamation mark. Hugo knew what he meant. It was probably the shortest conversation they ever had. (It's a pity they couldn't have kept up such economical modes of communication since).

Buoyed up with enthusiasm, Hugo asked me if I'd be interested in nipping over to France with him for a few weeks before the Uni opened. I was all on for it. He'd seen an ad for grapepickers in Bordeaux so that's where we made for. I didn't say goodbye to the manager. If I never saw him again it would be too soon.

We got the boat for France and a bus south from Normandy. It broke down half way to Bordeaux and we had to hitch the last part of the journey. We didn't mind that, we had no deadline to meet. One night we slept at a petrol station slumped over a gardening chair. The next we spent in an abandoned car down an alley.

When we got to the vineyard we must have looked like two tramps. The *patron* looked at us as if we had two heads but that was only because we had no French. When Hugo took the ad out of his pocket he went 'Oui, oui!' and ushered us into the farmhouse.'

We spent the next fortnight working our backs off from dawn till dusk and then guzzling the free wine our employers provided every evening as we danced in the village square. We were given a rickety little house to live in. It had only one room downstairs but that was all you needed. Each day at about six a.m., the son of the man we were working for almost kicked in the door to wake us up. Then we were driven to the vineyard.

The dew on the bushes looked like jewellery in the early light. They were freezing when you touched them so we asked for gloves. After we got into our working clothes we were given a set of secateurs each. We clipped with them until our arms almost fell off. At the end of each day we stood on top of the truck dancing on the grapes and stuffing our faces with them.

If you were a slow cutter your colleagues from the surrounding bushes all broke off from their rows to help you catch up – or to embarrass you. The boy who nearly took the door off the hinges every morning patrolled the vineyard on an old motorbike as if he was a supervisor checking your progress. If you said anything to him he just grunted. I tried to speak to him in my pidgin French and he replied in pidgin English. He didn't want conversation, he just wanted his grapes picked.

One night his father invited us round to the farmhouse for a meal. The table was done up like something out of the court of Louis Quatorze. There must have been twenty different varieties of cheese on display. Hugo and myself sampled as many of them as we could. We knew now what people meant when they said, 'The French live to eat whereas other nationalities eat to live.' At the end of the evening we could hardly stand up.

On the last night of our stay we were given a few extra bottles of wine. Hugo started to talk about how much he was enjoying his Arts degree after all those years in the 'priest factory'. He said I should give up Accountancy and go into Arts. 'You're not cut out for it,' he said. Did I need to come to France to learn that?

Up until now, all English had been to me was a subject I'd studied because I had to. In Muredach's I was given lines of poetry to learn off without having a clue what they meant. I'd got notes on prose essays to learn off in the same way. Enjoyment didn't come into it. But now I was talking about things I was interested in.

When I got back to Dublin I dropped out of Commerce and signed up for Arts. They gave me an exemption in Maths because it was a common subject to both faculties. That meant I had only two subjects to do, English and Philosophy. That gave me more time for dossing, and Arts was a doss anyway.

Most of the first term I spent in the Belfield bar, playing pool and getting drunk. I said to Hugo, 'After Christmas maybe you'll show me where the library is.'

Studying Philosophy after Accountancy was like going from Auschwitz to Butlin's Holiday Camp. We had great fun in the Belfield bar wondering if we really existed or not. We said things to one another like, 'Did I just come from a lecture or was it just in my mind? Do my lectures exist?' 'Maybe I'm not even having this conversation. Is there a me?' It went on and on. We were being childish but we made no apology for it.

Most of us went around talking about existentialism as if we invented it. We scratched metaphorical pimples and said 'I drink, therefore I am.' Then we went dancing at the Belfield Craze and tried to impress equally disaffected young women with our pretentiousness – even ones who didn't look like Ali MacGraw.

One of my lecturers was Desmond Connell, who went to become the Archbishop of Dublin. He used to go into pensive reveries as he discussed the finer points of Thomistic theology. During one of his lectures he told us about a philosopher who went to sleep one night and dreamt he was a mouse. When he woke up he couldn't make up his mind if he was a man who dreamt he was a mouse or if he was a mouse who dreamt he was a man. This led to a spirited discussion in the Belfield bar afterwards as myself and my fellow imbibers went down on all fours and started scuttling around on the floor to find out if we were truly men or mice. The truth of the matter was that we were neither: we were just idiots.

Was this supposed to be study? If it was I thought I could get used to it. At least if I didn't succumb to cirrhosis of the liver before graduation. We treated the lectures as preludes to the night's revelry. Debates were conducted about how many angels could dance on the head of a pin and then slumped home to the suburbs to sleep off the effects of beer.

Sometimes after a late night I wrote notes to my mother with messages like 'Wake me at two, I have a lecture.' Ballina had engrained this nocturnal lifestyle in me and university continued it. I hated going to bed early. It was as if you were letting the day away with something. My mind seemed to come alive after midnight. There were no distractions then. You could commune with your real self.

Our most noteworthy lecturer was Denis Donoghue. He was an authority on literary classics. He swept into the room like a ghost, as tall as a basketball player and whip-thin. The lectures were like extended poems, delivered in his urbane rhetoric. Most of us didn't have a clue what he was talking about but his classes were always full. 'Mind-blowing,' we'd say, 'truly mind-blowing.' But our notepads were usually empty after he'd departed the rostrum. It was like The Emperor's New Clothes. He could have been the greatest fraud on earth and got away with it. None of us wanted to admit we were stumped by him.

One of the people in my class was Harry Clifton, who went on to become a highly acclaimed poet. He was submitting his writing to David Marcus of the *Irish Press* when I knew him. 'The scrounger only gives me £2 a poem,' he complained, 'It's hardly the Guggenheim Fellowship.' But the thrill of seeing one's name in print couldn't be priced.

Harry and myself did night security work on the docks together at that time. We only earned pin money but a big perk was the fact that you could sleep on the job. We even brought our alarm clocks into the office with us. Anyone who tried to rob any of the premises we guarded would have had an easy time because we'd probably have been snoring like pigs as they made off with the loot.

One night when I was supposed to be minding a place I went off to the pictures instead on my bicycle. When I got back the boss of the premises was standing there waiting for me looking like thunder. 'Did you have a good time?' he asked me before handing me my walking papers.

That was the end of my night security work but I could hardly complain. I missed the money more than the mice that used to run up and down my sleeping bag every time I tried to grab forty winks.

America

In the summer of 1972 I went to Connecticut and stayed with Basil after the university closed down. He was renting a huge house outside the town of Stratford. A friend of mine from the university called Dom Hackett came with me. He had also been with me in Belvedere but I didn't really get to know him until I went to UCD. Dom and myself couldn't get a job for the first few weeks so we just sat around the house playing music and drinking beer. Dom looked older than me so he was able to get drink at the off-licence. Neither of us really cared if we got a job or not. We just soaked ourselves in the luxury of the house.

There was a painting of a flamenco dancer in the main room but the face hadn't been painted in. Basil told me it had been done by his last room-mate. He'd left in a hurry because the police were after him for non-payment of debts. I asked Basil why he kept the unfinished painting on display. 'It's a great conversation piece', he said, 'If it had a face on it nobody would ever ask me about my exciting room-mate.'

We weren't supposed to be in the house so whenever the landlady called we had to hide in a cupboard. One night Basil threw a party and about a dozen people showed up. Most of them were too drunk to drive home so they slept on the floor or any available beds. The next morning the landlady was passing by and she saw all the cars in the driveway. When she called to the door Basil said to her, 'I'm having some people for breakfast' but I don't think she was convinced.

There were three other tenants in the house besides himself. The one we saw most was Paul Linton, a student from a well-to-do family in Philadelphia. He didn't talk to us much and looked disturbed a lot of the time. If you asked him a question he just said, 'What's your fuckin' problem?'

The second tenant we called Captain America because he wore trousers with stars and stripes on them. He used to get into these big discussions about legalising pot and about how nicotine was much more dangerous for you. He reminded me of someone out of a Peter Fonda movie. The third tenant was also called Paul. He had been married but divorced his wife when he realised he was bisexual. He was now dating a tennis instructor from Idaho.

I slept with Basil in a water bed for the whole summer. I'd never seen one of these in Ireland but they were quite trendy in the States. Basil said they were good for your back. That was fine in theory but the bed moved so much I could never relax in it. What was the point of having a healthy back if you were awake all night? I never really got a good night's sleep on it. If either of us coughed or sneezed it was about five minutes before it stopped moving. Even turning onto your back caused a big commotion.

Another thing that worried me was the possibility of a flood. Basil had the electric sockets in the room on the skirting boards. 'What happens if the water leaks out?' I asked him one night, 'Will we be electrocuted?' He just laughed. 'You worry too much,' he said. I was always nervous of electricity because Hugo had nearly been electrocuted as a child. He put his hand on a socket once and started to scream. It was as if his hand was glued to it. Keith grabbed him by the waist and pulled him away. He probably saved his life by doing that.

At night-time we used to go out drinking to a little bar a few miles away called Esther's Hacienda. They had a pool table there that I was drawn to, and some very pretty girls that I was drawn to even more. I think I proposed marriage to about a half dozen of them before the summer was out. One night I saw two really attractive women talking to each other at the bar and I asked one of them if she'd like to dance. She started to giggle at me and I wondered why. A few minutes later I saw her wrapped around her female friend, kissing her passionately. It wasn't the kind of thing that would have happened in Ballina.

Some nights we just sat in watching TV. I'd never seen so many stations in my life, having grown up on one or two channels, or none. Here you could watch about thirty movies a week. Keith would have been in his element. The only downside was the ads. Every few minutes whatever you were watching broke off for 'A message from our sponsors'. One ad in particular struck me. It said: 'Divorces From $50 Up.'

One night when we were watching a Paul Newman movie Basil told me Newman lived nearby. He said if you drove by his house on Saturday mornings you could see him out mowing the lawn. I thought I'd pass on that delight. I preferred to think of him as 'Fast' Eddie Felson in *The Hustler* taking on Minnesota Fats in the dark gloom of a seedy pool hall.

We spent a lot of our time in Stratford even though there wasn't much to do there. It was probably like every other small town in America. Everything was bland and plastic and the sun shone continually. At the edge of the town there was a massive theatre where they had Shakespeare plays on all the time, in homage to Stratford-on-Avon. I didn't go to any of them. I was no great fan of Shakespeare since Muredach's. The college had almost succeeded in turning me off him for life.

One weekend we drove to New York to see my mother's cousin Valerie, a widow who was living in an apartment with her son George. George had just come up from Washington where he'd had a bad car accident. He was driving home from a drugstore one night when a criminal on the way from a heist crashed into him. The funny thing was that the criminal sued George for dangerous driving rather than the other way round. (George was going about twenty miles an hour at the time).

There was a car around the back of the house that the tenant who painted the flamenco dancer had left behind him and I drove it up to Stratford sometimes, usually on the wrong side of the road (and without a driving licence). One day I had a near thing on the motorway and Basil confined me to barracks after that. He said to just drive it around the huge garden at the back of the house, part of which was tarmacked. I contented myself with doing figure eights there with Dom. The problem was that there was a 30-foot drop at the end of the garden.

'Don't go near the edge,' Basil warned me but one day I was reversing in a circular pattern when the steering wheel slipped out of my hand. The car careered back towards the drop and I thought I was a goner. Two wheels went over the ledge but the chassis somehow got stuck on the tarmac because it was at an angle. If I hadn't been going in a circle it would probably have toppled over. 'That's the end of your driving career,' Basil informed me.

After weeks of hanging around looking for work I ended up getting two jobs on the same day. One was with a building firm and the other as a busboy in a restaurant. They could hardly have been more different. Every evening at tea-time I'd wipe the grime off my hands and dress up in my busboy's uniform to bring food to the diners in the restaurant. After a while I was too exhausted to keep the two jobs on the go so I gave up the restaurant one. Dom got a job in a hamburger place the same week. He started dating a girl from Waterbury that he met there and we didn't see too much of him after that.

I worked hard for the building firm but it was enjoyable because we were in different places every week. One week we spraypainted a whole school. The son of the boss did most of the work. He was decked out like an astronaut to stop the spray getting into his lungs. He stood on a trolley and we pushed it down corridors where huge areas of glass had been blocked out by masking tape. When it was finished we all went into the gym and swung on the ropes. The next week we demolished the buildings behind a sports ground, knocking walls down with hammers and then throwing the rubble out a window onto a truck. After that we moved furniture and buffed floors in an orphanage. You never knew where you were going to be from one day to the next.

One of the men I worked with had a cast over his foot the whole summer. We called him Skil for some reason I can't remember. He was a big drinker, spending most of his evenings in the ginmill, as he called it. 'I got smashed one night and closed the door of the truck on it,' he told me. He was so drunk he wasn't even aware his foot was hanging out on the side. He hopped around the place all summer with torn ligaments but they didn't seem to bother him.

Skil taught me how to 'shoot' beer. This was done by puncturing a hole in the bottom of the can. You then held the other end at your mouth and when you jerked the ringpull it shot down your throat furiously and gave you a big hit. (I later heard someone had died doing this in another State).

Some nights Skil used to go to a place called Steak & Brew which gave you unlimited drink for a set charge. This was a chain that was all over the States. In the end they had to refuse him entry. He drank so much he even exceeded their 'unlimited' amount.

After being barred from Steak & Brew he did most of his drinking with us. I gave him a bottle of Irish whiskey one day when he covered for me on a shift and he didn't turn up for work for three days afterwards. He was one of the best workmen I ever saw but he drank whatever he earned. His wife walked out on him in the middle of the summer but he didn't seem too upset. All he cared about was earning enough to slake his thirst that night. 'I only work from the neck down,' he liked to tell people. It was a pity because if it wasn't for his problem he could have been running the company.

He was supposed to be my supervisor but he let me away with murder. Any time I wanted a breather all I had to do was go down to the local off-licence and buy a six-pack of Schlitz. As long as you paid for it yourself he'd let you have a 'liquid break.' We'd have three cans each and shoot the breeze. I learned more about him in these sessions than I knew about my own family. The day I left the job for good I gave him another bottle of whiskey. I doubt it lasted the night.

Hugo came over to see us soon after that. He arrived without notice just like he'd done in London. Clive paid us a visit at the same time. He was on sabbatical from Africa to study Theology at Fordham University in New York. Basil didn't tell me they were there. I was walking home from work one night and he stopped his car in front of me and beeped the horn. When I looked in the window I thought I was seeing things when I spotted the pair of them in the back seat. Clive was in mufti. It was the first time I'd ever seen him without his priest's collar. He had a check jacket and a big tie with a diamond design on it. 'I like the tie,' was all I could think to say. He said Basil gave it to him. I sat in the car and we drove back to the house. Keith was the only brother missing now from the five of us. It was like having Ballina in Connecticut.

We had a few drinks and I started talking about having the two jobs going together for a while. Clive said, 'What is it with you and all these odd jobs anyway?' He always thought of me as a scholar, full stop. Maybe I was but I got more out of doing things that didn't come natural to me than things that did. It meant more to me to be able to fix a rusty hinge on an old door than to pen any number of M.A. theses.

Hugo's first impression of Stratford was the brightness of everyone's clothes. 'Maybe you only think that because you spent so much time in the seminary,' I suggested. 'No,' he said, 'People in Ireland go around in dark clothes wherever you are. It suits the national feeling of gloom.'

He was also surprised at the way everyone shouted at each other in America instead of just talking. He came up with the reason for this after a few weeks. 'It's because the rooms are so big everywhere,' he said. 'If you spoke at the normal volume you wouldn't be heard because you're so far away from everyone.' (Maybe that was where the phenomenon of the 'loud' American came from).

We spent a lot of time together over the next few weeks. He loved wandering down to Stratford for a pizza and meeting the locals. Whatever story they told him, he was all ears. He would have talked to a lamp-post. He came home every evening with some new revelation or insight about life in the Land of Opportunity. Free of the cloisters of All Hallows he was like a child opening up his eyes to a new cosmos.

He had a battered old copy of *King Lear* in his pocket and every now and then he'd whip it out and read a soliloquy from it. He was preparing to direct it in Belfield in the autumn for a theatre group he was involved with. At night he acted out scenes for Basil and myself. Basil would usually be reading *Time* magazine or cutting articles out of magazines that he planned to send to people. Paul Linton just squatted on the floor and gazed into space.

Towards the end of the summer Basil brought us to see Neil Diamond at an open air concert in Saratoga Springs. He looked like Elvis in a white jumpsuit. Elvis himself was appearing in Las Vegas that year. It would have been the icing on the cake to see him but Basil couldn't get off work.

A friend of mine from Muredach's called Gerry Cowley was working in Philadelphia so I wrote to him asking if he'd be interested in going with me. He said it would be too expensive but that he heard of a scheme where you could drive a car from New York to San Francisco for someone who wanted one out there and then drive another one back from San Francisco to New York for someone else. All it would cost was the petrol, or gas as they called it. I was interested in this but we needed four people to make it work and we couldn't find another two. I thought of jumping on a Greyhound bus to go and see him but Basil said that would have been insane, that I mightn't even get tickets for the show when I got there.

This was one of the most memorable summers of my life. In some ways it was the year I grew up. America had been a huge part of my life from all my years watching Hollywood movies in the

Estoria and now I'd seen it for real. It wasn't as glamorous as the movies and songs portrayed it to be but what country could be? In some ways its ordinary side appealed to me more. On my last day in the house I looked out the back window at the car I'd written off. It was still dangling over where I'd left it, three of its wheels on the asphalt and the fourth hovering in mid-air over the 30-foot chasm.

The following summer I went to Washington D.C., this time working as a janitor in an apartment complex where Audrey and Jacinta were staying. The building was shaped like a giant Y. It had 13 floors but the 13th one was called the 14th because nobody wanted to live on a 13th floor. The room numbers went from 1200 to 1400.

Audrey was nursing in the Walter Reed Hospital. She got me the job because she'd nursed the wife of the manager of the complex when she broke her arm. He didn't realise I was staying in the building as well as working there. I had to dodge him like I'd dodged the landlady of the house in Stratford the summer before.

It was nice not to have to use public transport to get to work. Every morning I just took the elevator down to my little station, often being complimented for my punctuality. Things got more complicated when I went on unofficial breaks up to the apartment to watch TV. I was enjoying *Bonnie and Clyde* one night when a tenant's tap was left on and flooded the floor of her apartment. The boss tried to page me but I had the pager turned off. In desperation he called to the apartment and I had the misfortune to answer the door. I was in my bare feet and was munching a chocolate chip cookie. It took some explaining.

Another day I took the elevator up to the wrong floor. All the corridors looked exactly the same on each floor so when I opened the door of the apartment I got the shock of my life because there was no furniture in it. All I could see in the whole room was a phone on the floor. I thought we'd been burgled but it turned out I was in C411 instead of C311. We all had a laugh about that afterwards.

I didn't mind the work but the weather was a killer. It was so hot it sapped my energy. If you were working you had to stay indoors. On my days off all I could do was lie under the sun like a vegetable. One day I went up to the roof of the building to sun myself and fell asleep. When I woke up I was burned to a cinder. My skin was on fire and my ankles swollen up like balloons. I must have been five hours under the sun's rays. Every step I took was agony. Audrey and Jacinta managed to get me to a bed. If anyone touched me I screamed with the pain for the next week. I couldn't work so I had to own up to the boss about where I was staying.

I expected him to give me my walking papers but he didn't. When I went back to work I was demoted to the basement. Going from C311 to here was like going from heaven to hell. I shovelled up garbage the residents of the complex threw down chutes from each floor onto a steel ramp. Bottles would come hurtling down at all times of the day. Sometimes they shattered into smithereens, almost taking my eye out. I had to shovel it all together and then pitch it into a machine and tie it up with wire. When you pressed a button it was compressed it into a rectangle. Then you pressed another one and it was hoisted into the air by a pulley and put into a dumpster. It was a lousy job because the place was infested with beetles and rats. After a while I felt I was almost on first name terms with them.

Most of the other janitors were black. It was strange being in the minority as a 'honkie' but they were always friendly to me. 'Just don't say the 'N' word when you're talking to us,' was the only restriction they placed on our relationship. We smuggled in six-packs of Coors sometimes when the manager was away and had informal parties with dancing and soul music. They had a natural grace and breeding. Even when they were telling me to do something it was done delicately. They'd never say, 'Close the door.' It was always, 'How about closing the door, man?' Details like that impressed me.

They thought I took the job too seriously. One night the main janitor saw me sweeping the floor furiously and he let out a screech. 'Listen, man,' he said, 'there ain't no such thing as clean dirt.' It changed my attitude.

Jacinta was working in the Irish Embassy now. (Her visa had expired so she was blocked from getting any other job). This was a coincidence because Ruth had been in the American Embassy in Dublin for years. Basil joked that the reason so little diplomatic business was done between America and Ireland during those years was because Ruth and Jacinta were always on the phone to each other, clogging up the lines so the politicians couldn't get through.

After getting into the embassy Jacinta started dating Dan, a happy-go-lucky male nurse from Texas. He was working in the hospital with Audrey. Audrey was dating Dan's room-mate, Floyd, a student doctor. Dan came over to the apartment most days after work and threw himself on the sofa to watch TV.

He called Jacinta 'Jackie'. That made her more American for me. She tried to get him to study so he could get into hospital administration but he wasn't really interested. 'Chill out,' he'd say to her if she was working around the apartment, 'You Irish girls don't know how to enjoy life.' He thought I was too serious and read too much. He was always pinching Jacinta's bottom and winking at me. Then he'd go over and help himself to something from the fridge. She said she was going to put a lock on it if he kept up at that.

Audrey had a bad car accident at the end of the summer and got whiplash as a result. She was in traction for weeks and in agonising pain. After she got out of hospital she went back to Dublin. It was a pity because she really liked Washington but her time in hospital took all the good out of it for her. 'It's true what they say,' she admitted, 'Nurses make the worst patients.'

I came home soon after her and got back into my studies. I was in the final year of my degree now and the lustre was going out of it. Too much time studying books made them seem like work no matter how well they were written. I found myself going into such detail about masterpieces that they became tiresome; it was like dissecting corpses.

A few months into the new term I noticed a lump on my neck and went down to the doctor with it. He had only to take one look at it before he referred me to a specialist. . It turned out to be a TB gland. I thought I might have got it from my work in the basement of the apartment complex in Washington. (For that I had the lady with the overflowing sink to thank). I had it removed surgically and got the all-clear afterwards but I was put on tablets for a year and Audrey had to give me an injection of streptomycin into my hip once a week as well. I tried to inject myself to save Audrey the trouble but I didn't make a good job of it. I would have made a very poor junkie.

I got my B.A. in 1974. Everyone was getting excited about the graduation ceremony but I failed to share the enthusiasm. All I did was read some books and regurgitate them. The people who deserved the mortarboards, I thought, were the writers of the books we read - or the parents who paid our university fees.

I had no idea what I wanted to do so I applied for an M.A. It was really just a way of postponing going out into the 'real' world. There were only six of us in the class and I didn't particularly like the other five. I felt they were too precious about their studies. The tutors weren't much better. In our tutorials I felt we were all expected to make pronouncements about the state of the arts, pronouncements culled from other people. It was as if we somehow felt ourselves to be more important than the people we were talking about. Sometimes I felt like scattering all my books around the room to shake everyone up.

We had to do a thesis on some writer as part of the course so I chose Ernest Hemingway. Hugo had given me *For Whom the Bell Tolls* and I'd gone on from that to read almost everything else he wrote. He wasn't very much in favour at the time, being seen largely as a macho philistine. 'I like the stories,' people said to me. This became a kind of mantra in time. As a result I decided to ignore most of the stories in my thesis. I always liked doing the opposite of what people expected.

The M.A. went on until August. That meant I couldn't get away for the summer unlike all my other years. I didn't realise how long a summer could be until that year. It was nightmarish strangling books you loved into intellectual debates but you had to do it to get the piece of paper.

In September I decided to head for Europe for a while. I hadn't any destination in mind. Anywhere would do. A friend and myself headed for Paris first. We decided we'd spend a few days there and then do our own thing. Neither of us had a bean but that increased the sense of adventure.

We bummed around Paris, sleeping under the Eiffel Tower and doing all those other things students did like pilfering fruit from the stalls and getting our feet kicked by the gendarmes when we tried to sleep in the railway stations. After a few days we decided to hitch to Germany. Hitching was forbidden and if the gendarmes caught you they took you into their car and drove you in the opposite direction to inconvenience you. When we saw them coming we ran to the far side of whatever road we were on to confuse them. The upshot was that they unintentionally brought us where we wanted to go without realising it.

Over the next few weeks I slept in doorways and petrol stations. In the daytime I dossed, haphazardly thumbing lifts. It was as if I was trying to free my mind from thought after five years of heavy reading.

I ended up in Greece, doing some odd jobs to earn enough money to eat (and, more importantly, drink). In a hostel in Athens I met another student who was going to Israel to work on a kibbutz. I thought about joining him but didn't have enough jizz left in me. By Christmas I was back in Dublin, an 18,000 word thesis under my arm that was as useful to me as an ashtray on a motorbike.

Tales Out of School

At this point the question of what I was going to do for the rest of my life raised its ugly head. My mother thought I was showing signs of following in my father's footsteps. She reminded me that he'd spent eleven years studying law - or rather not studying law. I wasn't too much different. I'd spent the last decade of my life playing snooker, listening to Elvis Presley records and dreaming of marrying Raquel Welch – or even Rachel Welch.

Many people I knew in UCD were busily examining their bellybuttons after graduation. Some of them went to places like Argentina to join communes or do community work. More conservative citizens applied for positions in RTE or the Civil Service.

There was no particular ambition driving me. As Keith put it, I had a B.A. and an M.A. but no possibility of a J.O.B.

To help my mother sleep better at night I went to a Career Guidance Officer. He gave me a big speech about all the options available to me, 90% of which I felt were rubbish. He had a book called *The Directory of Opportunities for Graduates* which was about as big as the Bible. Wading through it was like eating porridge.

One night I visited a friend of mine, Glenn, in his apartment on the Stillorgan Road. He had four or five copies of the book on his sofa. He had a fire lit and every few minutes he'd throw one of the copies on it to keep it going. This was usually done with a hearty guffaw. 'Throw another DOG on the fire there,' he'd say to his girlfriend, having coined the acronym from the title of the book. Somehow I couldn't see him rising to the top of the white collar world.

My mother thought I should do teaching. I didn't agree. I thought this was where all disgruntled graduates went to die. I felt it was the last refuge of a scoundrel, a return to the scene of the crime. Considering I'd been so miserable in Muredach's and Belvedere it could hardly work out. 'Maybe you can make up for the mistakes made on you in these places by becoming a good teacher,' she suggested. It was a good theory but I wasn't quite sure it would work. The mistakes that were made on me were more likely to make me want to murder the children rather than redeem them. I was too damaged.

I couldn't envisage myself back in a classroom to save my life but then something happened to change my mind. John Wilson was the Minister for Education and he spearheaded a scheme where university graduates could do a short course in primary teaching in St. Patrick's Training College. Full-time Pat's students did a three-year course. This got them a Bachelor of Education but we were being offered basically the same qualification for just one year's study. It sounded like a good deal so I applied for it and was accepted.

A few months later I started in Pat's. I felt like I was going into the jaws of a lion. As soon as I entered the building I felt I was back in Muredach's. There were stained glass windows and meticulously scrubbed floors, a far cry from the plexiglass of Belfield and the litter strewn all over the corridors. People had a look of having had a good night's sleep the night before; they looked ready for the challenge of work. Everyone looked too focussed, too tidy.

I was given a list of lecture times. I doubted I would be asking my mother to call me at 2 p.m. here. It would be more like 7 a.m. We wouldn't be studying for the love of it but for the expectation of a job.

There was a big emphasis on Irish. We studied the language at university level to teach children how to say things like 'John likes Mary.' No wonder the language was in the condition it was.

At one point of the year we were all given a grant and sent down to a Gaelic school in Kerry to brush up on our command of the language. Most of us just used the opportunity to brush up on Smithwick's instead.

We started to skip lectures and head to the local pub for fun. One day while we were in there shooting pool – old habits died hard - the lecturer got wind of our location and followed us. We hid in the back of the bar and the barmaid covered for us but he spotted the cue of one of my friends and followed us into the back room. When he saw the four of us cowering there he said 'Caillfidh sibh an deontas', which meant 'You'll lose the grant.' As it happened we didn't lose it but that was the end of my pool-playing career in Kerry.

When I got back to Dublin I made a more genuine attempt to learn Irish. Many nights after the lectures were finished I went to the Conradh na Gaeilge club off Stephen's Green. Irish was spoken there by all the customers. The icing on the cake was the fact that you could get drink served up to you into the small hours. Before the bar closed I'd stock up on about half a dozen pints, standing them like soldiers on the counter. You had to speak Irish as you drank them or you'd be told to leave but that wasn't a problem for me. In those days if somebody offered me a pint after midnight I'd have been happy to converse with them in Swahili.

The year I spent in Pat's was enjoyable in its way but after the freewheeling atmosphere of UCD I felt like a fish out of water. I also suspected the full-time B. Ed. students believed that us 'Wilsons' thought we were superior to them. Or maybe they just resented the fact that we got to do in one year what they were doing in three.

They seemed more committed to what they were doing than we were. Many of the people I knew from UCD were suffering from a sense of displacement. We were in Pat's as a last resort. It hadn't come to us in a dream.

This led to some problems when we went out on teaching practice. A cartoon of the time had a straggly-haired teacher going into the Principal's office with a cigarette in his mouth and drawling, 'Sixth want to know who won World War Two.' He was like a Trotskyite version of a Wilson.

I knew the feeling. I'd never stood in front of a classroom of thirty children before and tried to impart knowledge to them. I asked myself why I was doing it now. Was it because I was the youngest of a family and had some kind of subconscious craving to have a younger brother or sister to take care of? Or was I idealistic enough to want to undo the damage Jacko had done to me, as my mother suggested?

The first place I was sent on teaching practice was, amazingly, All Hallows, the place Hugo left eight years before. (I looked for skid marks but couldn't find any). We were only there as a stopgap. A makeshift set of rooms were set up in what used to be the seminarians' quarters because the school we were supposed to be teaching in was being renovated. In theory I could have been cutting my pedagogical teeth in Hugo's old classroom. (By now Hugo was a teacher himself in a posh girl's school in Blackrock and getting on very well there).

I was asked to give my first lesson to Third Class on religion at Easter time. I chose the crucifixion as my theme but became carried away talking about Judas one day. I told the children the biggest sin he committed wasn't betraying Jesus but thinking that Jesus wouldn't forgive him for betraying him. The class teacher called me aside after I said that. He looked tense.

'That might be a bit advanced for them to take in,' he said, 'They're only nine after all.' I saw his point. He handed me a Catechism with questions like 'Who made the world?' on it. The answer, 'God made the world', had a big ring around it made with a felt marker. That was the end of my sermons about Judas Iscariot. The teacher was probably afraid I'd come in the next day and give a diatribe on the existential nuances of Marcel Gabriel's theology.

I tended to lecture pupils instead of teach them, a fault shared by many 'Wilsons'. In secondary school you taught subjects, it was said, whereas in primary you taught children. In one project I undertook, the inspector told me my workcards were so elaborate they would have been more suited to university students. I hadn't quite given them the binomial theorem to learn off but I wasn't far off that. 'You don't need a degree in Nuclear Physics,' he informed me, 'to tell children the cat sat on the mat.'

One of the other students in my class had an intriguing idea for an audio-visual aid. It was a box with holes cut out in the shapes of letters of the alphabet. He also cut out letters to fit into the holes. The box was wired electrically so if you put a wrong letter in one of the holes you got a shock. Somehow I didn't think the idea would catch on. 'The old man rigged it up for me,' he said. 'He's an electrician.' (Maybe, I thought, an electrician who'd suffered his share of corporal punishment in youth). I wondered what might have happened if someone accidentally turned up the voltage. Was electrocution justifiable punishment for pupils who didn't know their ABC?

My father was disappointed I'd entered Pat's. (If I wanted to be sarcastic I could have told him I was disappointed he'd entered another Pat's because that was also the name of the hospital he went into to be dried out). He looked on teachers as 'infra dig', especially Primary teachers. He'd dated one before he met my mother but didn't like to publicise that fact. It was as if she was a skeleton in the cupboard.

I told him I'd have preferred to do something else but there didn't seem to be anything out there. Law was the obvious option but he'd spent most of his life turning all his sons against that as a career. (He used to joke that 'lawyer' should be spelt 'L-i-a-r').

He went back to Ballina for a last case during my year in Pat's. It concerned the will of his first girlfriend. He was the executor but her husband wanted someone else to handle it. He was offered a fee to give up the executorship but he didn't want to take it.

From the start he felt distrustful about the way the case was being handled. Such distrust increased dramatically when he arrived in Ballina and was confronted by three men he didn't know sitting in the widower's office. One of them was reading a newspaper upside down. 'What are you doing?' he said, and the man nervously pushed it away. He smelt a rat and refused to walk away from the case. In the end he managed to retain the executorship. The old tiger still had some fight left in him.

He was on a high after coming back to Dublin. He regaled us all with anecdotes, some of them going back to the old days. I thought it might spur him on to other things but it worked the other way. In the next few weeks he became depressed. It was as if the case had given rise to an appetite he couldn't fulfil. It took him out of a rut he'd been in for many years but he couldn't sustain it.

I asked him if there were any other cases on the horizon but he only laughed. 'Do you know of any of my other old girlfriends on the way out?' he said.

He still wrote letters to the paper and still backed the odd horse but the life seemed to be gone out of him. He acknowledged that himself. 'I've crossed the Rubicon,' he said, 'From here on it's all downhill.' Now and again his spirits picked up if people called but usually he didn't want to see anyone. If the mood took him he might give out *The Green Eye of the Little Yellow God*, his favourite recitation, but such moods were few and far between. In the old days he'd do it with all his force, acting out the voices like a trained actor, but as he got older he faltered. He missed lines he'd said hundreds of times before and his emotion sometimes seemed laboured. If you praised him to make him feel good he'd say, 'Don't say that. I know I didn't do it right.'

He spent a lot of his time wondering what lay ahead of him in the next life. Most of his friends, he assumed, would probably be 'downstairs'. He liked to tell a joke about the gates of heaven being stolen from St. Peter by the devil. God sued but the devil won the case because God had nobody to represent him: all the lawyers were in hell.

My father died in the middle of my year in Pat's, suffering a massive heart attack one day after an argument with some men who were delivering coal to the house. They left him a few bags short and when he confronted them about it they became aggressive. He wasn't used to being taken on like that and got so worked up he brought the heart attack on.

He'd given me my breakfast in bed that morning. When I said I was going to town he asked me to buy him a book on Hitler that had just come out.

I was at a film when he got his attack. I was doing some reviews for a magazine in Trinity College at the time. It was a film about demonic possession called *The Omen*. As I was watching it I had a premonition that something was wrong. I had other jobs to do in town but decided to go straight home. I had the Hitler book in my pocket at the time.

As soon as I got in the door I knew something was wrong. The house was silent. I went into his room and he wasn't there. The clothes on his bed were tousled. There was a Super Ser heater in the middle of the floor with his red velvet dressing gown on top of it.

My mother was sitting in the kitchen crying. Audrey was beside her. (She was up in Dublin for an operation on a hammer toe). My mother got up and put her arms around me. She didn't need to say anything. Audrey was crying too. She said, 'I did my best to save him. We rang Dr McKeever and he came up. He said he had no pain. He was gone in a minute.'

We were all relieved he didn't suffer a lingering illness because he wouldn't have been able to deal with that. Neither would he have been able to deal with my mother dying before him. He often said that if that happened he'd have drunk himself to death.

By the time he died he wasn't drinking much. I used to smuggle in the odd six-pack of Guinness to him when my mother wasn't looking but he wasn't going on benders any more. He got over the depression after the case in Ballina and had become mellow, contenting himself with giving out about the state of the world from his bed and writing more of his irate letters to the *Irish Times*.

My mother accepted his death stoically like she did everything else in life. I heard her crying in her room sometimes but she never opened up to me about her grief. If I broached the subject she just said, 'Thank God he didn't suffer.'

Aunt Nellie thought he gave my mother a dog's life because of his drinking but she never saw it like that. She told me once that the thing that attracted her to him most was the fact that he gave her confidence in herself. She'd been painfully shy as a young girl and his outgoing personality helped her overcome that when they were in public. At home it was a different story. There she was the confident one. He seemed to be the superior person in their relationship but she was the one who was really in charge.

She went through some depression in the years following his death, mainly because she didn't have him to take care of any more. She told me once that she would have considered going into a convent if he wasn't alive and all of us were reared. I was now 24 so she could have done that. Or could she? Sometimes she acted as if I was 4 instead of 24. And maybe I acted that way too.

It was as if her whole life was a mission. She'd raised nine children - ten if you counted my father - but she still couldn't put her feet up. That would have been death to her. If she hadn't somebody to minister to she felt irrelevant.

I found it difficult to grieve for him. I felt he'd died at the right time. He'd lived a full life but in his last few years he hadn't had much to look forward to. 'We try to kill time,' he'd say, 'as we wait for time to kill us.' Or he'd quote the line from *Ol' Man River* about being tired of living and scared of dying. He'd always been terrified of getting 'the bug', as he called it, meaning cancer. At least he was spared that.

I tried to fill his absence with work but my heart wasn't in it. In another way I became relaxed in front of the pupils on teaching practice now that he was gone. It was as if his death hardened me. Suddenly I didn't care what way I taught them anymore, or how I was coming across to them. In the evenings I brooded about him just as he'd once brooded about his own father.

Where was he now, I wondered. Would he be putting God in the witness box as he'd always promised?

Another hero of mine, Elvis Presley, died on August 16th of that year. I was out the night it happened so I didn't know about it until the next morning. Keith poked his head in the door of my bedroom on his way to Unidare and said, 'Elvis is dead.'

I only heard him from a half sleep. When I woke up I wasn't sure if I dreamt what he said or not. It was only confirmed to me when I went downstairs and saw my mother reading about him in the paper. She knew how badly I'd take it. 'How are you?' she asked me. I said I was all right but what I really felt was that it was like a second death in the family.

I walked into town and bought all the papers of the day in Eason's. I went into a café and read stories about him giving cars to people, chartering planes to get a particular peanut butter sandwich he liked. Back in my room I looked at all the posters of him on my wall. There were so many of them that Audrey called it The Elvis Room.

My mind went back to 1972 when I had a chance to see him in Las Vegas and didn't take it. I always hoped he'd come to Ireland but in one of the papers I read that his manager wouldn't have allowed that because he was in America on an illegal visa and was afraid to leave the country. That meant he didn't want Elvis to leave it either.

I could only have him through his music now. I played it non-stop and at ear-piercing levels, either out of anger or grief. When people told me to turn the volume down I ignored them, lost in a sea of self-pity.

June got married later in the month and that helped me get my mind of myself a bit. She married a Physics lecturer from Bolton Street called Pat. She'd been dating him for a few years. They were going to live on the south side of the city so it was a big change for her.

The ceremony was quiet until a friend of the family called Donie O'Donohue arrived. Donie was a huge Elvis fan and just as devastated as I was by his death. After a few glasses of wine he jumped up on one of the tables and started singing 'Blue Suede Shoes'. He hadn't a great voice but he did the movements brilliantly and when he curled his lip he looked just like Elvis. After he came down from the table he asked me if I was going to tell him he didn't exist. He was always teasing me about the fact that I studied philosophy. I told him that was all in the past, that I was back on the planet Earth now and about to embark on a teaching career. 'Maybe you're only imagining that,' he said.

After I finished the course in Pat's I started applying for jobs and after a few weeks got one in a small school in Clonsilla. I was given fifth class which felt a bit like being thrown in at the deep end but the pupils were high achievers and it was easy enough to get them to work. My classroom was a prefab that the Principal called 'The Horsebox' because of its small size but in time I grew attached to it. I felt the wind could have blown it over but even that gave it a kind of cosiness.

I often came in early to prepare classes and stayed late after school cleaning up when the children had gone home. The other teachers were friendly and the community closely-knit. The downside was that you felt on display all the time because everyone knew everyone.

The fact that it was a country school meant we were always close to nature. Birds often flew into the cloakroom that adjoined the prefab and trapped themselves in there. I always wondered why they didn't fly out the way they came in - through the open door. They usually kept banging into the window-pane instead, doing themselves untold damage in the process. The headmaster told me to get a cloth and wrap it around them so I could then lead them out myself but I was useless at that. Whenever I got anywhere near them they panicked, probably because the pupils were panicking (and more than likely the teacher too).

Another source of consternation was field-mice. They were always running into the classroom when the weather got cold. One day I saw one of them on his tip-toes hugging the radiator. I pointed it out to a pupil and he started screaming. Then everyone else joined in. They ran around the room manically and probably gave the mouse a coronary. The next time I saw one scurrying along the skirting board I decided not to mention it. Instead I announced, 'Everyone outside for PE.' This came as something of a surprise to thirty students in the middle of a Maths lesson.

A bigger source of tension by far was the arrival of inspectors into the school. In our first two years as trainee teachers we were on probation. The inspector could knock on your door at any time and expect you to perform for him. Everyone was on their best behaviour on such days. Afterwards he'd join us in the staff-room for tea.

You could usually cut the atmosphere with a knife. There were no blue jokes told on these days. Everyone would be running round looking for the best cup in the room for him and exchanging pleasantries about the weather. If he said black was white or two and two was five we'd probably have agreed.

On an allocated day for each of the first two years he spent the entire day in a classroom. This was the day he awarded teachers their diploma or (on the odd occasion) refused to do so. It was supposed to be a typical day in your teaching life but in reality was anything but. My main hope on such days was that the space cadets in my class, the ones who could usually be relied on to crawl up the walls, would be indisposed.

This was unlikely. Misbehaving children usually loved coming into my classroom, probably because they knew they'd get away with more there than anywhere else.

They also seemed to know how important such days were to us teachers. In the middle of my second inspection one bright spark tugged at my shirtsleeve and said, 'Sir, is it us that's being examined or you?' He was nine years of age. Not in a month of Sundays would I have asked such a question in Muredach's.

I could have done with a few tranquillisers that day. The inspector sat at the back of the class furiously scribbling down notes. I felt like I was being X-rayed or psychologically raped. Miraculously he gave me a pass. When I went to go home that day I saw one of the other teachers had put a note on my windscreen. 'We're up in the queer place if you'd like to join us.' He meant the local pub. I didn't need to be asked twice. I can't remember how much I drank that day. All I remember is crawling into my bed a few hours later feeling like a dead man walking. I don't know how I got home.

In my first years of teaching I couldn't get into my room quickly enough in the morning. It was as if I had the task of forming a generation of minds. I loved what I did but I found it hard to get the pupils to obey me and they were also incredibly noisy because I was such a soft touch. As I drove home every day I was already thinking of the next day's classes. I studied books on child psychology and racked my brains to think of new approaches but nothing seemed to work.

The headmaster used to say, 'It's them or you, Aubrey.' He had a business-like attitude to the pupils that shipped them into line like robots. If one of them had an accident in the yard he'd say 'Dry up your tears' as he put them up on the 'operating table'. If they lurched at the sight of blood he'd laugh and say, 'You won't die this time.'

I couldn't get them to learn their lessons like the other teachers. The harder I tried the less they did, probably because I was never any good at delegating chores. I tied shoelaces and peeled oranges and they were happy to let me be their lackey but if I asked them to do something educational they tended to just gaze into space. If I ever threatened to get tough with them they just laughed at me.

The headmaster told me I got too personally involved with them. 'I'll watch that,' I'd reply, but at the back of my mind I knew I was going to continue to make that mistake. We had to be who we were.

One year I decided to do the H. Dip. to give myself the option of becoming a secondary teacher if the primary school got too much for me. A big plus was that I was allowed to do my teaching practice in the school I was working in. This meant I could have become a fully-fledged secondary teacher without ever having stepped inside the doors of a secondary school – a weird situation..

It sounded great in theory but it turned out to be a nightmare trying to get to the lectures in Belfield after a tough day in the class. Fighting the cross-town traffic at rush hour on Fridays to get to a boring lecture on Piaget was enough to give anyone road rage. After a while I started to skip the lectures, getting a friend to forge my name on the attendance sheet that was handed around. I felt I was going to get caught out sometime and I was.

I ended up failing the 'Dip', which was quite an achievement. I never met anyone else who did afterwards so I felt quite special. 'Any idiot can pass that exam,' I boasted, 'it takes a particular type of genius to fail it.' I knew how my father would have felt about it. If he was alive he'd probably have given me some kind of reward. I'd finally become a member of a very prestigious club, the club of losers. It was an immense relief.

Hugo thought I would have made a good secondary teacher. For proof he cited some study guides I'd written for the Leaving Cert. for a publisher in the mid-seventies but I was anything but proud of these publications. They fossilised learning, turning it into bullet points that killed spontaneous responses. I preferred Hugo's story about the day he asked his pupils to write an essay on Shylock from *The Merchant of Venice* in his school in Blackrock. He wrote on the blackboard, 'What do you feel about Shylock?' and asked them to write an essay on the theme. They were all expected to come up with long-winded interpretations of his character but one little girl just wrote: 'I feel sorry for him.'

To me that was worth any number of study guides..

Wanderlust

One thing that kept me going though all the tough times in teaching was the thought of the long summer holidays. Like a lot of teachers I spent more time thinking about my vacations than my so-called vocation.

A holiday I went on in 1979 was about the most adventurous of them. It was a 'fly-drive' package that involved myself and three other lads I knew from Pat's. The idea was to fly to Barcelona and drive to Athens in a car we collected at the airport, having lots of exciting experiences on the way. But life doesn't usually work out the way we plan it and this was no exception.

The day after we got to Barcelona we were robbed of most of our money when we left the car unlocked to go down and have a look at a beach. Two days later in Milan most of our clothes were taken from outside a hotel in the middle of the night. Everyone but myself wanted to go home but I suggested we hang on. I thought that by the law of averages things couldn't get any worse. How wrong I was.

When we got to Trieste it was discovered my passport was four years out of date. (I don't know how many borders we'd crossed without the problem being spotted). We had to go to Rome to have it renewed. We went down through the boot of Italy intending to cross to Yugoslavia that way but there was a two-week waiting list for the car ferry from Brindisi to Igoumenitsa so we ended up driving back through Italy again and re-visiting Trieste. This time we were let through but on the way back the car over-heated so we had to drive at snail's pace wherever we were going. .

Nothing else went wrong afterwards but we were broke most of the time so couldn't really enjoy ourselves. Of the thirty or so nights we were away we spent over half of them sleeping in the car because we couldn't afford hostels. It was more of an endurance test than a holiday and we decided we wouldn't repeat it in a hurry.

The summer after that I got a job as a barman in the Bronx. This was more fun by far. The bar had a sign over the counter that said 'Give Vietnam Back To The Irish' so I felt at home right away. I was less impressed by the bullet holes I spotted in some of the walls. .

I was relieving another barman who was drying out. I hoped I wouldn't become a casualty like that but I was aware of the temptations from my time in London. We stayed open until the last customer left and that was often after 3 a.m. I made more in tips than my basic pay but earned it listening to emigrants bending my ear with painful stories about how they wanted to go back to The Old Country.

The owner of the bar was from Kilkenny. Many of the customers hailed originally from there as well. Hurling was a big topic. You didn't dare venture an opinion on this for fear of being hit over the head.

There was a juke box in the corner and at a certain point of the night it came to life with old Irish airs. Drinkers left their seats to twirl their lady friends round the floor during these numbers. Sometimes I didn't know whether I was working in a pub or a dance-hall. (When I was left with the depressives drinking on their own after midnight it was more like a confession box).

We had no draught beer because the owner never bothered to put in taps. The most popular beverage was ice-cold Schlitz. Most of the customers drank it straight from the bottle. Every third drink was given to them free. They were fond of saying 'Have one for yourself' with an order, an offer I found hard to resist.

Once you accepted a drink you left yourself open to hear the story of their life. It was usually the same story: they once had everything and now they had nothing. Sometimes I ended up being drunker than them at closing time, as had been the way when I was a barman in London. I slept off my hangovers in the pub toilet until the first drinkers of the day woke me up by threatening to break the door down if I didn't.

After a while I grew to prefer the customers who came in to drink rather than talk. There was one man who drank like there was no tomorrow. He took his whiskey neat. All he said was 'Hit me again' after each shot. He had so many back to back I wondered how he was able to walk out the door without falling.

Another customer was rumoured to be in the Mafia. Needless to say, his every wish was adhered to religiously. One night when he leaving the bar I saw him having an altercation with a woman. The next morning there was a pool of blood on the spot. We talked about it in the bar but did nothing as regards the police. We liked living too much.

After I came home from the Bronx I was restless in the same way I'd been after the fly-drive to Barcelona. It was hard to settle into the routine of teaching ten-year-olds their sums after seeing 'The Big Apple' up close. To keep my mind occupied I wrote about some of my experiences in short stories and sent them off to magazines and newspapers. Some of them were printed but more often they came back. I wasn't too bothered by the rejections because I was enjoying the activity of writing itself so much.

In 1980 I published a book of my stories with a tiny publisher from Raheny. It was cheaply put together and we had practically no distribution facilities. I went down to Listowel that year to launch it at Writers' Week.

Hugo came with me. He was writing a lot himself too at this time. On the journey down he pulled various poems out of his back pocket and recited them to me. I asked him had he sent them anywhere but he said he hadn't, that he just liked writing them. I said nothing existed for me unless it was in a book. He thought that was a ridiculous attitude, that if that was the only reason someone did something they were prostituting themselves.

I was in among all the heavyweights in Listowel - Brendan Kennelly, John B. Keane, Bryan McMahon, Neil Jordan. On the day of the launch I started drinking early as I had to talk about my book to a group of people and I was looking for some Dutch courage. I stood up on the stage but found it difficult to balance myself. John B. Keane looked up at me and said, 'You have a fine stink of porter off you, boy, you'll obviously make a great writer.' I survived the speech without falling off the stage and that night was out-drunk by Keane himself, who wasn't too bad a writer either. Hugo was amused by us all. 'I thought I was coming down to a writer's festival,' he said, 'not a drinking one.' But in Ireland maybe they're the same thing.

Back at school I found myself becoming restless again. I seemed to be like that after every trip away, no matter how short. I still couldn't stop thinking about the summer holidays. I hadn't enough money to go to the States that year so I decided just to go to London instead. One of the reasons was that Bob Dylan was playing in the Earl's Court arena there and I'd never seen him live before. (After Elvis died, Dylan had become my new idol).

The concert was on the last day of term but I still bought a ticket for it. I thought the headmaster would let me off a day early but when I put this to him he said it wouldn't be a good idea. 'If you got sick I'd have to accept it,' he said, 'but you're telling me you're going to be out in advance and that makes it awkward for me.' I asked him could he not forget we had this conversation . He said he could lose his job for that.

'If you're absent on the first of September as well,' he warned, 'strictly speaking you'll have been indisposed for the whole summer. That could affect your summer pay.' It all seemed ludicrous for just one day. (A half day at that as we always took off early on the last day). When I asked him could he mark me present he gave a wry grin. I had to re-book my flight for the following day and change the ticket as well.

Earl's Court was one of the biggest halls I'd ever seen in my life. It seemed to be about the size of County Mayo. I sat glued to my seat as Dylan came on. He was going through his religious conversion at the time and had a lot of negro spiritual singers with him. Together they nearly blew the roof off the auditorium. I had a hip flask of brandy with me and was fairly flying by the end of the night. I spent all the way home singing 'Knock Knock Knockin' on Heaven's Door' to nobody in particular. It got me some funny looks from the other strollers.

The following day I went to Wimbledon to see John McEnroe playing in the final of the tennis championships. When I got there I saw Princess Diana getting out of a car. She'd just got married to Prince Charles and everyone was talking about her. When I got to the entrance the security man told me my ticket wasn't valid. A huckster had sold me a forgery and that put a total damper on the trip.

When I got back to Dublin it was still only mid-July but many of the shops were already advertising 'Back to School' clothing. Such ads didn't do much for my state of mind. I wandered around town like a misfit, realising it had been a bad idea not to go to the States. The idea of teaching suddenly seemed very drab to me.

I was losing interest in it and when that happened the children lost interest too. I tried to prepare some classes but couldn't get motivated. My book was reviewed poorly in some of the papers and that dragged me down further. The sun beat down on me and I kept running into the shade, burying myself in books to get my mind off myself.

When term began I made an extra effort to adrenalise myself, bringing the children to films and shows and the occasional roller disco. I also took them to football matches. They responded to things like that but for some reason my own heart wasn't in them. I seemed to be trying to hypnotise myself into believing I was fulfilled.

To keep my energy level up I tried to focus my mind on the following summer, my familiar therapy. Ruth and Jacinta issued invitations from America but I never liked going to the family except for a night or two. It was too easy to fall into their rhythms and then you wouldn't be inclined to travel.

One day after school I met some people from my class in Pat's. They said they knew a guy in Denver who liked the Irish and who would give me a job for the summer and maybe even a place to stay. He was a carpenter called Tiko. I took down his number and rang him. 'Sure,' he said, 'Come on over, I'll sort you out.' That was it.

The month after that I was in Trinity College. On the way out I saw an ad in a glass panel on the wall. It was from a veterinary student looking for someone to go with him to the States. I rang the number and arranged to meet him the next day in The Buttery. His name was Fergus. He was from a big family in Donegal. I told him about the man in Denver and he said he'd be delighted to come with me.

When summer arrived we got a flight to America together. It was Fergus' first time outside Ireland so he was full of excitement on the plane, taking in everything like a child at a circus. Basil met us in New York and took us up to his house in Syracuse for a few days, giving us the royal treatment. He was married to a girl called Janet and they had a son, Barry, that he doted on. Fergus was fascinated by his stories of life in General Electric, the high-tech world of conferences and international flights. He said if things didn't work out in Denver to come back to him.

We got a flight to Denver a few days later. As soon as we touched down we phoned Tiko. He said to meet us at one of the local hotels but when we got there we looked like something the cat dragged in. The hotel manager wasn't too keen about us leaving all our bags in the lobby but we said it was only for a short time. About twenty minutes later Tiko arrived in his pick-up truck. He had mud on his shoes which impressed the hotel manager even less. 'What the hell are you doing here,' he roared out 'when you should be at my place?'

He had a dog with him. He let him run alongside the truck all the way back to his house. 'It's the lazy man's way of exercising him,' he confessed.

The house was ramshackle but roomy. He said we could stay as long as we liked and we could also do some work for him if we wanted. I wasn't much of a carpenter but I sanded some doors for him over the next few weeks and held his ladder when he went up on heights. Otherwise we just sat around and chatted. Sometimes his friend Don joined us. Don had been in Denver University but dropped out to set up a food business. (Tiko built an enchilada stand for him).

Tiko's dog had granuloma. He had pills to stabilise this condition. Fergus usually gave him these. Being interested in animals, he was good at that. (Every time I tried to give them to him he nearly bit my hand off). My main job was watering Tiko's sunflowers. They must have been about twenty feet tall. He had so many that it took hours to get through them. You could only water them every second day by law because there was a shortage of water in the city. If you were caught on an unappointed day you could be arrested.

Most nights we sat out on the verandah drinking beer and telling each other stories about our pasts. Afterwards Tiko would usually go off and make some phone calls. He seemed to have a lot of girlfriends. He spent hours talking to them, walking from room to room with his phone. Mobile phones hadn't come in yet but his cord was so long he was able to make calls even from the bath.

One night one of them rang him up and said, 'Talk dirty to me.' Tiko put the phone down and asked us if we had any suggestions. Fergus blushed. He wasn't used to this kind of thing. Tiko enjoyed his embarrassment. He knew Fergus wouldn't say 'Shit' if his mouth was full of it. I told him to introduce this girl to me as soon as he could, she sounded like my type. 'I'm not sure I could do that,' he said, 'What would Mrs Malone think?' He was always joking about 'Mrs Malone' ever since he handed me a letter from my mother one day. (She'd signed herself as that on the back of it).

Tiko liked telling us stories about old-fashioned Irish girls who went wild in Denver. There were a lot of 'holy Mary' types who were daily communicants back home but as soon as they touched down in Denver they turned into Jezebels. 'The quiet ones are always the worst,' he assured us.

I'd witnessed some of that myself in previous summers. Maybe it was something in the American air. 'If you want to see the two sides of life,' Tiko said, 'Go into Denver any night. You'll see hookers on one side of the street and doomsday preachers on the other.' He wasn't joking. (Such extremism even seemed to apply to the way people looked. Half of Tiko's friends were obese and the other half stick-thin.

Fergus and myself usually left Denver at the weekends to do some travelling. One weekend we went to a rodeo show in Cheyenne. At the end of the show the country and western singer Merle Haggard sang some songs with a tribe of Indians from the back of a flatbed truck. The atmosphere was riotous. When I was leaving the grounds I entered a competition that offered the prize of a holiday to Las Vegas. A few days later I got a letter to say that I'd won. I could also bring someone with me. I asked Fergus if he wanted to come and he was over the moon.

Tiko said to beware of gift horses and he turned out to be right because when we got to Vegas all we were offered was two nights in a fifth-rate motel and vouchers for free meals in the middle of the night. The reason for these was to keep you gambling your money away in the casinos. I fell for that trap, getting addicted to blackjack and blowing all the money I earned with Tiko after a short winning streak hooked me in.

When you were gambling, the pretty waitresses patrolling the tables offered you free beer. The only problem was that you were expected to tip them twice or three times what the beer would have cost, especially if they showed their vital statistics. This they were more than willing to do. Most of them had legs up to their shoulders.

Fergus was out of his depth with all the glitz. I think he was happier playing with Tiko's dog than in this plastic paradise. One night when we were walking home from the casino a sports car pulled up beside us and two scantily-clad ladies asked us if we'd like to go to a party. I figured they were hookers but Fergus took them at face value and started to get into the car. 'It's not Donegal,' I said, 'they don't mean that kind of party.' When he heard that he panicked and ran back to the hotel we were staying in. For the rest of the week he hardly put his nose outside the door.

When we got back to Denver Tiko teased him about the hookers almost every day for the rest of the summer. Fergus went beetroot every time he brought the subject up. Tiko said he was going to write to Fergus' mother in Donegal to tell her the sad pit to which her son had descended in pagan Vegas. Fergus was gullible enough to believe him and was a wreck for the rest of the trip.

After I got back to Dublin I told my mother I was thinking of leaving the teaching. She said that would be insane, that I was good at it and that it put bread on the table. When I said I wasn't happy at it she said most people were unhappy at their jobs. It sounded like Keith talking all over again. 'Is there not something artistic I could do?' I asked her.

She must have taken me seriously because she cut out an ad from the paper soon afterwards about a drama group that was looking for new recruits. When she showed it to me I didn't show much interest as I'd never seen myself as an actor. Anytime I was ever asked to do anything public as a child – except for that day with my father's keys - I hid behind the sofa. 'It might fill in the nights for you,' she said so I told her I'd give it a try.

It was a small group and most of the people in it hadn't acted before. Maureen, the director, favoured authors from the old days for the plays she was in the habit of putting on. Lennox Robinson was her favourite author. On the first night I met her she handed me a copy of a few of his plays and said to read through them and see which of them appealed to me most. I thumbed through them but found none to my liking. The next time I saw her I said, 'Why don't you try something modern?' She didn't want to hear that. I realised afterwards that she already had her mind made up about the play she was going to put on next, another dreadful stage-Irish piece of drivel.

She offered me a tiny part in it. When I expressed dissatisfaction about this she said, 'There are no such things as small parts, only small actors.' It was the classic cop-out line.

I did that part for her and many other equally negligible ones in the following months. I didn't understand why she never wanted to give me anything better. Sometimes I thought she was threatened by me. I often reviewed plays for magazines and papers and I thought she might have wanted to pull me down a peg or two as a result. She wouldn't admit to this of course. When I drank too much it gave her an ideal excuse to sideline me. When she did that I had little motivation to behave. I generally saw rehearsals as glorified boozing sessions. It's a miracle I was never breathalysed on the way home from these, or on the way from the plays themselves. (We also staged these in pubs).

Nobody in the group was ever going to threaten the Abbey Players with their acting. Most of them were practical sorts. That suited Maureen. She gave us the old maxim: 'Show up on time, know your lines and don't bump into the furniture.'

We put the plays on in Old Folks Homes as well as pubs. Here we could afford to make mistakes as they were getting the shows for free and hardly likely to complain. Maureen let me drink as much as I wanted in places like this. I also replenished her own glass with whiskey fairly often. Whenever I did this the other members of the group would accuse me of trying to sweeten her up to get bigger parts for myself.

My mother noticed me getting too fond of 'the gargle' around now and tried to gently wean me off it. For her it must have been like looking at a repeat of my father. The only difference was that I was younger than him and to that extent I got away with my indulgences without my body showing too many signs of metal fatigue.

On the mornings after rehearsals she'd squeeze orange juice for me from a contraption she kept on the breakfast table. It was like an antidote to the booze and I guzzled it down in my dehydrated state. 'What's the point of giving you this,' she said, 'when you cancel it out with the Smithwick's every night?' I had no answer for her.

I eventually infected the rest of the cast with my drinking. We had some wild nights where we mangled the collected works of vintage

Irish playwrights in the basement of the Lincoln Inn. The best parts of such nights were the chats before and after line readings. I got to know about the lives of dozens of people who came and went, transient thespians like myself who wanted to have a go at 'treading the boards' in the protected environment of pubs and clubs where you didn't run the risk of being heckled even if you were the hammiest deliverer of a line in Ireland's theatrical history.

Every time I went to the counter of whatever establishment I was in for a round of drinks I'd usually have an extra one for myself that I'd gulp down before going back to the company I was with. As well as Smithwick's I was also getting fond of Stag cider, 'the madman's drink' as it was called. It gave me a quick high and also released my inhibitions, usually too much so. With enough of it inside me I tended to insult the other members of the group, telling them they were lousy actors.

I spent many days after these rehearsals phoning up people to find out who I'd offended the previous night. It got to the stage where I'd arrive at the pub and say, 'Can I apologise to you all in advance before I start drinking?' Some of them thought I was obnoxious but because I was having a go at everyone, not too many of them took my barbs seriously. My consistency gave me a licence to be obnoxious.

I knew I needed a few drinks to get the courage to face an audience but the booze was also giving me amnesia when it came to memorising scripts. I often quoted lines from the wrong place or gave people a faulty cue. They learned to improvise around me. I'd look pleadingly at the prompter behind the curtain (my eventual best friend) to rescue me any time I corpsed but after a while it was as if she was feeding me the whole play. Sometimes she whispered the cues so loud they were heard by the people in the first few rows at the premieres. After that I was left on my own to sink or swim - and I usually sank.

One year we did a John B. Keane play called *The Buds of Ballybunion*. Amazingly I was given a fairly decent part in it as a farmer. I told Maureen I'd stay sober to repay her faith in me and worked hard at learning my lines. On the night of the dress rehearsal I gave everything to my performance, probably because I had the best part of a bottle of whiskey inside me. I definitely thought it was next stop Broadway for me but unfortunately the audience didn't seem to share my enthusiasm. They just sat there transfixed. A few hours later one of the other actors told me 90% of them were senile.

The society doubled as a kind of unofficial dating bureau. I found it easier to relate to girls in settings like this than in dance-halls or discos. I always hated the whole game-playing that went on in these places, the way you had to try and sell yourself to make yourself sound more interesting than you were. I used to fortify myself with liquor to deal with all that pressure, often ending up being footless when it came to the point of the night when a woman asked me something about myself that might have proved meaningful. In the dramatic society at least you were seen for what you were, warts and all.

One night before a performance the prompter said to me that I was the most intense person she'd ever met. I didn't know whether to take it as a compliment or an insult. I thought I'd been super-cool but she knocked that perception on the head. Maybe I was trying too hard after a lifetime of avoiding social engagements.

I dated another member of the group for a few months after that. She was from Mullingar but living in a flat on the North Circular Road. We used to go drinking every Monday night. It was an unusual night to go out but it suited us. She always had the same drink, a gin and tonic. After two or three she got merry. She did great impersonations of the other cast members as well as some public figures like Margaret Thatcher.

Sometimes we acted out scenes from the plays we were in, changing the lines to make them funny. I enjoyed these nights because they relaxed me but there was something missing between us. Maybe we were just playing at being boyfriend and girlfriend, parts that suited both of us because we could make up our own lines and let them lead us where they might.

'Could you not live a more simple life?' my mother used to say to me. 'Why do you drive yourself so much?' 'I'm like a shark,' I replied, 'If I stop moving I'll die'. I liked the image of myself as this inquisitive creature in love with change but deep down I knew I was chasing my tail. I knew there had to be something I was trying to escape with all of my excesses – and most likely it was myself.

Embattled

Writing was a continuous problem for me at this time of my life. In one way it made me feel more alive than anything else I did but in another way it was a distraction. 'I hope I don't see you doing any of your reviews during the Maths class,' the headmaster said to me one day. There was no danger of that but my mind was often on other things besides teaching when I was in the classroom. I seemed to be trying to split myself into two halves and giving neither of them their proper due.

Many Irish writers had been teachers at some point of their lives but for me the mix didn't gel. I found myself becoming self-conscious in conversations with the other teachers at break-times. I felt I was always expected to have something interesting to say. This bothered me because I didn't want to be on display all the time. I wasn't paid to write during my teaching time any more than I was paid to teach during my writing time. I wanted the two sides of my life neatly segregated but that wasn't always possible.

The writer John McGahern lost his teaching job in a primary school not too far from where I was teaching for writing what was deemed to be a pornographic novel, and marrying a Finnish woman in a registry office. I couldn't write like he could but maybe I was better off. Neither was it likely I'd hare off to Finland during the summer holidays.

In teaching as in everything else I attempted to do in life I felt I fell short due to a lack of concentration. In the company of snooker players I might be thinking about the next Irish class I had to prepare and in the middle of an Irish class I might be thinking about my next snooker match.

'You're spreading yourself too thin,' people would say to me, and they were right. I found myself only enjoying experiences because there was something else over the horizon to intrigue me. I identified with Marlon Brando's statement, 'I become fanatically interested in everything I do for approximately seven seconds.' That was me too. Except I never won an Oscar, or bedded half the population of Western California. (On the bright side I didn't weigh as much as a whale and I didn't have a son who killed his sister's boyfriend).

I played snooker to a moderate standard but got more interested in the professional game than my own one as the years went on. I also started to transfer my loyalties.

Jimmy White got into the semi-finals of the world snooker championship in 1982 and gave me a new hero to replace Alex Higgins. He was beaten by Higgins that year and Higgins went on to win the title but it was Jimmy everyone was talking about after their match. I watched it in a house in Iona Road that was being rented by three of the people from the drama group I was in, all of them nurses. Jimmy had the ability to make snooker look so easy I was glued to the set. He reminded me of the young James Dean with his carved features and hungry look.

I spent the next few months trying to meet him, ringing him countless times to London without getting on to him. I gobbled up anything I could find to read about him and went to see him play in Goffs at the Irish Masters. I brought my mother to one of the matches but got so excited I couldn't watch it, spending most of my time standing by the close circuit TV in the foyer with my hands over my face.

After his last match that year I drove down to Kildare with Hugo to try and get an interview with him. He was staying in the Keadeen Hotel. He passed us by almost as soon as we went in but his manager wouldn't let him talk to us. I went out to the car in a state, slugging back a baby whiskey I had in the glove compartment. Hugo doubled back to the hotel and had a few words with Jimmy and Kirk Stevens, another player, in the hotel restaurant without the manager knowing. This enraged me further. On the way home in the car I took the two sides of the road with me and almost killed the pair of us.

Two years later Jimmy reached the world final but was beaten in a close match by Steve Davis. Davis had become a hate figure to me by this stage. I saw him as the Margaret Thatcher of snooker, a player who tried to take any living thing from the game. Anytime he lost a match it nearly meant more to me than Jimmy winning one. When he lost back-to-back finals in 1985 and 1986 I almost danced jigs in celebration.

My concentration started to dip more and more in the classroom as I started to get more and more interested in other things besides the job. I wondered whether I might be doing the pupils a favour if I walked away from it. The class I had in my first year performed excellently but the ones I had afterwards came nowhere near, either due to my falling standards or theirs.

The children also got cheekier as I got older and I was less able to deal with them. I felt talk and chalk couldn't compete with television or their latest video game.

I wasn't the only one to suffer. A joke started going the rounds about a person being called for school by his mother. 'I don't want to go in today, Mammy,' he said to her. 'Why not?' she asked. 'Because everyone hates me,' he replied. 'The teachers hate me, the pupils hate me, and I'm afraid of everyone.' 'You still have to go in,' she said. 'Why?' he asked her. 'Because you're the Principal,' she replied. I would have enjoyed that joke more if I wasn't suffering so much. In many ways, I was that soldier.

Another joke of the time had two pre-school children in a kindergarten. One said to the other, 'There's a contraceptive behind the radiator.' The other replied, 'What's a radiator?'

Children got wilder with the years as well. A teacher I heard of in Ballymun left his classroom each day carrying a bin-lid over his head to shield himself from flying missiles thrown by his pupils. It made *The Blackboard Jungle* look tame. With the advent of technology, the pupils were also losing their innocence. In a video store one day I saw a 'revisionist' version of the Cinderella story: 'Then Cinderella divorced Prince Charming and she got custody of the children and he got the slippers and both of them slept around and signed on and he saw the kids at the weekend and they all lived happily ever after.'

Sometimes we had in-service days. The good thing about these was you got time off school to go the seminars. The bad thing was the amount of bullshit that was talked.

The seminars advised us of the importance of motivating the child, of lighting the flame of their enthusiasm. I couldn't help feeling some resentment over the fact that nobody had seen fit to try to light that particular flame when I was a child. My own schooldays were characterised by fear rather than fulfilment but now I was expected to do somersaults up and down the classroom to inspire my pupils. 'You came from the swinging sixties, didn't you?' one psychobabble expert said to me. I replied that the only thing that swung for me in the sixties was Jacko's bamboo cane.

Far from wanting to motivate the children, my main fantasy was finding someone who might *de*-motivate them for me. If I could have found somebody to put a set of tranquillisers into all of their bowls of cornflakes every morning before breakfast he would have been worth his weight in gold to me.

The progressive textbooks advised us to grow up with the children. I didn't find that too hard to do since I felt like a child myself a lot of the time. Sometimes I felt like an extra pupil in the classroom – the one they didn't let graduate. I was the nut behind the wheel, making it up as he went along. Or as happened more frequently, losing the plot entirely.

I felt like a robot in charge of thirty other robots, all conspirators in the same gigantic scam, a perpetration of formulas trotted out to satisfy governmental departments or somebody who might one day offer a job to these children on the strength of them, a job as insane and irrelevant as the one I was trying to do here.

'I wouldn't worry too much about Head-the-Ball if I was you,' the headmaster would say to me now and again about such-and-such a child, 'He's going into the family business. All he needs to know is how to write his autograph on the back of cheques.' And I'd think: So what am I doing here?

The unruly children were the ones I liked best as people. They were a nightmare in the classroom but I knew they were the people I'd like to share a pint with a few years on. The swots were only my friends from 9 until 2.30. After that real life began again.

Sometimes I told my mother I was going to explode if I didn't get a different job. She didn't like that talk. She feared the unknown if I left. 'You could be going from the frying pan into the fire,' she said.

It was her attitude to everything: the devil you knew was better than the devil you didn't. When I complained that I wasn't getting anywhere with my writing she'd bring up an article or story I'd published months or even years before. I hated this sitting on the fence and looking back into the past. It might have been an article she hadn't even encouraged me to write in the first place. 'You have no ambition,' I'd say when she was in this kind of mood. It reminded me of the old joke: 'How many Irish women does it take to change a light bulb? None. They just sit there and say, 'Aren't we all right here in the dark?"

That was cruel of me. I knew she was out for my welfare but things weren't happening fast enough for me. I didn't want to end up crying into my pillow about what the what-might-have-beens like my father,

Most days after school I went into the Greyhound Bar in Blanchardstown with two other teachers from the school, David and John. After a few months we became fixtures. The barman would have three drinks standing to attention at the counter at 2.45 even before we walked in the door. We joked that we should take out shares in the place, that our names should be engraved on the seats. After a few years maybe our three cars could have found their way to the pub on their own.

John drank Guinness and I usually had a pint of Smithwicks. David liked Bushmills whiskey with red lemonade. It was always the same order. 'Two pints of the usual and a Bush and red.' As we swallowed them down, suddenly the world seemed a rosier place. Suddenly it didn't matter all that much that Dessie O' Connor didn't know his seven times tables or Kevin Phipps hadn't done his essay on the life of a penny or the class project on world hunger in Africa turned out to be a disaster. That world was irrelevant now. This was our time. Set them up again, bartender. Down the hatch.

It was strange going into this cavernous womb in the middle of the day to give ourselves intravenous injections of whatever potion we were imbibing as we rehashed the day's trivial events. Many people would be leaving the pub to go back to their offices for the afternoon as we went in but we were now free for the whole day. It was too much of a temptation to resist.

I always wore my best clothes to work on the mornings after lengthy sessions in the Greyhound to disguise my hangover. John picked up on this after a while. 'How's the head?' he'd say whenever he saw me dressed sprucely as I made my bleary-eyed way into the classroom. After which I'd tell him to do something physically impossible with himself.

David was married and John was going steady so they were usually more in a hurry to get out of the pub than I was. They'd talk about having 'One for the road' after a few but every tipple I had just meant I wanted to sink deeper into my seat and forgot all my worries outside this pleasantly-lit womb.

When I got home there would be the familiar lecture about what I was doing to my insides from anyone who happened to be around. My mother had hardening of the arteries and various members of the family were always worried something might happen to her. 'You're never here when we need you,' they'd say. I knew they were right but I couldn't admit that, even to myself. I was the classic spoiled brat of the family who wanted his mother to cool his porridge in the morning and then act Jack the Lad for the rest of the time.

'I worry about you driving home with drink on you,' my mother would say and I'd mutter something about being a better driver when I'd had a pint or two because I was more cautious then. 'If you lose your licence that'll be the end of your job,' she'd warn, and I'd tell her not to nag me, that I had a life to live. Then she'd say something like, 'I'm only saying these things because I care about you. We all worry about you.'

Audrey used to tell me my mother feared I'd end up with as big a problem as my father if I wasn't careful. I always gave her a smart answer back but it was usually out of guilt rather than self-righteousness. She spent her day trying to save lives in the hospital and then came home to see me apparently trying to prematurely end my own one.

I was drinking not because I wanted to but because I had to. The AA manuals said you had a problem when you had a drink even when you didn't particularly want one. I'd reached that stage long ago. 'Please don't leave your seat while the bar is in motion' said a sign above the counter in the Greyhound, and I didn't. For about five years.

I also used to drink in another pub nearby called the Clonsilla Inn but I became barred from that. I was sitting there one day with David when a man walked in with his girlfriend. He went to the Gents and she sat down beside me. We started talking and then the man came out of the toilet and said, 'Are you chatting up my girlfriend?'

When I said she wasn't my type he became aggressive. I told him to cool down but he refused. I even offered to buy him a drink. It was then I realised he was drunk already. He said he was going to carve me up and I pushed him. Suddenly I became the aggressor. The barman came out from behind the counter at that point and told me to go, that he wouldn't serve me anymore. I told him it wasn't me that started the fight but he didn't want to know. The other man was a stranger but I'd been going to this pub for about five years, day in and day out.

I went back the next day and apologised but the manager said he ran a tight ship and wasn't going to lift the ban on me. I was shocked at his stubbornness after all the custom I'd given him over the years and found myself resenting him deeply. A few months later he was shot through the knee by another man he barred, a hunter who came in from the woods one day and slung two rabbits across the counter before asking for a pint. He refused him and the man came back that night and shot him at blank point range. I tried to feel sorry for him but I couldn't. A few months later I was barred from the Greyhound as well, this time for using bad language.

The more I fell foul of barmen the more I drank. Because I'd been quiet growing up I needed to go crazy for a while. I said ridiculous things to people just to get a rise out of them. I had fights with strangers I didn't even remember until I woke up the next morning with some injury or other, the alcohol having acted as an anaesthetic at the time.

I went on some weird dates at this time as well. I remember coming out of a pub with a woman one night and not remembering where I parked the car. (Eventually it turned out I hadn't brought it with me at all). I also walked out of films and plays under the influence. I remember going to three different concerts one night and leaving all three before they were over. I thought I was being cool and living life to the full but to the people who were with me I was really just being a pain in the neck.

Just as acting gave me a new identity, so did drinking, for a while anyway. But when you came down from the high it was even harder to live with your dull self than it had been before. I went from craving the spotlight to finding any stone I could to crawl under.

I used to be able to get nicely drunk on three or four pints but now it was taking double that much to get the same effect. That's why I started taking chasers. I was finishing whiskeys as soon as the barman could pour them. Some mornings I came into the classroom still high from the night before. It was the only way I could cope with the job now.

Then one day the inevitable happened. I was on a boozing session with David in the Strawberry Beds on the banks of the Liffey when he said there was a party in the Meeting Place, a pub we both liked to go to off Dorset Street because of the brilliant music sessions they had there. Never one to refuse an excuse for more booze I told him I'd see him there. I was offered a lift but didn't take it because I wanted to get my car home. I left the car park looking forward to hearing music from the jazz guitarist Jimmy Faulkner who'd been drinking with us earlier and Freddy White, a blues singer David also knew.

I was about a mile down the road outside the Phoenix Park when it started to rain. I was doing a fair speed in my rush to get to the pub when the traffic lights in front of me went red. I hit the brakes and went into a skid, careering headlong towards a car that was in front of me. I knew I was going to hit it about ten seconds before I did. There was nowhere to swerve because there was traffic on both sides so I hit it head on. A moment later a woman dashed out of it roaring at me. The damage wasn't great but she was hysterical. I tried to cool her down but she got worse when she saw I was drunk. I asked her if she'd settle the matter privately if I paid the damages but she said no, that she was calling the guards.

At that point I made a run for it: up over a gate and into the nearby Phoenix Park. For a few minutes I thought I was making good progress but then I heard a voice behind me and when I turned round I saw a blue uniform. A garda wrestled me to the ground and asked me where I was going. When I told him I was on the way to a party he seemed more amused than anything else. 'How were you going to explain the car?' he asked me.

I was bundled into a Maria and brought to Navan Street Garda station. Here I added insult to injury by hitting the man who arrested me because he wouldn't let me go to the party. (At the time this was much more important to me than the prospect of losing my licence.) I also refused to give a blood sample.

They put me into a cell for throwing the punch at the guard. It was the first time I'd ever been locked up. I always had a horror of closed spaces but that didn't bother me now. I spent the next few hours doing little but emptying my bladder. Around the middle of the night they let me out and I walked home. For one mad moment I contemplated doing a detour to the Meeting Place. The party was probably still going on.

When I woke the next morning my head felt like World War 3. I told Audrey what happened and she said she'd see if she could do anything. I wasn't sure what she meant by that. She drove to the Navan Road and told the arresting officer what a lovely person I was and how this incident had been a one off but he didn't fall for it. 'We're talking about the law of the land here,' he said, 'Are you trying to pretend last night didn't happen?' He said the best thing I could do now was get myself a good lawyer.

After a few days I phoned Donie O'Donoghue, the family friend who'd impersonated Elvis at June's wedding. Donie had been something of a wild man himself in his youth and knew all about lowering drink. (He once flew to New York for a pint of beer when the barman of a pub in Dublin refused to serve him and then flew back to Dublin again the next day). He'd qualified as an accountant and had many business interests as well as being a barrister.

He'd been dating Jacinta for a while and also knew everyone else in the family. He spent so much time in our house he actually called my mother 'Mammy'. He also had a lot of chats about the law with my father over the years and my father had given him some of his books when he was in the King's Inns studying to be a solicitor. I said to him, 'Maybe you can use some of the stuff in Dad's books to get them to go easy on me.'

He did his best. After telling me what an idiot I'd been to try and escape over the wall he got down to the hard business of putting forward a case for me. He managed to get me off on fleeing the scene of the crime so I was just charged for drunk driving. I ended up paying a fine and being banned from driving for a year.

'I hope you'll cut down on the drink now,' my mother said as she watched me getting up at the crack of dawn to get the bus to work and I told her I would.

I kept the promise for about three weeks.

Orphans

My mother died in 1985 after a series of illnesses that would have killed a lesser woman many years before. She had a lot of circulation problems as well as hardening of the arteries. One day she had more trouble than usual walking and seemed to know something was wrong. When she went to sit down in a chair she slipped and I could see the agony on her face.

She passed it off as she always passed everything off but Audrey persuaded her to see a doctor. She was given an appointment card for a specialist but she didn't go. She put the card in the pantry where all the others had been put over the years, most of them ignored. When the pain got worse we brought her down to Casualty.

They took her in on the spot. 'How did you let this go on for so long?' the doctor said to her. She said she didn't think it was worth bothering about, that you had to have something at her age. He said it was a clot and they'd have to investigate further.

Over the next few days they ran a lot of different tests on her. I visited her in the hospital and she was her usual self, hardly concerned about the results. 'You hear some wicked coughs in here,' she said. As was always the case, she spent most of her time looking around at all the other patients instead of thinking about her own problem.

At home we feared it might be serious but we didn't say anything to her. There were lots of calls to America and Audrey came up from Cork. Eventually the surgeon told us what we all feared but were afraid to say: she had cancer.

He said her general health was good and he hoped to get all the tumour out. An operation was arranged and she was as casual as ever about it. 'That old cancer,' she said, 'sure they have great treatments for it now.'

On the day of the operation we all went to Jervis Street to get the results. Clive was home from Africa by now as well. We sat in a room waiting for the surgeon to come out of the theatre in his green outfit. Clive said the rosary and we all joined in like we used to as children when my father gave it out. We were hoping against hope.

When the surgeon appeared, though, he gave us no hope at all. 'I couldn't operate,' he said, 'The tumour was too big. The operation would have killed her.' He tapped a wooden table beside him. 'It was that hard,' he said.

He was sympathetic but factual. We all stood stunned before him. Nobody could think of anything to say. June and Audrey broke down crying and Clive looked as if he was about to. Hugo and myself just sat there. I felt as if I was beyond emotion. 'I'm very sorry,' the surgeon said, 'I know how hard this must be for all of you but she's had a good innings. She's 74, isn't she?'

I couldn't understand him saying that after what he'd just told us. What did it matter if she was 74 or 84 or even 94? What right had he to say that anyone had reached their time to die?

I don't remember walking out of the hospital. I felt strangely relieved now that there was nothing left to hope for any more. A part of me knew all along that she was seriously ill but wouldn't admit it to myself.

We went to a cafe. Clive said he thought she should be told her position when she was out of the anaesthetic but the rest of us were doubtful. 'Her faith will get her through this,' he said. He had tears in his eyes. Maybe it would be like everything else in her life. Maybe she'd get through it but we wouldn't.

When we got home Clive phoned the three of the family who were in America. Ruth was hysterical. Basil and Jacinta said they'd expected the worst from the original diagnosis. All three of them said they'd arrange flights home as soon as they left down the phone.

I went in to see her after she came out of the anaesthetic and she was bright as a button. I tried to be bright too but I wasn't a very good actor. Maybe she saw through me. She probably knew the truth the moment she woke up.

If she didn't she had to be suspicious when she saw Basil and Jacinta visiting her in the following days. Then Ruth came in and broke down at the bedside. 'Don't worry,' my mother said to her, 'I've beaten this before.'

We said the rosary for her every night at home. One of the doctors said something about remission one night but it was a slim thread. Maybe she could still live for a while even with the tumour, he said. I felt he was just trying to console us. Now that she'd been opened it would be that much more aggressive. It would go haywire once the air got at it. We were clutching at straws.

She had strange visions in the following days. At times she almost seemed to be hallucinating. I heard her screaming as the physiotherapists tried to get her to cough. They were afraid of a build-up of fluid in her lungs. But what did that matter now? If she was going to die would she not be better off to go soon?

As she got some of her strength back we sat by her bed watching her pulling at all the tubes that were coming out of her. The nurses had to hold her hands down to stop her doing it. 'It's because of the painkillers she's on,' one of them explained, 'They're making her reactions a bit strange.'

Everybody was kind to her but it couldn't take away the horror of what was happening. I looked at the scar that ran across her stomach like a zip. It was perfectly sewn – but for nothing. She'd have been better off not to have had any operation. Why hadn't the doctors seen it on the X-ray? Keith said they were like amateurs, that we were all guinea pigs in their hands.

I tried to talk to her but only platitudes came out. I'd lived with this woman for over thirty years of my life and yet I could hardly remember having a conversation with her about anything beyond the details of the day. Maybe all our best relationships are like that. But it didn't make the visits to her any easier to bear.

She was the woman who did everything for me but I'd never gone to the trouble of finding out what made her tick as a person. She was always there so I took her for granted. But now that she was about to be taken away from me I thought of all the hundreds of nights I spent getting drunk with people I thought were my friends when I could have been with her. She tried to stop me going out on these nights but I never listened, just as I'd never listened to her frantic attempts to get me to accept my job or my writing or anything else that worked me up. Was this my punishment for such cavalier behaviour or was there still time to undo some of the damage in the time that remained to her?

She became neither worse nor better as the days went on. At home we got on each other's nerves because of our tensions, falling out over stupid things like who'd go in to see her on a given night. We tried to get our minds off her but our efforts were pathetic. She'd ruined all of us by being the dominant person in our lives, a quiet woman in the corner of the room who ruled by love.

I prayed for her to come out of the hospital and then prayed that she wouldn't. It was a selfish wish. Her pain grew worse and wore all of us down with it. After weeks of visits there was nothing to say any more. We argued among ourselves about how much she should be told and this seemed to get back to her. Even in her terminal state she seemed to be running the house from her bed. 'Don't fall out among yourselves,' she said. And then, turning the conversation back on me as she always did no matter how sick she was, 'You don't look well. Are you eating at all? Who's doing the cooking now?'

Any time I asked her a question about herself she ignored it, quizzing me about my own eventless life instead. After leaving the hospital I'd feel as if I was the patient rather than her. I knew this was the way she preferred to play it so I went along with it but it had all the hallmarks of a black comedy.

During one of my last visits to her she started asking me about how I'd be if anything happened to her. I wasn't able for this kind of conversation even if she was. This time it was me who changed the subject. Just this once I wanted her to talk about herself. I wanted to ask her if she was afraid or if there was anything I could do for her.

I never got the answer to either question because she died soon afterwards. It was on a night when we'd almost stopped believing she was dying. She'd lingered so long I had got to almost believe the doctor might have been right about the remission after all. But when the phone rang one wet Monday night and it was the hospital, the very ringing itself seemed like a death knell.

The message was short and brutal: she was sinking. We all piled into a car and said the rosary as we drove to Jervis Street, breaking all the red lights on the way. When we got there she was unconscious. Her eyes were closed but we talked to her in case she could hear. After a few minutes she stopped breathing and the monitor was turned off.

I went out to the corridor with Hugo and he put his arms round me. 'Don't worry about her,' he said, 'She's gone straight up. She's the lucky one. It's the rest of us who are in the gutter.' I sat down beside him on a window sill and we looked out the window. People were buzzing around the streets and I thought: How could they be going about their normal business when my mother had just died?

She donated her body to medical science for research. My father had done that too. 'Come in to Trinity some day,' he used to say to me, 'and you'll see my skeleton dangling in the air.' There was a service at the church but I didn't go to it. Neither did I go back to the house afterwards. People came from all over Ireland to pay their respects but I knew I couldn't face them. I drove out to Howth instead and sat on a cliff for hours. I knew a new chapter of my life was about to begin. Suddenly I was an orphan.

She never cut the umbilical cord for any of us, forcing us back to her even against our will. Hugo said, 'She made us love her,' and I knew what he meant. I didn't deserve her love but I still got it. God tempered the wind for the shorn lamb.

Now that she was gone I felt the family was going to splinter. It would have no centre any more. She was the glue that held us together and now that she wasn't there we'd have no reason to keep in touch. We'd keep telling each other we should meet up but in all likelihood we wouldn't. That was the pattern in families after parents died. They got on with their lives and became more involved with their own children. When we visited each other now it would be more formal, more like visiting a cousin or a friend. We wouldn't just arrive on someone's doorstep anymore without announcing it. There would be phone calls, arrangements. The spontaneity would be gone from our lives along with the person that created that spontaneity. No matter how at home we made each other feel, the home itself wouldn't be one.

Audrey watched me sinking into a stupor in the following nights. She said, 'Don't let it get to you. This is the hardest time. If you come out of it, everything afterwards will be less of a challenge.' She thought my mother's death was going to reform me but I assured her no such reformation was in the offing, or any trek down the road to Damascus. 'Will it make you pray more?' Ruth asked, but I couldn't answer that. How could prayers help me now? What good had the rosary done us on the way to the hospital? God – if there was a God – had betrayed me.

Basil said to a priest he knew, 'How is it that our father, an admitted sinner, had such an easy death while our mother, a saint, had such a painful one?' The priest said God allowed her to do her Purgatory in this life because he loved her so much. It was a neat answer, maybe too neat. I was more inclined to think it was part of the absurdity of all our lives, the way the dice fell.

I sat in the empty house for months afterwards blaming myself for all the nights I'd deserted her to go out with women or play snooker or drink – or all three together.

What did these activities have to offer me now? Where were the women I'd left her for, the ones who promised to realise my dreams for me? Where were my career prospects or my adventurous lusts? I couldn't recapture them because something died in me too that day in Jervis Street. No doubt I'd come up with other things to fill the vacuum in time but they'd only be stopgaps. Everything meant less now, every involvement and every dream.

When my mother was alive I neglected her, putting her last in everything and probably sending her to an early grave with my drinking. On one of the days she was in Jervis Street I even went off playing snooker with Keith's son David instead of staying with her.

The memory of details like this haunted me in the following year. I wallowed in my guilt, that very Irish disease. It was a negative form of remorse. I punished myself for my selfishness with a woman who spent thirty years worrying about the drunken excesses of her husband and then, when he died, continuing the same kind of fretting about me.

'Would you not even go off the drink for one night?' she asked me often and I told her I would, maybe believing the words when I said them but never carrying them through.

Would I do so now that she was gone? Hardly. What would be the point now when she wasn't there to be relieved?

A portrait of my mother   My mother in her riding breeches

My father, second from left, with friends

My father as a man about town

My grandfather P.J. Malone

The family in the fifties

June and Ruth outside Norfolk   A rare photo of my mother

My parents with the 'novena' of children

Keith and Clive as young men

June and Ruth growing up

Clive, Ruth, Keith and June in Dublin

Norfolk

My parents and Clive at his ordination

My father and June at Enniscrone

Clive blessing our cousins the O'Gradys

Basil with June and Ruth in the sixties

Hugo and Kathleen on their wedding day

The family at Iona Villas in 1985

Myself and my pupils in Clonsilla

With snooker ace Ronnie O'Sullivan

Meeting John McEnroe with Mary, Hugo and Basil

A passport photo of Mary

My father in 1976

Christmas 1975 at Iona Villas

Family gathering at Hugo's wedding day

My parents at Keith and Clive's graduation

The family all together in the fifties

Auto-Pilot

I moved out of the house in Iona Villas the following year and into a flat in Claremont Court. It was basic but it had everything I needed. The absence of furniture suited me because it also meant the absence of memory.

There was a pub down the road with a pool table and I went there most nights. I made a new set of friends. We talked about everything from sex to soccer but rarely anything about our personal lives. I was still going by the name of Peter and in time began to believe it was my real name. If someone called it out in the street I turned by reflex to answer.

I was drinking as much as ever but I didn't have to worry about driving now because the pub was within walking distance of the flat. Most of the people I knew were big drinkers and they also liked pool so I spent many of my nights playing with them. Every time I lost a game I went into the lounge next door and watched TV until my name came up again on the blackboard. I played until I lost or until closing time was called. Then I rolled home and fell into bed, sometimes without even undressing myself.

The teaching got harder. Whatever chance I had when my mother was alive was gone now. There was nobody to tell my troubles to or advise me. My motivation was practically nil and I was also having some health problems, most of them accelerated by a poor diet and too much Smithwicks.

The children became more demanding in class and I was less patient with them. They seemed to get cheekier every year and also to challenge my authority more. Corporal punishment had been abolished in 1981 so there was nothing you could threaten them with except sending them to the headmaster's office. (More often than not that was like a treat for them. They just sat there drawing pictures).

I felt if I was teaching younger children they wouldn't be as disruptive. (I had fourth class now). I asked the Principal if he'd move me to a more junior class for that reason. He said he would if I could get someone to swap with me. John agreed to do that and for a while I had some peace. But then the old problems started. It really didn't matter what age the children were if you couldn't handle them, and I couldn't.

I had taken on the job because I liked children but now that affection was slowly being eroded. Parents told me about their delight at their fledglings taking their first step and saying their first word but I couldn't share their enthusiasm. I wondered if my own parents had been this ecstatic when I had negotiated these stupendous milestones. It seemed to me that when I was a child there was nothing special about it. There was nobody around to talk about oedipal conflicts or separation anxiety or any of the other trendy terms you heard on shows like the ones featuring Oprah Winfrey or Sally Jesse Raphael that I watched in my flat on the satellite channels, or between pool games in the pub.

When I was a child in Ballina I was given a football and told to disappear until tea-time and that was happiness. If a visitor called to the house I wasn't shown off like a prize turkey or oohed and aahed over as I scored the winning goal in a five-a-side. Now the goalposts had shifted.

With the child-centred curriculum the pupil was king. It was he who made the world spin around. He was the centre of gravity, the prime mover and shaker, the dream of the future. My status as a teacher was to be a monitor of his achievements. As such I felt more often than not like a eunuch in the harem. The 'N.T.' after my name didn't stand for National Teacher anymore, it stood for National Tramp.

My own daily traumas didn't matter. As an adult I'd outgrown my relevance in the world: I was like yesterday's sour milk, an orange peel to be cast into the bin. But if I could get Junior into the A-stream of the secondary school then maybe, just maybe, the Lord would save my soul on Judgement Day.

I expressed such notions to David and John in the Greyhound. They saw my point but were probably more amused than impressed by my excessiveness. We all had stories to tell about the little darlings in our care but I knew I was feeling the pressure most. The headmaster's words from years before came back to me: 'It's them or you'.

I scrawled words on a blackboard and set homework for pupils that I dreaded having to correct. I became the thing I once vowed I never would: a clock-watcher. As terms wore on I also started to get sick with the stress of it all, to fall prey to any bugs that were in the air because of my own failing powers of resistance. I came into the classroom some days feeling hungover even on the occasions when I'd had nothing at all to drink the day before. The chalk slipped from my hand sometimes as I tried to write on the blackboard. I started to forget simple tasks I'd set the pupils. Parents came up to the classroom asking me why I hadn't corrected such and such an exercise and I'd hardly know what they were talking about.

Sometimes it felt as if my mind wasn't only on a short fuse but a short circuit. I'd ask the children to do some task but when they presented it to me I'd have lost interest and be on to another one. The only way I could maintain an interest in what I was doing was by shifting the emphasis every day, every hour.

I hated the noise in the room but I seemed to hate quietness even more. It made me nervous. I'd excite the pupils with some story or activity and then get frustrated when I couldn't calm them down again. It was like when I used to play with Deezer back in Ballina. I liked the adrenalin but then he got too wild and I couldn't tame him.

Eventually the pupils stopped responding to me at all. I realised I was giving my classes to myself, like a ham actor rehearsing lines in front of a mirror that he'd never get the chance to say to a paying audience. I listened to my voice issuing dictates and it seemed to be coming from somebody else, from a part of my psyche I wasn't acquainted with anymore.

There was a stranger inside me occupying my body and asking it to pretend things like running a tight ship were important, or keeping off the grass at playtime, or learning off irregular verbs by heart. It was as if I'd been brainwashed into such schizophrenia by my own pathetic craving to hold on to a job I hated instead of severing the ties and making that bold leap into an uncertain future. I kept thinking the summer holidays would give me the respite I needed but they acted as little more than temporary reprieves for me. Every September I'd report back for duty like a deserting soldier who'd been nabbed in a foxhole and dragged back to the frontline for more battle with an enemy he didn't even recognise any more.

The noise in the classroom was also tipping me over the edge. The teaching handbooks recommended an 'industrious hum' but in my room it was more like a permanent hornet's nest. I banged a ruler on the desk to try and stop it but it only made it worse. As I ranted and raved to the pupils I thought of the old adage: 'The only problem about giving out to a six year old is that in no time at all you begin to sound like a six year old.' If they insisted on behaving like infants, I told them, I'd have to treat them like infants. But in the process I became one too.

I watched films like *To Sir with Love* where pupils responded to tenderness rather than cruelty but the older I got the more I seemed to go backwards instead of forwards. I reverted to a primitive form of child psychology, throwing out the new curriculum and all my old idealism. I started to act hysterical if a child dropped a biro on the floor or stood up without permission, to become the kind of teacher I'd always reviled: a bully. The classroom became a bit quieter as a result but I didn't feel the children liked me anymore and I didn't like myself either.

Hugo said he knew what I was going through. 'There are two kinds of teachers,' he told me, 'good teachers and nice teachers. You can't be both.' In actual fact *he* was both even if he didn't know it but I knew I couldn't be.

I became like a schizophrenic, treating the classroom like Dachau one day and the next back to my old self telling funny stories, the actor in me unable to resist the entertainment value of my anecdotes. And then the noise would start again, and the misbehaviour and the wildness. When I tried to stop it I only made it worse by raising my voice.

One night June asked me how the job was going. I said, 'If the children feel like working, we work. If they don't, we don't'. She let out a laugh. 'What kind of a school is that?' she said, 'I wouldn't mind going to it.' She certainly wouldn't have had to be brought to the Convent of Mercy by a guard in Ballina if there was a teacher like me in there. But that was the way I felt education was going, or at least my brand of it.

By December every year I felt I'd already done a full year's work and yet I was only a term into it. I ticked off days in my diary like a prisoner putting notches on his cell wall telling him how much more time he had to serve, counting frantically towards the Christmas holidays in the hope that this fortnight might recharge my batteries.

Some years I didn't even get that far, coming down with mysterious bugs in the first few weeks of September that I couldn't even put a name to. I'd get a feeling like a hoof in the chest going into the classroom and start imagining I was in the early stages of a coronary. In the staff-room my head throbbed as the other teachers chatted excitedly about grades or the Christmas concert or a threatened outbreak of lice. Were they the insane ones or was it me?

The infections I kept getting were resistant to antibiotics. That made me think they might have had a psychological root. But the symptoms were physical. As well as a pain in the chest I'd get a parched feeling in my throat that seemed like dehydration. The only thing that seemed to cure me was sleep but I was usually too uptight for that. Some days after school I put a towel over my head and soaked myself in a basin full of boiling water with a liquid called Friar's Balsam in it. It was an old folk remedy I heard about. By now I was willing to try anything.

My doctor told me I was suffering from depression. I told him I felt more uptight than depressed. Maybe the name didn't matter. I also thought I might have the seasonal affective disorder SAD that sapped people of their energy in wintertime. Some days I crawled into the car at 2.30 feeling I could hardly turn on the ignition and drive home. 'You're burned out,' he said to me, 'It's an occupational hazard of the job you're in.' Maybe it was as simple as that.

He gave me sick certs as I needed them but I couldn't relax even at home because I knew I'd be facing the firing squad again soon. I dosed myself with Panadol and Lemsip and whatever other concoctions were lying round the house, usually finishing the night with a few hot whiskeys. The doctor told me I was wasting my time with all these, that I was only making myself worse. He prescribed Valium for me for a while and I swallowed them like Smarties. On the bottle it said, 'Keep Away From Children'. I said to the doctor, 'If I did that I wouldn't need them'. Ha ha.

'Rest is the debt you owe to your body,' he told me, 'Your tiredness is the way it's punishing you for ignoring that. You keep pushing yourself beyond your limits. You've been working on your reserve for a long time now.' I said I knew that but it wasn't something I invited on myself. 'The kids are doing my head in,' I told him. 'Then maybe you're in the wrong job,' he said.

If I was, I felt trapped in it. Ever since the age of four I'd been in educational establishments of one sort or another. Primary school, secondary school, university, training college, teaching in a primary school, and then back to university to do the H. Dip. I was terminally institutionalised. It was like a vortex that sucked you in, like those Russian dolls that kept opening and leading to a smaller one inside.

'I like the teaching itself,' I told him, 'but in the last few years I've had to spend more and more of my time trying to keep order in the room.' 'How much is more and more?' he asked. After thinking about it for a minute I came to the conclusion that it was probably up to half. 'There's something wrong there,' he said, 'you're supposed to be working in a school, not a prison.' Sometimes it seemed like one, with me as the main inmate.

At the tea-break in the staff room one day I said, 'Let's get the head-bangers from all the classes and put them in a special room that's supervised by Arnold Schwarzenegger. He'll walk around banging a chain on the desk to let them know who's boss. The room will have no windows or doors or toys or televisions or anything else and no teaching will go on in it. Arnie will just stand there laying down the law. Then he'll let them out at 2.30 and they'll go back to their lives.'

Everyone looked at me with their mouths open as I finished speaking. There was a silence and then some nervous laughter. They weren't sure if I was serious or not but I thought it was a good idea. Why should a handful of pupils in each class be allowed to sabotage the education of the rest? I couldn't think of any other job where someone who tried to stop you doing your work got away with it. Imagine if a mechanic was trying to fix your car and someone else kept dragging him away from it. The idea that the person would be indulged was anathema to me. But it was happening in education.

On one of my visits to the doctor he said, 'I think you're a perfectionist.' I thanked him but then he said, 'I didn't mean it as a compliment. That's what's dragging you down. You want the world to conform to your way of thinking but it won't. You have to learn to adapt.' He was right. Ever since I was a child I'd had to have things done a certain way. It bugged me if a picture was hanging sideways on a wall or if a box or drawer wasn't fully closed. If I saw something crooked in a room I'd have to straighten it.

Claustrophobia was another problem. Sometimes I had to ask to be let out of buses when there were crowds on them because I'd feel a panic attack coming on. That happened to me once on a bus in the Midlands. I had to be let off and hitch a lift to where I was going as a result. I also got feelings of panic in high places like cliffs or the top storeys of buildings. Maybe I inherited this from my father. He used to feel the urge to throw himself off the balcony in the Estoria sometimes.

The children in the class drew confidence from my problems and turned this against me. One day I asked a pupil to do a simple task and he said, 'Fuck off.' I can still hear those words. That was probably the day I left teaching in my mind even if it was years later before I actually walked out the door for good.

In Pat's we'd been given loads of lectures about loving the badness out of children, about appreciating the fact that there was a reason behind everything they did. Rousseau talked about children's innate goodness. But what would Rousseau have said if a child told him to fuck off? Would he still have cuddled him? If he did he was a better man than I was.

If someone said 'Fuck off' to me in a bar I know what I'd have done to him. If I said it myself to a barman I'd have been kicked out by the bouncer. There were no such things as bouncers in schools. All you could do was report children to the principal if they misbehaved. If you did this too often it looked like you had a problem yourself.

In my first years in the staff-room I listened to the other teachers talking about 'bold' children. I usually had a soft spot for these terriers but now I was starting to dislike them because they were making me feel old before my time.

One day Basil rang me from work. He said he was just back from a conference in Vancouver. Next on the list was one in Lausanne and from there he was heading to Montreux. I marvelled at his energy. 'How are you?' he asked me then. I told him I was having trouble making it up to the Artane shopping centre for a loaf of bread.

The talk in the staff-room now was mainly about falling numbers, the necessity for all of us to pull together to keep the ship afloat. There were frequent conversations about trying to haul in children from surrounding estates to increase our catchment area. My own preferred discussions would have been about how to get rid of some of them, especially the ones who reminded me of Charles Manson or the Yorkshire Ripper.

To clear my head after school, some days I used to walk all the way from Blanchardstown to Howth, a distance of about twenty miles. I played pool there in a pub called the Pier House. One night I ran into Phil Lynott there. He was sitting at the counter looking wasted. I asked him if he had a coin for the pool table. 'No,' he said, 'but I can buy you a pint.' I couldn't take him up on his offer because

I already had a barrel-load of them inside me. 'If I have any more drink I''ll explode,' I said and he laughed. A few months later he was dead. Would I follow him to an early grave?

I slugged back pints during my games and went for walks by the sea if I lost. In school I moved white chalk across a blackboard to teach children and in the Pier House I used a different kind of chalk to write my initials on a different kind of blackboard for permission to move a white ball up and down a cloth of green baize.

In the first guise I was Mr Malone, an offbeat teacher on the verge of a nervous breakdown; in the second I was Peter Murphy the unpredictable pool shark who sometimes spilled drinks over his cue. The following morning I taught Irish verbs to the beat of a metre stick on my desk, desperately trying to whip up the kind of enthusiasm in the children that I myself had lost. 'Chuaigh mé,' I'd say, 'chuaigh tú, chuaigh sé, chuaigh sí,' And they'd chant in unison, their shrill voices puncturing the air, only one of us realising the absurdity of trying to drum boring verbs into the heads of children who'd have preferred to be out playing hopscotch on the tarmac.

Afterwards we wrote it all down, me on the blackboard and them in their copies. And then we went on to other conundrums: the mysteries of mathematical equations, the rigours of English grammar, the civic pride we should take in our lives. I had them for five hours a day, their tiny faces gazing up at me curiously as their lives were about to begin while I wondered if mine had already ended. Each passing year I'd see these same faces walking along the road to the nearby secondary school and feel left behind, as if I was the one pupil who failed to graduate.

One day a pupil said baldly to me, 'You're not as good a teacher as the one I had last year.' When I asked him why he said, 'Because you're not hard enough on us.' What saddened me wasn't the criticism but rather the fact that an eight-year-old child would have such a yearning for being disciplined. When I told one of the other teachers about the comment he laughed heartily. 'Some days,' he said, 'don't you just feel like taking it out and pissing all over them.'

Things got worse after that. I tried to do everything that was expected of me but my mind felt a million miles away. At a parent-teacher meeting one year I told a woman her daughter was 'smack bang' in the middle of the class academically. She replied, 'I want her smack bang at the top.' But how could you make a silk purse out of a sow's ear?

The days passed by in a blur. I looked out the window of the classroom and envied the birds pecking at the breadcrumbs on the tarmac. I even envied the caretaker picking up the leaves that fell on it. I told David I'd have changed places with him in a minute. He said, 'The funny thing is, he'd probably love to be where you are.' Was it funny or tragic, the fact that none of us ever seemed to get what we wanted in life?

I went back to the classroom afterwards and put on the projector for the Irish lesson. I said the words without conviction and the pupils parroted them. They had to know I didn't really believe them anymore. I was a dead man trying to teach a dead language. They'd study it as I had, from the ages of four to seventeen, and after that time would probably still be unable to put two sentences together to save their lives if push came to shove.

A child asked me if he could go to the toilet. I felt he didn't really need to go but I still gave him permission. How could I blame him for wanting to get out of the classroom when I did too? Both of us were victims. As a pupil I'd hated teachers and now as a teacher I was starting to feel the same way about pupils: I'd lost out on the double.

The last straw came for me the year my classroom was burned down. It was a day when I'd been even more stressed than usual. My patience snapped with a pupil when he started fighting with the boy sitting beside him and I read him the Riot Act. A few hours later he lit a match in the classroom and threw it into a cupboard when I was at my lunch. One of my other pupils came into the staffroom in a panic and said the prefab was on fire. I ran towards it but when I got there I couldn't get in the door. As I watched it go up in smoke I thought to myself: 'Somebody is trying to tell me something about this job.'

. The fire brigade was called and they fought valiantly to save it but it was too late; it had gone up like a tinderbox. In the middle of it all, the headmaster came out and said to me with a hangdog expression on his face, 'Look on the bright side, Aubrey – you'll probably have tomorrow off.'

For that luxury I'd nearly have torched it myself.

Between Two Stools

Things were never the same for me after the fire. I was angry at the boy who did it and also at myself for giving rise to a situation where something like that could happen. Was it an act of revenge against me? I never knew but people told me I should stop thinking like that. No matter how many of them tried to console me, I still blamed myself. I wasn't good at getting over things or stopping myself brooding on them. 'You didn't do anything wrong,' they said to me, but their words meant nothing. 'It's a bad workman who blames his tools,' I said, 'or his pupils.'

I had to move into another building for the next few months. In time a new school was built and all the other prefabs pulled down as well as my one but this seemed to only make things worse for me. The new school was state of the art and it had a gym in it as well. All the other teachers were excited about all the luxuries but I missed The Horsebox. I was always my own boss there.

I would have parachuted out of a snake's backside to get out of teaching by this point. In the new school I felt part of a factory of learning, the last thing I wanted. We had to give PE lessons in the gym as well and I felt ill-equipped to do that. The children always ran wild on me the second we got in there. Whatever chance I had of disciplining them in the classroom I had none there. I also kept thinking one of them was going to do themselves an injury and sue us.

I finally left teaching in 1988. I should have been delighted but I still felt a tinge of nostalgia leaving the classroom for the last time. Whatever else, it had been my second home for eleven years. The teachers also gave me a very generous cheque as a farewell gift and that touched me deeply. It was in a card that said 'Congratulations On Passing Your Driving Test'. David had bought it. 'There were no "Going Away" ones in the shop,'' he explained, 'and I had to take something.' In a way it was appropriate with its drawing of someone whizzing off to new frontiers. I hoped I could do justice to it.

He told me the Greyhound would probably have to close now after losing my custom. The more serious teachers said I should have been a remedial teacher, that the one-to-one would have suited me best. That was probably true but it was too late now. The die was cast.

Sometimes I met pupils on the road to the school afterwards and they said I was wise to get out of the 'Torture Chamber'. One of them told me I was the best teacher he ever had. 'It's a pity you didn't say that when I had you,' I said, 'I might have stayed.' 'Then I did you a favour,' he joked.

The family was apprehensive about me leaving. 'Are you sure you've thought this through?' was the usual comment. It was as if I was still the baby of the house and couldn't make up my own mind. I told them I'd have ended up in the funny farm if I didn't get out. 'But what will you do?' they kept asking.

It was a good question and I didn't have an answer to it. Over the next few weeks I made phone calls to most of the editors I'd worked for as a freelance journalist since I left university but none of them had anything for me. Writing had always been a part-time job for me in the past, a hobby that brought in a few pounds. Now that I started actively looking for work my outlets seemed to dry up. It was as if editors sensed my need for them and backed off.

I was now dating a girl from Galway called Mary. I'd known her since we were in Iona Villas. Her family had moved up to Dublin shortly before mine in the sixties. Her father actually worked with June for a while in the Irish Permanent but we hadn't known each other in those days.

We met at a party in Bird Avenue in Dundrum. 'It was well named,' she joked afterwards. She'd come to it with a friend of Hugo's. She thought I was dating another girl that night because I arrived at the party with one on the back of my motorbike but that was just a friend I was giving a lift to. One of the people living in the house, amazingly, was Sean McDonnell's brother Joe. My life seemed full of coincidences like that. Sean was now living in England with his wife Betty. He told me he owned a pub in Poole but someone else said he was only working there.

Mary was trying to get off cigarettes when I met her. She had a match in her mouth when I saw her first. She was going through the motions of 'smoking' it as a way of satisfying the 'hand-to-mouth' movement smokers seemed to need to wean themselves off the habit. 'It's a poor substitute,' she said. I asked her what she did for a living then and she said she was a legal secretary. 'As opposed to an illegal one,' she added. I seemed to be destined to be associated with the law in some form or other.

As the night went on we stayed talking. We found we had a lot of common, not only because we were both from the West but also in our interests and attitudes to life. At the end of the party I asked her out and she agreed to meet me the following Wednesday. We met in a pub on the Quays and that set a trend. Once a week became twice and then it was nearly every night. Other parties followed, and then trips away together. Mary had an easygoing personality that acted as a contrast to my tense one. It was almost like a continuation of my mother and father into a new generation.

The two of us were also interested in writing. She'd had a few stories in David Marcus' 'New Irish Writing' page in the *Irish Press*, as I had, but hers were more spontaneous and less wordy. She wrote in a kind of stream-of-consciousness style. When I said that to her she said she didn't know what it meant. I told her that was probably why she did it so well. University study, in contrast, had nullified whatever spontaneity I might have had.

I told her she should write a novel but she said she didn't have the discipline. Any writing she did was done in moments snatched at the office between legal letters. She stuffed pages into her typewriter surreptitiously and whisked them out again just as fast when she had to do something official.

Mary was born on Christmas Day. She was disappointed that she hasn't been called Christina. That would have been much more exotic to her than Mary. I told her I had a different kind of gripe because I was born on Patrick's Day and should have been called Paddy instead of Aubrey, which was too exotic for me by far. We concluded that children should have the right to choose their own names, that names were monkeys on your back that you carried around with you all your life, despite being thought up on a moment's whim (or from the bottom of a bottle of whiskey).

She also felt cheated out of Christmas presents. Most people just gave her a birthday present on Christmas Day. It meant a lot to her when she got two different cards on December 25th. But at least both of us always had our birthdays off work.

We shared many of the same interests in music as well. Leonard Cohen was a particular favourite. Whenever I visited her in her house we played his music on her little turntable until it came out our ears – if that's not the wrong expression.

When I asked her what kind of books she read she said *Jane Eyre* was her favourite novel of all time. I'd never read *Jane Eyre* but *Wuthering Heights* (by Charlotte Brontë's sister Emily) had been on my B.A. course. I practically knew if off by heart. 'Emily was for the intellectuals,' she said, 'I always preferred writers who wrote from the heart.'

I mentioned some famous ones that I admired. She was familiar with them but didn't really like any of them. When I asked her why she just shrugged her shoulders. 'I can't put it into words,' she said. In subsequent conversations she was similarly tightlipped. 'I can't speak about books like the people in UCD,' she said, 'I just know what I like and what I like isn't always what these people think I should like.' She made a point of not reading writers who were 'highfalutin'. 'I don't care if it's *Finnegans Wake* or *Mills & Boon*,' she said, 'as long as it gets me through the night.'

She was more in touch with life than me. I dissected texts but she took them in more. When we watched a film together I would be checking out camera angles but she was immersed in the story. Maybe we learned a bit from each other.

When we came out of a film I usually asked her what she thought of it. If she said she enjoyed it, I'd ask her why and she'd say, 'Why do you have to analyse everything? I just liked it, that's all.' She always felt I was cross-examining her on such nights and that took all the fun out of the films for her. I tried to stop doing it, but found it difficult and had to bite my tongue every time I felt like saying something 'intellectual'. In time that became a dirty word to her – and to me.

She missed Galway a lot just as I missed Ballina. We talked about the fact that one day we'd love to go back to either place to live. The two of us had too many ties to Dublin for the foreseeable future but that didn't stop us thinking we might go back to either place to live some day.

Mary became friends with my family fairly quickly. She connected with us as if she'd known us all her life. My mother took to her in an instant and looked forward to the days she'd be calling over. She always knew Mary was relaxed when it came to the point of the night when she took her shoes off. That was a habit of hers that made her into a kind of Sandie Shaw figure.

Basil was home on holiday from New York the first time she came to Iona Villas. He was dressed in a Hawaiian shirt and spoke with what she took to be an American accent. She didn't think he was one of the family because he was so different to the rest of us. 'He's very outgoing,' she said. 'Basil is the odd one out in the family,' I explained, 'He's normal.'

One night Mary and I were nearly killed. We'd been invited to a function in the Devil's Glen in Wicklow that was organised by her boss. I drank too much and on the way home it started to rain. As I came down a hill I saw a rock in the middle of the road in front of me. I tried to swerve but the bike skidded and we ended up in the ditch. Mary was all right because she was wearing a helmet but I didn't have one on me. I got a gash on my forehead because of that. I was gushing blood but was too drunk to realise that. I thought it was just rain. When I got home I went straight to bed. The next morning my forehead was stuck to the pillow.

Mary and myself decided to get married in 1989. Neither of us was into big ceremonies so we did it like my own parents had done, without telling anyone. The only two people who knew were the priest and our two witnesses. One of them was a friend of Mary's from Artane. The other was Keith's son David. It was the priest's first wedding so he was almost as nervous as we were. Afterwards we went for a meal in a pub and from there to St Anne's Park in Raheny to take some photographs. We honeymooned on 'Costa del Dollymount' as we jokingly referred to the local beach.

I always thought of myself as a bachelor so I was apprehensive about living with somebody, even someone I cared for as much as Mary. I was also worried that I'd miss being out at night.

After a while I got used to staying in. 'Where's the wild man now?' Hugo asked me after seeing the transformation. But maybe that man had already got his marching papers. Mary said she didn't mind me being out the odd night but I told her that wasn't the way it worked. If I got the taste of pub life again it would be like a drug fix. It was either all or nothing with me. In the following months she became the social butterfly while I house-hatched.

I needed some ready cash now so I looked up the papers for jobs. The main ones advertised in the 'Situations Vacant' columns seemed to be either courier work (about a dozen offers daily) or hairdressers (about twenty). I told Mary that if I became a courier to a hairdresser I could clean up on the double.

After a few weeks I applied to one of the courier firms, presenting myself at a dingy office in the centre of the city one wet Monday morning. A group of rough diamonds in leggings were discussing the vital statistics of a secretary in Dublin 4 who wouldn't let them wash their hands in her front office. 'I gave her a French letter,' one of them said, 'and she wouldn't even sign for it.' There was raucous laughter at that.

The man behind the desk introduced himself as Trevor. 'Do you know Dublin?' he asked me. I said, 'Pretty much'. That was effectively my interview. 'This is your radio,' he said, reaching behind his desk, 'you'll get the hang of it in no time.'

He rigged me up with rain gear and gave me the address of a pick-up. Five minutes later I was on my way. It was a slightly less rigorous induction procedure than becoming a teacher. When my father said he wanted me to be a 'man of letters' I doubt this was what he had in mind. As I drove through the rainy streets looking like a hobo I wondered what he would have thought of me, the son with the brains supposedly bursting out of his head togged out now like the Michelin Man to earn a crust.

There was a pleasant mindlessness to the work. You didn't have to talk to people if you didn't want to and when you were finished you were finished. It wasn't like teaching where you brought your work home with you. You didn't have copies to correct or you didn't need to fret about the next day or the one just gone. You just did your drops and that was that.

I got up every morning at the crack of dawn and reported in, or hung around the Quays waiting for a message on my radio. It was so cold some mornings my hands tingled but then the sun would come out and the feeling would come back into them. I weaved my bike in between traffic on a hundred and one different detours, carrying everything from lampshades to umbrellas to hairdryers in my outsize bag.

The bike rarely stopped once I turned on the ignition on at first light. From then until six or later I had my foot on the gas. I only got fifteen minutes for lunch, if even that, but that made the time off sweeter. There was nothing to equal the elation of 5.30 on payday when you'd get skulled in the pub and then go home with a six-pack and watch the late-night movie, sleeping like a baby afterwards and then being a different kind of vegetable over the weekend. It was dog's work for dog's pay but heaven compared to the tensions I'd been exposed to in the previous decade.

Sometimes I had so many packages on the bike Trevor told me not to have my lunch until I'd delivered them in case I got a puncture from the extra weight. I tied them up with an expanding strap that had a hook on each end.

A lot of my time was spent going through red lights and parking where I wasn't allowed to. I'd lash up flights of stairs to offices at the top of high-rise buildings, desperately hoping there wouldn't be a ticket on the windshield when I got back. Often there was. That meant the day's earnings were basically gone. Other times I'd run a red light and pass an anxious few moments looking over my shoulder to see if there was a garda car around. Sometimes I drove on footpaths when the traffic was bad. The only thing that mattered was getting to your destination. I had to convince myself great treasures lay in the jiffy bags I carried in order to work up the enthusiasm to deliver them when nobody answered a door or a baying dog threatened to bite my leg off.

The courier work gave me more of an interest in playing snooker in the evenings. I'd done this when I was teaching as well but I was usually too wired up to enjoy it properly. Now it was different because my mind was free. It made the nights that much more relaxing hitting balls around.

In a way it was like being in the Hibs all over again. The flipping of coins over the cloth, the abstract tussle between you and a stranger, the spectral quiet of a back alley hall at midnight. You chalked your cue and feathered the cue ball, willing it on that extra inch to make your task easier. You cleared the table and then you started again, putting fifteen reds in the triangle and the six colours on the spots, over and over again like Krapp's Last Tape, picking them off like a sniper.

I was still doing journalism on the side and some days I found myself being asked to deliver parcels to newspapers and magazines I was actually writing for. I didn't like to be recognised in these offices so I kept my helmet well down on my head when handing in the material. Some of the offices had a policy whereby you had to take off your helmet before entering for fear of robberies. That made things awkward for me. I often found myself waiting outside these offices with deliveries I couldn't bring myself to carry in for fear of the journalists inside recognising me. When a courier arrived from a different company I'd usually ask him if he'd take my package in with his own one.

Sometimes I gave them money to do this. When they asked me why I was asking them to go in for me I made up some excuse about having had an argument with an editor or a secretary. The situation became complicated when letters got lost. The boss would be on my case and I'd have to forge a signature or tell a lie about the person I was supposed to have given the letter to. These circumstances led to some tense moments for me, making me seriously consider throwing my hat at it all. Mary said it was insane putting myself through this with all the education I had. She wanted me to look for a job as a remedial teacher but I told her nothing could be worse than teaching, not even this dead-end existence as a Third World writer trying to disguise himself as a postman to make ends meet.

After a few months of Arctic freezing I told Trevor I wanted to ditch the bike and get into a car instead. I thought it would give me bit more respectability if I ran into anyone I knew. 'You won't make much money on four wheels, Peter,' he told me. I knew what he meant. You couldn't turn a car around as easily in traffic as you could a bike. Some of the provincial runs were good earners but he only gave those to his 'inner circle', or the people he drank with. I hadn't attained that status yet, nor was I likely to.

I got the car anyway. If nothing else it got me in out of the cold. But he was right about the money: I only earned buttons now. There was also a lot more stress involved if you got into a traffic jam at rush hour and couldn't get to your destination. Trevor would be roaring down the line at me as I sat paralysed in a 20-car tailback. The second I got out of the gridlock I'd have to put my foot on the floor to make up for lost time.

The upside was that between drops I didn't have to face the elements. I could read *War and Peace* in the comfort of my Fiat Uno if I wanted. Not that this was advisable. The other couriers preferred *The Sun* and *The News of the World* to while away the time between drops. Anything more highbrow was frowned on. One day I was caught reading a Hemingway book and Trevor screamed out, 'What in the name of Jaysus is *that*?' as if it was a bomb. I had to apologise that it wasn't a motor magazine or the latest edition of *Playboy*.

That was the level we were at. The talk had to be about either cars or sex. Nothing else was permissible except maybe the weekly rant about money, or where you were going later that night to get slaughtered. That was the cycle upon which my life revolved at this time. I was expected to get drunk every night so I'd have funny stories to regale everyone with at the base the next day but also to be so full of energy that I did my work without a hiccup. That might have been possible for some of the people I was working with who didn't look as if they were long out of the cradle but I was pushing forty now. When I punished my body I knew all about it the next day.

Some weeks our pay cheques bounced because Trevor was on such a thin line of credit with the banks. 'We're stretched to the wire,' he kept saying, but someone told me he had a string of properties that he was renting in the Algarve.

A lot of the people I worked with were also 'signing on' so they buffeted up their income that way. At least that's why I imagined they disappeared at the same time every Wednesday morning to sign their autograph in the dole office in Gardiner Street. I didn't have such an outlet so when the cheques bounced I was left with a frugal weekend.

'This can't go on,' I said to Trevor every other week. He promised me it wouldn't but it did, time and time again. I knew I was a fool to let it happen. I also knew some of the others were getting backhanders on the quiet.

One morning I psyched myself up for a confrontation with him. I went in to the little room he had behind the office and said I wanted a word. He was on the phone at the time and he told me to wait outside. At that point something snapped inside me. Almost without realising what I was doing I took the phone out of his hand and throwing it at the wall. Then I took another one that was sitting beside it and did the same with that. He sat there looking at me, neither of us believing what had just happened. Up until now I'd been behaving like someone who wouldn't kill a fly on a holy picture.

'What do you want?' he said, looking at the two phones on the floor. I took a piece of paper out of my pocket. On it I'd written a list of the drops me owed me for. He read it slowly and went over to a box on a shelf in the corner of the room. He opened it with a key and took out a billfold that was wrapped in an elastic band. He counted seven £50 notes and handed them to me. I took them without saying anything and walked out of the room.

I later learned he'd been a policeman before going into the courier business and that he kept a gun under his desk. I wouldn't have put it past him to have shot me in another mood. But not that day. He knew I'd reached breaking point. It wasn't even about the money. I just needed to let off steam on someone, on anyone. Maybe the ten years I'd spent taking abuse from children was finally catching up on me.

That was the end of me in that company. I was no sooner out of it than I applied to other ones. There were still loads of them advertising themselves in the papers. You could get into them literally by just knocking at the door. In the next few months I did that a number of times, doing a few weeks here and there and then chucking it in for little or no reason. After so many years in a white collar post it was a novelty to be this frivolous. Maybe it was as close to Jack Kerouac as I'd ever come.

I didn't know who I was working with half the time in these companies. Someone might do a few days just to pay an ESB bill and then you'd never see them again. Most of them had something else going on in the background. Some of them were waiting for insurance claims to come up on accidents they had so they could retire to the Bahamas. We all just took the money and ran, earning it and then blowing it away like snow. It was what we called 'Fuck you money.'

One day when I was carrying a can of paint in the car I left it on its side under the seat to stop it rolling from side to side. The top of the container came off and it destroyed the carpet of the car and also a little tape recorder I used to keep under there for listening to music as I drove. I went back to the paint manufacturer and told him what happened but he wasn't interested. All he offered me was a fresh can of paint.

I'd probably have accepted that if he'd been polite but he wasn't. Maybe I was still fired up from my phone-throwing escapade because I ended up taking him to the small claims court for damages.

I had nobody to represent me there so I tried to think how my father would have handled it. I wasn't a performer like he was so that wasn't really much help. When I went into the courtroom I felt I was up against a stacked deck.

A solicitor from their side pleaded the case that I was responsible because I'd put the paint can on its side. I said there was no message on the can telling me not to do that. After that one sentence I stepped down. I think the judge was impressed with my casualness because he awarded me damages. The next time I was in Berger Paints I noticed the cans of paint carried messages on the top saying 'Not To Be Turned On Its Side'. Nobody rushed up to serve me. I could feel people's eyes burrowing through me.

Another incident happened not long after that. I was dropping some building materials into a factory but they were too heavy to lift so I asked the manager if I could drive inside to unload it. He said I could but a few minutes later a forklift operator who was working near me hit the edge of my Uno, causing a fair bit of damage to the wing. I showed it to the manager and he said he'd pay for damages but the next day he changed his tune. 'I never told you to come into the factory,' he said. 'It's your own liability'. I told my boss what happened but he was hardly surprised. 'People tell me lies every day of the week,' he said, 'What planet are you living on? Next time get it in writing.' It was a long way from studying Jean-Paul Sartre and Albert Camus on the Belfield campus or worrying about being and nothingness. I said to Mary, 'I've just swapped Rimbaud for Rambo.'

Any writing I did at this time was sporadic. The only regular slot I had was in a magazine called *Image*. I'd been doing film reviews here since the late 1970s. My father helped me get the job shortly before he died. The editor had been married to my cousin Paddy.

Paddy was a business consultant whose heart gave out at the tragically young age of 42. He was in France on a lecture tour when it happened. I only met him once in Dublin. It was the year we left Ballina. He was very quiet that day. 'I'm sorry I'm so anti-social,' he said. I didn't even know what that word meant then.

I remember him calling to our house one day in Ballina when my father was complaining that some of the locals were trying to tarnish his father's reputation by saying he was of lowly origins. (Even though P.J. Malone eventually became a magistrate, he started life in the 'rag trade'.) Paddy listened patiently to my father's problem and then said in his best Stoneyhurst accent, 'Uncle Hugh, what you have to do with these people is use reverse psychology. Don't just tell them your father was involved in the rag trade. Say he rode into town in an ass and cart.'

My father laughed so hard at that, the floor shook.

Into Book Writing

I started writing books in the mid-1990s. One of the main reasons was because any journalistic jobs I got were so uncertain. I did a lot of journalism during my teaching years but little enough of it was published. As a freelancer you were always on the outside looking in; you were at the tender mercies of editors. There were jobs for the boys (and girls) in in-house positions but I never quite succumbed to applying for a staff job. The idea of spending eight hours a day in the proximity of other journalists to me was like a working definition of hell.

The process of writing always appealed to me more than writers themselves. Maybe I knew too many of them who wrote like angels and lived like devils. Reading their material I'd imagine they were the very souls of sensitivity and then at a function or some trendy party I'd see them shafting a colleague and think: Could this really be the same person who wrote that wonderful tribute to Goethe in yesterday's paper? Basically I agreed with e.e. cummings, who said once that he preferred the company of ice cream salesman to that of writers. (I would have agreed with that even if I didn't like ice cream as much as I do).

I also lacked ambition as a writer. Jack London said he'd rather win a water-fight in a swimming pool than write the Great American novel. I always thought I'd prefer to win the World Snooker Championship than write the Great Irish one. (I realised at this stage of my life that neither of these eventualities were very likely.)

I often had my articles bowdlerised at this time, or even pulled from publications at the last minute for little or no reason. Family members told me I was great but it was as dangerous to believe this as it was to believe the Dublin 4 critics who were lining up to take pot shots at me every time I put pen to paper. As Ernest Hemingway put it, 'If you listen to the good stuff about yourself you have to listen to the bad stuff too.'

One day the editor of a magazine I'd sent something to informed me that my submission was winging its way to the waste paper basket as we spoke. Other disgruntled souls seemed to relish telling me that I was a substandard clod who really should never have given up the day job. Sometimes I took these comments to heart but more often I felt they were being made by people who were either jealous of me or resentful. There were times when I thought that even if I got an interview with God, they'd say something like, 'Nice piece but I think we did Him last week. And isn't He a bit dated?'

Most of the articles I did were published in the *Evening Press*. Eventually they came to the notice of the NUJ and I had to join the union to be allowed continue. I'd always been waiting for a phone call from them when I was writing for *Image* but they didn't mind the occasional column. In the *Evening Press* I had too big a profile for them to ignore.

To join the union you had to prove that two-thirds of your earnings were coming from journalism. About a tenth of mine were so I had to dummy up receipts to get in. Most people who dummy up receipts are trying to pretend they earned less than they did so I was in an unusual situation.

After I was accepted, the inevitable happened: I started to get less work in the *Evening Press* so I really didn't need to be in the union at all now. In future years I paid back to the union everything I'd ever earned from that paper in my monthly subs. (That was probably God punishing me for the false receipts).

. When things weren't happening for me on the journalistic front I went up to the attic and unearthed some old stories I'd written when I was in Iona Villas and tried to dust them down. I had so many of them written since the seventies I felt I should do something with them. I had sent a lot of them to David Marcus in the *Irish Press* and he published some of them in his New Writing page.

Marcus was a shrewd critic and an inspired developer of unknown writers. More than anyone else he was responsible for me becoming one. (To that extent he has a lot to answer for.) One of the first stories I sent him had a scene in a country railway station where a woman was about to throw herself under a train. The way I wrote it, there were about a hundred people milling around her. He called me into his office in Burgh Quay and said, 'This is a railway station in the middle of nowhere. It's 8 a.m. What are all the people doing there? It reads like a scene from *Anna Karenina*.'

Seduced by the early acceptance in a national paper I started to send him a story almost every week. Many rainforests could have been saved had I resisted the temptation to be Artane's Samuel Beckett. He tried to be kind about my work but it was inevitable that the quality would vary inversely with the quantity. As my lachrymose diatribes continued, his responses grew more intemperate. One day he sent a story back with a little note that said, 'There's less to this than meets the eye.' I got the message and stopped sending him things.

As I got to know the literary scene better I realised it was much easier to get journalism accepted than fiction so I ditched my Tortured Adolescent persona and tried to become Steve Martin instead.

Writing wasn't really about what you wanted to do, I knew, it was about what the public wanted. I didn't want to end up shooting myself like Vincent van Gogh because my work wasn't being bought by the public. Instead I went out into the marketplace and dumbed myself down to meet the horse-traders.

After my work in the *Evening Press* thinned out I tried other outlets for it without much success. I rarely even got to speak with editors I tried to contact. They seemed to be permanently in meetings. All you'd get was their voicemail. I was reminded of Woody Allen's comment, 'It's not just dog eat dog in this world; it's dog won't return dog's phone calls.'

Sometimes the excuse for such laxity was inspired. One editor apologised for not returning my phone call because he had to go to Australia the previous day. 'I'm not talking just about yesterday,' I said, 'I'm talking about the way you've been ignoring me for the past ten years.' (That caused an interesting pause on the line).

Publishers often sent me novels to review in the very same post as a rejection slip concerning one of my book proposals. This was a bit like getting a 'Dear John' letter from a girlfriend accompanied by a request that you write something nice about her new beau. I took no small degree of pleasure in making bonfires of such novels – a bit like Glenn with his DOGS in the flat in Morehampton Road during my university years.

I decided to try my hand at writing books in the early nineties. I needed to get my teeth into something big to take my mind off the daily grind. I knew I was leaving myself open to abuse by doing so. I'd made some enemies over the years as a result of things I'd written about their own books in reviews. People in Ireland also had long memories. Not for nothing had Brendan Behan once referred to Dublin as the largest village in Europe. The longer you spent in it, the more you met the same people at functions. Sooner or later, unless you were a saint, you were going to rattle sabres with some of the more irascible ones. As Ulick O'Connor once put it, 'Irish Alzheimer's means you forget everything but the grudges.'

I had my first book published in 1995. It was a collection of funny facts about celebrities that I called *Hollyweird*. The publishers flew me over to London and arranged a schedule of over twenty interviews for me with various radio stations. I thought I was going over for a holiday but I never worked so hard in my life.

Every day there was some publicity person talking to me about it. I stationed myself in a booth in the offices of the BBC for some of the interviews. In the evenings little pieces of paper were slipped under the door of my hotel room naming places where I had to present myself at different times. I duly turned up and gave them the patter they wanted. Most of them asked me the same questions. When the tenth interviewer asked me what the previous nine had, i.e. was it true that Melanie Griffith had a pear tattoo on her left buttock, I began to suspect something strange was going on. Eventually the penny dropped. The location of Ms Griffith's tattoo placements were in a press release the publisher had sent to all the interviewers. They'd read this but probably not the book itself.

The next book I wrote was *The Guinness Book of Humorous Irish Anecdotes*. It came about through an agent I had in London called Chelsey Fox – a good name for an agent. (I'd met her when I was promoting *Hollyweird*). When I was researching it I wrote to about a hundred people in Irish public life asking them if they'd like to contribute an anecdote. About six replied, all in the negative. Ireland's future Taoiseach John Bruton (whom I would interview when he attained that office) wrote to say that the only anecdote he had was that he had no anecdote. This amused me slightly so I decided to put it in – especially since most of my other leads were being deafeningly silent.

After a few weeks of such silence another letter came in the door. It was from the comedian Brendan O'Carroll saying that he'd like to help. A phone number was given at the top so I rang him. I told him I'd be delighted to have him in the book but seeing as Guinness was a conservative publishing house he might be better off to avoid some of his more racy humour. If there was a four-lettered word in the anecdote I told him he could substitute another word instead if he kept the gist of the story. He didn't appreciate that approach. A few days later I got a letter from him. It said, 'You want me to lie but not say 'fuck'. I'd prefer to say 'fuck' and not lie.' That was the end of my involvement with Brendan O'Carroll.

Another book I did at that time was a small hardback about the film *Ryan's Daughter*. There was a series of books on the shelves called *Movies Made in Ireland* and I felt it would slot into that. They were published by a company called GLI but when I approached Pat Neville, the owner of the company, he told me the old story: he had no money. If I wanted it out I'd have to fund it myself.

He suggested publishing it in conjunction with a book on the film *Michael Collins* that Neil Jordan had just made. I thought this was a good idea so I approached Jordan for permission to use some stills from the film in the book. His father Michael had been one of my lecturers in Pat's and I'd also met Neil himself at a party one night. He hadn't been too friendly to me on that occasion, greeting me with the line, 'Not another fucking teacher.'

Time hadn't mellowed him. He refused to allow me to use any stills from the film and Warner Brothers were looking for $500 a shot so that was clearly out of the question. I ended up going out to *The Star* newspaper where a young man in the photography department gave me about twenty location shots he'd taken when the film was being made. They featured all the main stars in period garb but they weren't from the film itself so they weren't the property of Warner Bros. I was deeply indebted to him and asked how I could pay him. 'Just get me three packets of fags from the newsagents across the road,' he said. The few pounds the cigarettes cost saved me the ten grand Warner Brothers were looking for.

I wanted to print 3000 copies of the books but the man running the company said that was a bad idea, that even if they sold out we wouldn't make any money with that kind of a print run. He advised me to run off 10,000 copies instead to try and make a kill. That meant going to the bank for a loan.

Over the next few months I priced the job. The quotations I was getting from Irish printers were off the wall. In desperation I approached a company in Budapest where a man called Istvan Lukacs told me in his pidgin English - I needed an interpreter to intercede in our conversations - that he could do the job for a fraction of the cost Irish printers were looking for. Ireland were charging me the same amount for the covers as Istvan was for the entire books. They sold well for a while but after paying off my overdraft and the interest I barely broke even. I ended up with over 3500 unsold copies of *Ryan's Daughter* in my attic.

One year when I was down in Dingle on a holiday I went for a walk on Inch beach. At the edge of the beach there was a café called Sammy's and a bookshop attached to it. As I walked in the door I saw a huge lithograph of *Ryan's Daughter* on the wall. I suddenly thought: This is where the movie was filmed.

I asked Sammy if he'd like to buy 3500 books from me. When he picked himself up off the floor – questions like that have a habit of giving booksellers premature coronaries – he said he'd think about it. He eventually took the whole 3500 off me, albeit for a knockdown price. He also said he'd take some of my unsold *Michael Collins* books if I wanted. I threw them all into the back seat of the car a few weeks later and made off for Kerry. Mary was with me. She said, 'I hope Michael Collins behaves himself with Ryan's daughter in the back seat.' (On first inspection they seemed to be compatible).

Sammy was shrewd in his dealings with me. He was also the only Iranian I've ever met who spoke English with a pronounced Kerry accent. 'You should realise it will take me about ten years to sell these,' he told me. I did, but I also realised he'd probably become rich in the process.

My main problem had been getting photos of *Ryan's Daughter* for the book. 'This series isn't about words,' Pat had advised me at the outset, 'it's about pictures.' This wasn't exactly music to a writer's ears but I'd heard through the grapevine that a man called Peter Vollebreght had a huge collection of stills from the film. I met him in a bar one day and gave him £100 for a selection. He was delighted with that as he was out of work at the time. Before we left the bar he dropped a clanger: 'I can't give you permission to use the photos.'

That was a stumbling block. I decided to write a begging letter to Ted Turner, Jane Fonda's ex-husband. (Turner Entertainment held the rights to them). He must have been happy with Ms Fonda at that point because he went easy on me, only charging me $120 for the lot.

I think we sold about 1500 copies of the books overall, at £4 a pop. 'The ignorant Yanks buy them in the tourist shops,' the rep told me, 'It's only when they start reading them on the plane back to Martha that they realise they're crap.' (You wouldn't want to be sensitive to be a writer.)

The following year I offered Duckworth Publishing another book I was working on, a collection of quotations from Brendan Behan. The Tessa Sayle Agency represented the people who held the rights to Behan's estate and they dug in their heels about releasing copyright. I secured the services of an octogenarian Russian agent, Vernon Futerman, to liaise with the Italian woman who worked in the agency to get the permission to use the quotes. So a Russian met an Italian in England to release rights for an Irishman. I felt quite important. (But I didn't make a penny from the book).

My interest in Behan increased following this. A few months later I suggested collecting a bunch of funny stories about him to a publishing friend of mine called Gus Smith. Gus said he liked the idea but it was dependent on Sean Penn taking on the role of Behan for a forthcoming movie of *Borstal Boy*. Penn was spending a lot of time in Dublin at the time with his new love Robin Wright. He became so immersed in the Behan project he even had some of his teeth removed in order to feel more like him. (It gave the expression 'getting one's teeth into a role' a whole new meaning).

Penn also spent a fair amount of time drinking in Mulligan's pub that year to try and feel more like Behan. (I'd have liked that part of the research myself). I felt he'd take the part but he jumped the ship at the last minute, leaving me with a book that now looked to be a dead duck. I decided that if he ever came back to Dublin I'd gladly remove the rest of his teeth for him, with or without the Behan project in mind.

A few months later I was watching Pat Kenny's talk show on the television when Brendan's brother Brian came on it as a guest. After the show was over I rang the TV station and asked them what hotel he was staying at. I was surprised when they told me. It turned out to be on Stephen's Green so the next morning I went there and ambushed Brian over breakfast. 'How would you like to work on a book with me about your brother?' I asked him. He jumped at the idea.

For the next year or so Brian and myself collaborated on a book that came to be called *The Brothers Behan*. It was partly a biography of Brian and partly a collection of the anecdotes I'd amassed for Gus Smith from the aborted Sean Penn project. It fell between a lot of stools but still somehow came together.

When we had it finished we launched it in the only place possible: a bar. We chose McDaid's, where Behan had done most of his drinking. Brian came to the launch with his third wife, Sally. She was younger than me even though Brian was now in his seventies. The next day we brought the two of them down to Glendalough and went for a meal afterwards. Brian became a close friend to myself and Mary during the writing of the book but Sally died tragically the year after it came out. Brian was heartbroken and didn't live long after that.

I remembered him with fondness. Like his more famous brother he was an eccentric to the core. He once set up a society for distressed women on a boat. 'If they're not distressed going in,' his mother warned, 'they will be coming out'. After the paedophilia scandals broke out among the clergy in Ireland Brian phoned me in an agitated condition one night from Brighton. He said he was worried that he hadn't been abused in the Artane Industrial School where he spent his early years. 'Was I not attractive enough?' he said, 'All my friends were abused.' It wasn't a subject to be joked about but with Brian different rules applied.

He was a joy to work with and a joy to know. At the time of his death he claimed to have set up a society for the abolition of marriage and to have 300-plus paid-up members. All you could do was laugh. A sixties child out of his time, his *joie de vivre* was inimitable. He hated dour writers like Samuel Beckett, whom he described as 'a long string of piss'. After Beckett wrote a play called *Breath* (which lasted only a minute) Brian said he was starting an equally short one called *Fart*. At the beginning of our collaboration he plagued me with calls about when I thought I could get it done. 'Rome wasn't built in a day,' I said to him, to which he replied, 'I wasn't on that job.'

Most of the journalism I was doing at this time was for the *Evening Press*. One day I got a call from John Boland, the features editor. He said he needed a photo of me for a new column he wanted me to be a part of called *At Wit's End*. I told him that could be awkward for me because many of my friends knew me as Peter and I didn't fancy the idea of my identity being revealed. I told him I hated the name Aubrey and rarely used it with people I knew. 'Why the fuck do you use it for writing then?' he asked.

I tried to explain my predicament to him. 'Engelbert Humperdinck's real name is Gerry Dorsey,' I said. 'That's fine for him but I'm different. I'm not looking for attention. If I was born with a name like Engelbert Humperdinck I'd want to change it to something like Gerry Dorsey.' 'That sounds like inverted snobbery,' he said, 'If you weren't looking for attention you wouldn't want a byline. You'd have a pen name.' He had a point. What was funny about my situation was that my pseudonym was the one I used in real life while my writing one was my actual name.

The column couldn't be sacrificed so I knew I was going to have to disguise myself in some way for the photo. The next day I went into a theatrical accessory shop and bought myself a wig and a fake moustache. When I got home I tried them on. Then I added a hat and an old pair of glasses that had belonged to my mother.

I set out for a photo booth with a tartan scarf draped rakishly around my neck to complete my disguise. With a kooky hat and a Groucho Marx moustache I felt I could just about swing things. What I didn't bank on was running into an old friend as I came out of the booth. 'Aubrey?' she said tentatively. This made me feel my disguise wasn't as good as I imagined. She was somebody I knew from my acting days. After an initial moment of panic I told her I was appearing in a play shortly and was trying to get 'in character'. She didn't look very convinced.

I sent the photo in to John Boland. He wasn't over the moon about it but accepted it grudgingly. The day my first article appeared with the photo I showed it to Mary. She said I looked like an Iranian terrorist. I didn't mind that if I was unrecognisable. Later that day I called into the snooker club. I was chatting to the owner for a few minutes when I noticed he had the *Evening Press* open on the counter before him on the page where my article and photo were.

As we finished talking he started reading my article. I felt like someone in a movie under the Witness Protection Scheme in the scene where the hero infiltrates the hoodlum's gang under an assumed identity and then one day they find a photograph of him with his real name under it. When I said this to Mary she said, 'That's a bit dramatic. You're not in a James Cagney film. You're in *The Evening Press*.'

A few months later *The Star* newspaper interviewed me about one of my books. I was again faced with the old problem: They wanted a photo of me for the article. This led to another minor panic. I raided the biscuit box where I kept all my photos and tried to find one where I didn't look like myself. Mary said, 'Are you still going for the Iranian terrorist image?'

I chose a photo Basil had taken of me a few years before. I was in a group of about ten people in it. We were standing beside a statue of James Joyce in the city centre. My head was about the size of a pea in it so I felt safe. What I didn't realise was that the picture department would blow the photograph up and cut everyone else out. The result was that my face looked like I had the worst case of acne in recorded time. The even worse part was that I was still recognisable. I didn't leave the house until it got dark for days after this for fear of someone asking me about it. The next time the situation arose I vowed to send the relevant newspaper a photo of Basil instead. The interview in *The Star* had been done over the phone so no one would have known what I looked like. 'What about

Basil' Mary asked, 'how will he explain it to his friends?' 'Maybe he'll be delighted,' I said, 'He loves photographs.'

To avoid further problems I decided to write for places that would have little or no interest in what I looked like. In some ways I felt as if I was under house arrest. I thought I might need to consult with someone like Salman Rushdie for advice. He obviously had a more sophisticated set of disguises than I had.

I went through a brief period of sending articles to the *Irish Times* in the following months. They used to take book reviews from me in the old days and I also had a feature printed there once commemorating Walt Whitman's centenary but after that I could have wallpapered my room with their rejection slips. The Whitman piece must have been read widely because for ages afterwards people came up to me telling me they liked it. Had it become a collector's item, I wondered? People who hadn't even seen my books, or the hundreds of articles I wrote for *The Evening Press*, came up to me in the street and said, 'I liked your Walt Whitman article.' Maybe Walt himself even got reincarnated to read it.

One night during a radio interview for a book I was promoting a few years later the interviewer said, 'Are you still writing for *The Times*?' I told him I hadn't had anything in that newspaper for about eight years, a comment that floored him. Afterwards an innumerable number of people still continued to come up to me enquiring about my *Times* features, so much so that I was eventually tempted to write a letter to the editor saying, 'Dear Madam, This is to state that in my entire life I have never had more than a half dozen articles in your newspaper, and nothing at all within the last decade. I would deeply appreciate it if you advised the people of Ireland of this statistic so I can go about my daily life in peace.'

When we lived in Ballina my father was always writing letters to *The Times* on anything that upset him over the years. Only rarely were they printed. A man I knew who worked in the paper informed me one day that they had a Crank File devoted to his outpourings. With my own humble missive, I thought, I'd be carrying on a hallowed family tradition.

Elvis and Other Headaches

The biggest problem I ever had with a publisher was in 1997. That was the year I decided to write a biography of Elvis Presley to commemorate the twentieth anniversary of his death.

I did it in conjunction with the Elvis Social Club, a spin-off from the official fan club. We used to meet in a pub on the Quays and under the influence of too many pints of Smithwick's dance around the place like idiots to karaoke versions of songs like 'Mystery Train' and 'The Wonder of You'. It was run by John Kavanagh, a very nice guy who was also an Elvis impersonator. His girlfriend at the time was Dee Maher, an equally friendly lady who'd seen Elvis live over twenty times. Dee actually got a letter from Elvis once thanking her for all her work on behalf of the club. She allowed me to reproduce it in the book.

We launched it in a pub on Thomas Street and everyone got suitably sozzled. At the end of the night Mary and myself tried to sing 'I Can't Help Falling in Love With You' from a rostrum John set up for the night. By that stage I could hardly stand never mind sing. Some sadist captured the moment on video and presented it to me afterwards. It cured me of any desire to be an Elvis impersonator. (Maybe that was his intention).

On the anniversary of the night itself, August 16th 1997, I rang up a bar in Camden Street where an Elvis impersonator was doing a show. I asked the manager if he'd let me set up a stand with my books on it. He said he thought it was a good idea but he wanted 10% of my earnings for giving me the stand. I had no problem with that. Later in the evening I brought a few hundred books into the bar and set them up at the top of the stairs, just outside the room where the Elvis impersonator was doing his show. I had posters of Elvis all around the stand and the books were displayed prominently but I didn't sell even one copy that night. Everybody just wanted to hear the music and get drunk.

The night was a sobering experience for me, if that's not the wrong expression. It taught me that it made about as much sense to try and sell a book in a pub as it would have to try to sell a pint of beer in a bookshop.

The book was originally supposed to have been published by a man in Bray called Terry Rowan, but Rowan led me a merry dance, dropping out of the deal just a few months before publication. The deal was just a verbal one but I trusted him so I wasn't too fussed about not having a contract.

Coming up to publication, though, I got a bit nervous when the contract still hadn't arrived. It was like the proverbial 'cheque in the post', always on the way to you but never quite there. On the eve of publication he said he'd had some problems and was sadly waving goodbye to my manuscript. This caused me to have a major panic attack. I told him what I thought of him in language I wouldn't like to repeat here. (Let's just say it made Bob Geldof sound like a Reverend Mother).

By this stage I'd had numerous meetings with him and had also employed a man to format the book. When I asked Rowan for compensation for these expenses his reaction was simply to say, 'This conversation is now over.' I couldn't take this lying down so I went to a solicitor for legal advice. He told me I was on shaky ground seeing as I had no contract but I had enough other documentation to make him sympathetic to my plight. He agreed to employ a barrister and we went to court. I was only looking for £700, a mere fraction of my overall costs. I told the barrister it was a question of principle with me rather than anything else, that what I was seeking was a moral victory rather than a financial one. My father had often told me of cases where plaintiffs were awarded a penny as a token. I thought I'd even be happy with that.

Rowan didn't show up when I appeared at the District Court on the appointed day so I was awarded damages. I thought that was the end of it but then he appealed the case to the Circuit Court. I now realised he was trying to make himself into something of a nuisance.

When we got to the Circuit Court I saw that he'd employed a solicitor. He looked very imposing. My star witness was my typesetter, Jimmy Lundberg. Jimmy had been in touch with Rowan about the book and felt he could shake him with his testimony but he was less gung-ho when he saw the solicitor dressed up in his finery. As the solicitor took the stand, Jimmy tapped me on the shoulder and whispered, 'Do you mind if I say something to you, Aubrey?' I said 'Go ahead.' He said, 'In my opinion, we're fucked.' I thanked him for his vote of confidence.

The solicitor tried to give me the third degree when I took the stand but I kept my cool. Jimmy was next up and he testified well, letting the courtroom know just how deep we were into the project before it was called off. John Kavanagh also wrote a letter for me that we gave to the judge. It testified to the fact that he'd spoken to Rowan on the phone and was assured by him that he going to publish a significant print run of the book.

A part of me felt the whole business was absurd. Six months of my life and two court cases for a few measly pounds. How Elvis would have laughed. Or would he? I suddenly remembered the fact that a book had probably caused his death. It was the one written by his bodyguards, spilling the beans on his excesses. Two weeks after it came out Elvis was in his grave. John Lennon put it well when he said, 'It's always the courtiers who kill the King.'

Despite my doubts I won the case and was awarded the compensation I asked for. It was pittance in comparison to what I would have made if the book had actually been published but as I told the barrister it was never about that for me. Outside the court he said to me, 'Well, you've got your moral victory.'

A few minutes later a photographer from the *Irish Independent* approached me and a crowd began to gather. Before I knew where I was I found a media circus around me. Microphones were thrust in my face and I was asked for my reaction to what had gone on. I couldn't believe it. I thought this was a trivial case nobody would have been bothered about.

'Let's get a shot of you,' the photographer said, raising his camera. 'If you click that,' I said, 'there'll be another court case here, with you in the dock. Either that or I'll break your jaw.' Suddenly I felt like Frank Sinatra.

My father would have been amused. It was the twentieth anniversary of his death, just as it had been of Elvis'. In one sense I felt I'd done it for him. I remembered his last case, the one he went down to Ballina to fight, and how he'd seen the man reading the newspaper upside down. I'd had a similar sensation one day when I went out to Bray and asked Rowan for the contract. 'It's around here somewhere,' he said, making as if to look around his shelves. That was the day I realised something was fishy.

I was standing there savouring my victory when he passed by me. I was tempted to say, '*Now* the conversation is over,' but I didn't.

A journalist came up to me and said, 'Could I have a few words from you about what just happened?' 'No comment,' I replied, 'This isn't for the papers.' 'Really?' he said, 'Did you not know it's already in the *Evening Herald*?' I was stunned. They'd obviously heard about it in advance and had the piece pre-set.

The man with the camera told me it was going to feature in the following day's paper as well. When I heard that I panicked. I ran down the stairs from the courtroom, frantically looking for a phone-box. I found one just outside the building and rang the features editor of the *Independent*.

'Please kill the story,' I pleaded down a bad line, 'it's not the kind of publicity I want for the book.' But he said he couldn't, that it was the sort of thing people liked to read about. 'I've been writing for your paper on and off for over twenty years now,' I said, 'I'm asking you this as a favour.' But he was unflinching.

The next day the story was everywhere – in the broadsheets, the tabloids, you name it. The headline in the *Independent* read, 'One for the Money', making me feel totally misrepresented. These were the very papers that had pointedly ignored me over the years when I was looking for reviews of my books. Now they were putting me on their front pages with all of the wrong kind of publicity. Suddenly I knew how film-stars felt when interviewers didn't want to talk about their work as much as some trivial titbit in their private lives.

I felt the whole media slant was totally unbalanced, making me out to be litigious and mercenary. The truth was that a man had broken a gentleman's agreement a heartbeat away from publication of a book. The whole business made me more cynical about journalism than I already was, which was saying something.

The book was well reviewed but some of the people in the fan club didn't like me saying Elvis had a drug problem, despite the fact that twelve different substances were found in his body after he died. Or that all his films weren't masterpieces.

One night at a function I'd been asked to attend to donate some copies to the Friedreich's Ataxia Society a woman came up to me with a growl on her face and said, 'So you're the horrible man who the book on Elvis. Well let me tell you this: I burned it.' 'Good for you,' I said. I felt strangely complimented that someone would have such strong feelings about something I wrote. As my father used to say, 'Love me or hate me but don't ignore me.' I learned afterwards that she was the wife of the man who ran the Elvis fan club that was in competition with our social club. Once again politics had raised its ugly head. When a radio programme devoted specifically to Elvis failed to mention it and I learned that the same man was behind this I realised what a cauldron I'd fallen into.

Whether out of masochism or some other reason I now started another book on Elvis, a spoof where I pretended to have found Elvis' hidden diaries in a disused shed near Tupelo. I sent it to a publisher in London, Simon Mitchell of Quince Books. He said he was interested in it but he needed a sugar daddy to fund its publication. He got in touch with a man he knew called Ray Santilli. Ray had become famous – or infamous – for a spoof he'd done some years before. He pretended to have performed an autopsy on an extra-terrestrial being – as you would. (This went on to become the subject of an Ant 'n Dec movie, *Alien Autopsy*).

Ray also had hundreds of rare photographs of Elvis, and a letter he wrote the day he died - about, of all things, American football. Simon and Ray flew over from London one day to show me all their stuff. They brought me for lunch and we discussed publishing the diaries with a big media splash. Ray said he had connections in Japan that he hoped could fund it.

Hugo was doing Elvis impersonations in bars for free pints at this time. I thought it would be good if he could launch it dressed up in Elvis gear. We could go into a theatrical shop and buy him a jumpsuit with a high collar and a rhinestone belt. My idea was that as Elvis Hugo would say he hadn't died at all in 1977. Instead he flew to Dublin from Memphis in 1977 and got work stacking shelves incognito in a supermarket in Donnybrook. Hugo could do interviews where he said my discovery of the diaries blew Elvis' cover and made him come out of hiding to declare who he really was. (I knew all about double identities from my years as Peter Murphy).

Ray told me to put all my ideas on hold as he tried to get the book off the ground. The first thing that had to be done was to get it 'legalled'. He gave it to a lawyer he knew in Los Angeles and he went through it with a fine toothcomb. Then he showed it to Joe Esposito, the best man at Elvis' wedding.

Esposito liked it but he thought there were some parts of it that might be sensitive to living people, like for instance Elvis' widow Priscilla, or some members of the so-called Memphis Mafia, Elvis' entourage. When he showed it to Priscilla she insisted on a number of cuts. The lawyer also told Ray it couldn't be endorsed by Graceland so we'd have to plough a lonely furrow. Ray said he'd have to take a raincheck on it at this point because there were too many complications so the book stayed in dry dock. The upshot is that, for the moment at least, Elvis can go on stacking shelves in Donnybrook to his heart's content without fear of being 'outed'. (At the time of writing he would be 78 years old so I hope they're not giving him too much overtime).

I found it hard to get motivated on new projects after the Elvis book was sidelined. I kept writing books and articles but my spirits were at a low ebb and maybe publishers sensed that. No more than Elvis I was also getting on in years. John Kavanagh said to me, 'Ain't it funny how time slips away'. (He had an Elvis line for every situation).

A whole new generation of whizz kids with laptop computers seemed to be taking over the journalistic scene. I felt like something out of the ark with my bockety old Canon typewriter. I started to think the only way I could get something published was to become a news story myself, as happened with Terry Rowan. (Though I hardly wanted a repeat of that).

For a time I considered putting myself about on the social scene and getting to know the editors personally. 'That's hardly on the cards,' Mary said, 'considering you make Howard Hughes look like a party animal.' An editor I knew came up with a good suggestion one day. 'Why don't you stand on the top of Liberty Hall with an Uzi and start blowing people away. That should get you some good publicity.' I said I'd get back to him on his suggestion but it would be dependent on him providing me with a state-of-the-art Uzi. I wouldn't want to miss my targets.

The frustrating thing was sending out articles you'd worked hard on and not knowing if they were being read or dumped because you got no feedback on them. Editors tended to hide behind secretaries. If they weren't in meetings or at funerals or weddings or parties or conferences they were either missing, presumed dead, or on their summer holidays on Jupiter.

One night at a party I ran into an editor who'd been studiously avoiding replying to my suggestions for many moons. 'So you actually exist,' I said to him as he passed me on the stairs with a glass of brandy in his hand. I thought I might have embarrassed him but his numb reaction suggested he didn't even knew who I was. This made me realise the truth of the old saw that there was a Yes list and a No list in Dublin's social scene and I wasn't even on the No list. The following morning I said to Mary, 'I was at a party last night and there were so many famous people there, I was the only person there that I didn't recognise.'

I felt the best way of keeping my sanity was to keep writing books. They had a longer shelf life than the journalism and no matter how many rejections you got there was always some light at the end of the tunnel (even if it was only a train coming the other way).

A literary agent told me humour book had a better chance of being accepted than anything else so for the next few years I concentrated on these. I compiled quotation anthologies on every subject I could think of – drink, sex, politics, sex, sport, sex, and, er, sex. I also decided to re-work Ambrose Bierce's *Devil's Dictionary* into a modern context, calling it *The Cynic's Dictionary*. This went on to become my best-selling book, going from hardback into paperback in both Britain and the United States and even coming out in a Spanish edition called *El Dictionario de Los Cinicos*. This was the first time I ever saw one of my books in a foreign language. Whenever I went to parties now and people asked me what I was working on, I was able to draw myself up to my full height and say in my most self-important voice, '*El Dictionario de Los Cinicos*.' That was usually enough to make them depart the room in record time.

Robson Books published a biography I wrote of Ernest Hemingway to coincide with his centenary in 1999. I had hoped to re-work the thesis I'd done on him in 1975 but when I went out to UCD and asked for it they sent me into a room where there were about 500 other theses and basically told me to dig if I felt like it. (I didn't).

After writing the book I sent it to over a hundred publishers and they all rejected it. I was just about to give up hope when I casually mentioned it to a man I knew in Northampton who'd published some of my quotation books. He said, 'Try Jeremy Robson,' as Jeremy was a friend of his. I did that and Jeremy accepted it. I'd sent it to over a hundred people before him without any success. I don't know whether this demonstrates the fact that most things in publishing come about by accident or the fact that it's who you know that counts more than anything else. Probably both.

Working with Robson plc was my first experience of the impersonal nature of publishing. So impersonal was it that they didn't even inform me when the book was published. I was sitting in the offices of *The Phoenix* magazine on Baggot Street one day with the features editor, Paddy Prendiville. We were talking about the writer Colm Toibin. Paddy had asked me to write a piece about Toibin because he'd just been nominated for a prestigious literary award.

In the middle of the conversation he said to me, 'I see you have a new book out on Ernest Hemingway.' 'No,' I said, 'that's not coming out for a few weeks yet.' With that, he pulled a copy of it down from a shelf. Robson's publicity department had sent out review copies without even telling me the book was out. The author is always the last to know.

When I was writing it I tried to contact Hemingway's third wife Martha Gellhorn for an interview but she didn't get back to me. Gellhorn committed suicide a few years later, at the ripe old age of 89. When I told Mary this she said, 'When she got that far, wouldn't you think she'd have stuck it out?' I could see her point but suicide was almost a religion for people associated with Hemingway.

His father killed himself, as did Hemingway himself, his sister Ursula, his brother Leicester and possibly his other sister Marcelline. The father of his first wife Hadley also committed suicide and, more recently, his grand-daughter Margaux. 'I'm curious to know how long a Hemingway can last in the natural way,' his son Jack speculated after the last tragedy.

After I finished writing the book I learned that Hemingway's other son, Gregory, also died in strange circumstances. He was dressed as a woman on the night he passed away and arrested under the impression that he was one, dying in the woman's section of the prison in which he was placed after being arrested.

Gregory had been a doctor for most of his life. He was married to Valerie Danby-Smith, an *Irish Times* journalist who met Hemingway in Spain towards the end of his life and went on to become his secretary. There were rumours he had an affair with her when he was married to Mary, his last wife. Valerie met Gregory at Hemingway's funeral and the following year they married. They had five children.

I was intrigued to find out that Gregory was a cross-dresser, and also that Danby-Smith had a child by Brendan Behan. I got her phone number from a person I knew when I was writing the book and rang her up to ask her if she'd help me with my research. 'Who are you?' she asked me in the middle of one of my questions to her. When I told her my name she hung up.

Not everyone was as unfriendly to me as Martha Gellhorn and Valerie Danby-Smith. Editors asked me to interview various people around this time and some of them proved very charming. Interviewing John McGahern about his book *Amongst Women* was like talking to a kindly country farmer – which he was, of course. I rang him off and on in the following years and he never played the writer. He liked me telling him stories about my mother's people in Roscommon, some of whom he knew.

The snooker player Ronnie O'Sullivan was also a pleasure to meet. Mary heard on the radio one day that he was going to be in Bewley's Hotel in Tallaght that afternoon so we jumped in the car and headed out there. He chatted to me like an old friend when I asked him if I could interview him. He even asked me to drive him from Tallaght to the Airport when we were finished. It was the first (and probably last) time I had a world champion in my car. On the way he took a phone call from his father, who was in prison for murder at the time. (It was also the first time anyone in my car made a phone call to a convicted murderer).

Ronnie was easier to talk to than Jimmy White, my other snooker hero. I spent most of the 1980s trying to get Jimmy to talk to me and finally got him to agree. By then, though, I think he was almost afraid of me because I'd been ringing him so much. Mary said, 'Maybe he thinks you're gay' and she was probably right. He would have been entitled to think that as I almost stalked him all through the 1980s.

I finally met him one morning at the Keadeen Hotel, the place I'd tried to talk to him so many years before without success. I put a pint of Smithwicks before him as well as one for myself at 11 a.m. one Monday morning and waited for his reaction. Either I thought that was what he would have wanted or I was trying to be streetwise. He was dressed in a scruffy jumper and Levi's and probably thinking about his life back in London. (He'd just lost a match and was about to head back there). I put about twenty questions to him and he answered me in oneliners.

He wasn't being rude, that was just the way he was. The two of us sat sipping our beer but there was nothing to say: his playing style said it all. I'd chased him halfway round Ireland but now that I was sitting opposite him I went blank. It was as if the search had drained me. It was like the Paul Newman joke about the man who lusts after a beautiful woman for years and when she finally agrees to go out with him he says, 'Honey, I can't. I'm too tired.'

Another person I met during this time was Charlton Heston. He was in Dublin to promote his autobiography but he didn't like it when I pointed out a typo in it. I'd had the audacity to criticise Moses and he let me know it. I felt he was going to break the two tablets of stone all over again. (Suddenly I knew how Michael Moore must have felt when he confronted him about gun control in *Bowling for Columbine*).

I also ran into Billy Connolly one day. This wasn't in my capacity as a writer but when I was doing the courier work. He was on Stephens Green in the middle of a torrential shower and I was carrying about a dozen parcels and on my way to a drop in the Shelbourne Hotel. 'Let me shake your hand,' I said when I spotted him going into the hotel, 'I'm a journalist. I'd love to interview you.' He looked at me as if I was from outer space. I had about six layers of clothing on me as well as leggings and a balaclava. I also had my expanding belt strapped around my waist with a load of parcels inside it, making me look like a suicide bomber. He exploded into laughter and then marched into the hotel. Obviously he thought I was a nutter. Maybe he was right.

An earlier encounter with John McEnroe proved to be a tenser affair. When I heard he was staying in the Berkeley Court Hotel during an exhibition match he was playing for charity one year I recruited Mary and Hugo to come along with me and try and break bread with him. Basil was also home at the time and he came along too, with his camera. (Basil was almost undressed without his camera in those days.)

McEnroe was talking to his friend Mats Wilander at the time and didn't take too kindly to being ambushed in the middle of his conversation. He glowered at me with that 'You cannot be serious' expression on his face and I thought he was going to chew me out. He agreed to the photograph but didn't exactly tell me the story of his life when I asked him a few questions. It was like talking to the wall.

Two other famous people I met were Leonard Cohen and Tony Curtis. I later put them into a book I wrote about the psychological problems of famous people called *On the Edge*. The cliché about Cohen was that people put razor blades into the sleeves of his albums so they could slit their wrists after listening to them but in actual fact he turned out to be quite jolly. I was sorry Mary wasn't with me as she'd been with me from the very start of my obsession with him. Cohen's friend Irving Layton had even met Mary in the Aran Islands once and was so captivated by her he wrote a poem for her. (When I met Tony Curtis I made sure she was with me. 'Is this the missus?' he said when he saw her).

On the Edge was positively reviewed by most of the critics but it was heavily criticised by somebody in the *Sunday Times* who called herself Sue Denham. I didn't recognise the name and spent a number of days wondering who this snotty new journalist on the scene happened to be. A few weeks later I learned that Sue Denham didn't exist. The name was a pun on the word 'Pseudonym'. When criticism is anonymous it always makes you feel it's less trustworthy so that piece of news reassured me. (As Sir Boyle Roche once said, 'Anyone who has the audacity to write an anonymous letter should at least have the decency to put his name to it.')

Shortly after *On the Edge* was published, the Prion editor Andrew Goodfellow asked me if I'd like to write a guide to traditional Irish pubs. This didn't rate very highly on my list of priorities but I rarely said no to editors. As one of the older hookers on the publishing block I felt that work bred work. If you wrote the books you weren't madly excited about, the ones you did like had a better chance of following them. My main worry was that I'd be asked to 'cover' a pub I'd been barred from. That would have been interesting. (Thank God the Greyhound wasn't 'traditional'.)

For the next year or so I found myself in more pubs than I'd ever been in my life, with one big difference: I wasn't drinking in them. This was a severe test of my self-discipline. I'm sure many barmen were surprised to see me with a pen in my hand instead of a pint. Some of them would have known me from the bad old days when I was raising hell.

After the book came out it was reprinted by the Dublin publishers New Island in paperback. The irony of this wasn't lost on me. A British publisher had commissioned a book about Ireland which was then taken up by an Irish one. I had often approached New Island with ideas in the past and been given the cold shoulder. If I'd come to them with the *Historic Pubs of Dublin* idea on my own steam, I wondered what they would have said to me. Probably 'Not for us', their customary response to my suggestions.

New Island arranged an interview for me on TV3 one Bank Holiday Monday to advertise it. I'd only been on TV once before, when a friend from the Elvis Club brought his camcorder into the radio centre of Beaumont hospital and filmed me talking to a deejay there. I thought it was a good idea to have my first TV appearance in a hospital. If I collapsed from stress there would be someone on hand to give me mouth-to-mouth resuscitation. (Or, as might have been more likely, open heart surgery.)

The show was on at the crack of dawn so it was still dark when I got up. I set off for the studio with a new-found sympathy for TV-AM people. How could they have a social life when they had to be tucked up in bed shortly after tea?

My eyes were falling out of my head as Mark Cagney greeted me backstage. He was the man who was going to interview me. 'You don't have a thing to worry about,' he said to me, probably spotting the fact that my knees were shaking and my face chalk-white from fright. I told him he reminded me of an anaesthetist. (I was still locked in the hospital idea). When the interview began he threw questions at me like bullets and I stuttered my way through the answers like someone on drugs. I felt if he asked me my name I'd have had trouble answering. (Maybe that's not a good example seeing as I was going by two different names now anyway).

Part of my nerves came from the fact that I was worried about anyone I knew from snooker or the courier firm seeing me. Mary tried to console me. 'It's a holiday weekend,' she said, 'They'll all be sleeping off their hangovers.' I forgave her for thinking all my friends were alcoholics – probably because they were.

After it was over I crawled back to the car feeling like I'd been dragged through a bush backwards. 'Never again,' I said to Mary. As we drove home I felt my eyes going. Most people were just on the way to work. When we got home I fell into bed but I couldn't sleep. Every minute I felt the phone was going to ring and somebody I knew from the wrong side of the tracks was going to say, 'Jaysus Pether, what the fuck were you doin' on the telly?' (They always added a 'h' onto the Peter).

Because the pub book sold well, Andrew Goodfellow now asked me to do another one for him. I had suggested writing one about the eccentricities of famous people and he said he'd like that – with one proviso: I had to write it on a computer. (All my books up to now had been done on my battered old Canon typewriter). He wanted me to be able to shift paragraphs around at the press of a button instead of working with selotape and scissors, my preferred tools of the writing trade.

I said to him, 'This book is about eccentrics, isn't it? Well I'm an eccentric so you have to let me do it the old-fashioned way.' He wasn't buying it. 'You're writing about them,' he said, 'but I don't want you to be one.' Obviously if Andrew was a film director he wouldn't have got on well with Method actors.

I eventually burned the thermal head out of my Canon. Or maybe it committed suicide. I couldn't blame it after years of being battered senseless by the middle finger of my right hand and the middle finger of my left. That was the only way I knew to type – it was a style I learned from my father - but I got so fast over time I could nearly take down The News as it was being read..

Canon told me they couldn't replace the thermal head. The machine was still typing but every letter had a crack in the middle that made the typing look like bad photocopying.

I got a new one but a few months later the head went on that too. This time the problem was letters being chipped at the end rather than in the middle. So 'q' became 'o' and 'y' became 'v'. I now had two machines that were still typing but virtually useless. Canon now told me they were discontinuing the whole range. I was also informed that Canon ribbons were also being discontinued. The typewriters were useless to me without the ribbons so I bought about 1000 of these. Considering I got 100 pages from a ribbon this was a hefty purchase. I started wondering which would run out first on my third and fourth typewriters, the ribbons or the thermal heads. Either way I'd be snookered.

Whenever I cried on Mary's shoulder about my adventures as a Luddite she told me I needed to be dragged kicking and screaming into the 21st century. Whereupon I reminded her of all the times she'd lost precious documents on her computer simply by hitting the wrong key. That could never happen on a manual machine.

When I finally bought a computer it was like my final compromise to the world of modernity. One or two editors still allowed me to send in hard copy but they were exceptions. Most of them told me I was like the Kerryman who tried to erase his computer errors by applying Tipp-ex to the screen. I had a soft spot for this gentleman.

In 2002 I wrote a book for a small publisher who allowed me to present it any way I wanted. It was a humorous guide to dating. I wanted to call it *Sleeping with the Enemy* but the editor thought Julia Roberts mightn't like this as she'd made a film of that name a few years before. For safety's sake we changed it to *In Bed with the Enemy*. It was hastily cobbled together at the end but I could hardly complain: the editor had joined the British Army and was called out to sudden combat duty in Afghanistan just before it was due to be proofed. He even had to draw up a will before he left. Bad and all as writing was, I wouldn't have wanted to trade places with him. (It also sounded like more fun thinking of sharing a bed with Julia Roberts than having your arse shot off by terrorists in the Middle East).

I worked hard trying to drum up publicity for the book, picking media contacts out of dog-eared little notebooks that went back years. It got a lot of reviews in Ireland but none at all 'across the pond'. The publisher asked me what I thought the reason was for this but I didn't know. Some months later I learned that the publicist hadn't even sent out review copies to the British media. I think she expected them to review it clairvoyantly.

I was getting a lot of publicity around this time from the *Evening Herald*. When I rang them and asked if they'd give it a plug they said they would. The next day a photographer arrived at the house and I was again faced with the worry of trying to avoid having my picture taken. I tried to stave him off by saying I'd cut myself shaving. I gave myself a scratch on the cheek to bolster my case but he wasn't to be deterred and said he could shoot me in profile. I put a cap on my head to try and disguise myself and added my mother's glasses as he got his camera ready. I couldn't find my wig or my fake moustache but tried to hide my face behind a coffee mug before he said, 'Would you mind putting the cup down while I take the photograph, please?'

When it appeared I went into my old panic mode and resolved never again to let any of the paparazzi within an ass's roar of the house. 'Maybe the time has come for you to lose your camera shyness,' Mary said, 'Most people around here are so far into their dotage they wouldn't give a monkey's if you were a serial killer, never mind a writer.' She'd had her own photograph in a local paper a few times as a result of some voluntary work she'd done for the Vincent de Paul and enjoyed showing it to people. 'I realise you're the normal one,' I said, 'but you have to let me be myself. My books may be for sale but I'm not.' 'You and J. D. Salinger should get together,' she said, 'Maybe you could find a bunker for yourselves somewhere in Outer Mongolia.'

The *Evening Herald* photo, she said, made me look like a homeless person. Sadly, I looked like that for the rest of the time as well. Because I didn't meet people much I tended to mooch around the house in my bare feet. I wore crumpled trousers and shirts and a jumper I liked that was so old she suspected it must have belonged to my grandfather. 'You're like someone from the Simon Community,' she told me, 'That jumper will walk off you one of those days'.

This was in contrast to her own 'fashionista' persona. I used to call her 'Christina Dior' when she was on her shopping sprees. (Her middle name was Christina as a result of her being born on Christmas Day). She admitted she always got a thrill going into a clothes shop. It was her one vice, as was testified to by the wardrobes overflowing with her clothes. She also seemed to have more pairs of shoes than Imelda Marcos. We had to buy an ottoman and put some of her stuff in the attic to clear space for her 'Winter Collection'. Downstairs, meanwhile, the dishevelled Dickens clone sweated over his manuscripts.

'All your brothers dress like dandies,' she complained as I pruned my latest bolshie tome, 'How come I got the derelict?'

Division Four

As my career in writing continued its stop-go pattern I started to play league snooker seriously to take my mind off it. Mary knew I needed something to stimulate me when it was stuttering so she encouraged me to play more. She didn't mind me not dressing up to go to the snooker club because she felt nobody did there anyway.

The club I belonged to was in Drumcondra. The main match nights were Tuesdays and Thursdays but I went over there on other nights as well, for in-house competitions and practice sessions. Most of the members were from Dublin and many of them were heavy drinkers so we spent a lot of time in pubs as well. Mary hadn't factored this into the equation and neither had I. After leaving teaching (and, more particularly, the Greyhound bar) I'd become a reformed man but I should have known old habits die hard. The more nights I spent out the more I got fond of the bottle again.

In our away matches we usually played in dead-end dives. I met some hard men in these places and some hard women as well. We spent a lot of our time trading insults, usually about our snooker prowess – or should I say our lack of it.

When you lie down with the dogs you get up with the fleas. I made some bad friendships in these years, years I'd like to buy back now, years that wrecked my health and whatever tiny talent I tried to fine-tune. The odds were usually stacked against me by my opponents in these grotty venues. If they weren't cooking the scoreboard they were trying to cook me. After a while I stopped caring. If a victory meant that much to them, my attitude was: let them have it. It didn't matter enough to me and maybe that was the problem. To succeed in anything you needed to be obsessed by it. I used to be once but now my only addiction seemed to be an addiction to defeat.

I knew my life as an amateur player was going down the toilet. Maybe my life was going down the toilet, period. Who cared? With enough beer in your stomach it didn't seem to matter.

We played in Division 4, the lowest one. If there was a Division 24 I would have chosen that instead. I wanted somewhere I could make a lot of mistakes without them costing me matches – because I knew I was going to make them anyway.

I'd been in the team a few years but didn't always get to play. I was the weak link in the chain. 'They say you learn more from your defeats than your victories,' I said to the captain one night after I'd lost a match. 'In that case,' he replied, 'you must be very fucking educated.'

There were four of us on the team: Joe, Frankie, Bob and me. There were also a lot of subs who came and went as they pleased, playing every now and then to keep their hand in and then disappearing without notice.   Darren and Eddie were the two main ones.

Joe was the captain. He did some work as a fitter but only when he felt like it. This gave him time for all the paperwork. Bob was a barman with irregular hours so you never knew where you stood with him, or even whether he'd turn up or not. Frankie was our best player but he was unreliable too. It came so easy to him it meant nothing to him as a result. Darren was on the dole. He was studying for something in computers. Eddie never said what he did which made us suspect it was dodgy.

Sometimes the whole six of us went to the matches for moral support. Other times we were lucky to have two. We often gave 'byes' to the opposition, especially when Frankie let us down at the last minute. Most years we propped up the bottom of the league, giving us the nickname 'The Fawlty Towers of the snooker world'. (That was one of the more polite descriptions.)

The games I enjoyed most were the ones I played after the rest of the team went home, when there was nobody watching. On nights like this I tended to find something from somewhere, doing things on the table that I didn't understand as everything seemed to cohere into a plan. The next morning I'd remember snatches of the night but I knew I'd never be able to repeat it, like all those years ago in the Hibs.

I played my snooker like I lived my life: erratically. For a while I could be disciplined but then I always did something to up-end the gameplan. It had been the same in teaching. I'd throw myself into a match full tilt for a while but I didn't have staying power. There was always a part of my mind that was somewhere else.

The other players were different. They acted as if their lives depended on the outcome of these matches, even threatening violence sometimes if they didn't go their way. Arguments would develop over details like whether your shirt-cuff touched a red as you were bending over the table or whether you jabbed the cue-ball twice or played a push shot.

The free ball was another bone of contention. We often got half-blind referees giving decisions we knew were ludicrous but still weren't worth arguing about.   One night in a club out in the mountains in Tallaght I was docked 28 points because of the miss rule. I never thought I'd see the day the standards of top-flight snooker made themselves manifest at our little matches but they did. I wondered what would come next: white gloves?

Another night when I was on a break of 25 the referee suddenly noticed the blue ball was missing from the table. Instead of giving me the points he awarded them to my opponent as I was deemed to have played a string of foul shots. On nights like this I went home thinking I needed to take up a different game. It wasn't right for a 37-year old man to be losing matches to this kind of chicanery.

And so it went on, maverick airs counterpointed by discussions of how many angels could dance on the head of a snooker cue. It was childish but it was also corrupt. It made me wonder how much more corrupt it would be if there was actually something at stake. I knew about the rumours of drugs in the game and the allegations of match-fixing. Maybe there was a deeper kind of corruption practised every day by players who never fell foul of the WPBSA but were still guilty of gamesmanship. It would have been learned in halls like these and stored away for future use when the difference between victory and defeat hung on a knife-edge.

There was also a lot of snobbery in the game, even in those lower reaches. I went into the club one night and saw Frankie practising on his own. 'You shouldn't be playing with yourself,' I said, ' You'll go blind.'

He wasn't amused by the old joke. When I asked him if he wanted a knock-up he said no. He always thought he was too good for me. After he finished a frame he started wiping the balls with a cloth so he wouldn't get a kick. 'Will you be signing autographs later?' I asked. He didn't like that either. A few months later he dropped out of the team and I was flummoxed because he was our ace card. I asked Joe what happened. 'He got into the women,' he told me.

It was the old story. For years I'd seen the eyes blazing out of his head with a manic glare as he went for tricky reds down the cushion. Now all the big breaks and all the pub yarns, all the bravado and all the guile were going to be no more. Because he'd got 'into the women'. Was this maturity or a cop-out? I didn't rightly know but personally I felt he was better off out of snooker. And yet I hungered after the trophies he was turning his back on.

'Why don't you concentrate on things you're good at?' Mary said to me. 'You have a flair for tennis or even soccer. Why do you keep playing a game that you're not getting anywhere with?' I never had an answer for her. Maybe it was what I'd said to Clive all those years before in Connecticut: I liked it precisely because I wasn't good at it. It was a challenge for me.

I noticed the same thing happening with Alex Higgins and Jimmy White in the professional game. They seemed to get bored when things were too easy and let frames slip away from them. The only thing that fired them up was the challenge. But the competitive spirit tensed me up so much I often collapsed there too. There was no logic in it.

I hated playing in the in-house competitions most of all because the players I was up against here knew me all too well. They knew my weaknesses because they'd seen them on display every Tuesday and Thursday night in the league games away from home. They used this inside knowledge to routinely beat me, all sentiment being reserved for the pub afterwards, or the burger and chips takeaway after that.

After a string of defeats in the league the club players started to mess with my head. One night Joe broke off against me using the butt-end of the cue, spreading the reds every which way. 'Do you not respect me?' I asked, knowing only somebody who wanted to lose a frame would ever do that. In my anger at the slight I knocked in a 48 break. Joe's face was priceless. For a few days after that I walked around on a cloud but the next time I tried to make a 48 break it stopped at 9. And that pattern continued.

Alcohol was part of the reason. For a while I went off it when I was playing matches but then I started smuggling it into the club. I also got shorts in the pub up the road to tide me by. I even started to buy bottles of orange, emptying the contents down the sink and pouring beer into them. One night Joe saw one of these and said, 'Jaysus, that's an awful strange-lookin' orange crush you have there.' I'm sure he knew what it was from the smell off my breath but by now I'd stopped caring.

Drink was both disease and cure – disease because it made me miss my shots, cure because when a match was over you had a balm to put over the wound of failure. And maybe someone to drown your sorrows with. The bottle never argued, it never told you you should have put more side on the white or knocked in the easy yellow instead of taking on the hard blue.

In moderate doses drink relaxed me. The problem was knowing when I had enough. I'd take the first one to relax me but it was hard to stop there. Our matches were often played in clubs that had pubs attached to them and that added to the temptation. If the person playing me was drinking as well we could have a casual match with each of us taking chances. If he wasn't I felt I was setting myself up for a fall. He'd play with me like a cat with a ball of wool and then pounce from the long grass.

I usually started imbibing early on these days. It was like trying to gee yourself up before asking a woman to dance at a discotheque. There was one difference between the situations though: at discos you didn't have to negotiate tricky cuts on crystalline objects nine feet away through watery eyes. And putting your arms around a woman and whispering sweet nothings into her ear was a lot more enjoyable than trying to find the extended spider when your legs were going from under you.

The drink made me reckless. I jumped balls off the table sometimes, which infuriated Joe. He'd pour cups of black coffee into me to try and get me focussed. The caffeine probably did as much harm to my insides as the beer. Sometimes I'd order a pint with a coffee chaser. It was a bit like popping a Prozac and an Ecstacy tablet in the one go. I remembered my father being on tranquillisers and anti-depressants at the same time and thinking: That's no good

– they'll neutralise one another. But now I was virtually at the same thing myself.

Alcohol gave me an exaggerated sense of my ability. I remember one night when I'd had a skinful and thought I was playing like God. I lost the match but thought the reason was that I'd been out-classed. That wasn't the way Joe saw it. Coming home in the car I told him I thought I played pretty well. 'You played like a geriatric retard,' he said. That was the end of that conversation. It was also the end of me trying to combine my two favourite hobbies. Afterwards I was chaperoned, pumped up with Coca-Cola instead of any other kind of intoxicating liquid. I couldn't see the point of it all. I knew I was going to lose anyway so why couldn't he let me enjoy myself doing that?

I passed through many Garda checkpoints on these nights but somehow managed to bluff my way through them. One night when it started to rain I thought of the time I crashed into the car ahead of me outside the Phoenix Park. I had a litany of prayers to get me through such situations. I told God I'd never drink again if he let me get home without having my licence revoked. If I had to lower the window for a conversation I'd put on a posh accent to get myself waved on. In time I learned another ruse: if you left the window open the whole way home the whiff of booze didn't hit the Garda in a rush when he opened it. Chewing gum and polo mints took the smell off my breath as well.

Hugo told me I needed to cop on to myself if I didn't want to end up with a crowd around me in some street. One night I got legless with him in a karaoke bar in Smithfield and hit a bouncer. Hugo had just pulled me off the stage after I accidentally spilled a drink over a customer in the middle of a rendition of 'Goodbye Yellow Brick Road' that was about three octaves too high for my voice. I ended up being thrown down the stairs by the bouncer . Afterwards I conked out. When I woke up it was the middle of the night.

There was another madder-than-mad night when I went around a roundabout about fifteen times trying to find the exit. It was like something out of a Kafka nightmare. A plainclothes Special Branch man stopped me eventually. He said watching me was like looking at someone in the dodgems at a carnival. He took my keys off me but he didn't book me. Instead he told me to go for a meal and to collect my car the next morning. After he went away I doubled back to the car and drove off. A minute later he came up behind me and flagged me over again. 'I thought I told you to go for a meal,' he said. I couldn't believe he was letting me off the hook a second time. Another time after a rake of pints I was breathalysed and still let go. I was never able to understand the reason for that. Was I so drunk I turned the bag back to its original colour?

I knew I couldn't go on like this forever and I didn't. One night Joe came up to me and gave me the speech that had been about two years overdue. 'I've been hearing you're hitting the bottle pretty hard,' he said, 'I don't mind you having one or two but when it starts to cost us matches I have to draw a line in the sand. Darren said you were staggering round the table the other night. Obviously that can't continue so I'm taking you off the team indefinitely.'

I went easier on the booze after that but the atmosphere at the matches was never the same. Once you had a name it was hard to rid yourself of it. Frankie and Darren still gave me funny looks even if I was drinking tonic water. I won a few games when I was on the dry but I couldn't keep my place on the team. I'd be put in if someone was sick but as soon as they recovered I'd be dropped like a hot potato.

I never thought of myself as having a drink problem. As Brendan Behan said, my only problem was that I couldn't get enough of it. I used to read these quizzes that tried to find out if you were an alcoholic. They had twenty questions and if you answered Yes to more than five of them you were deemed too be one. The thing about me was that I usually answered Yes to about fifteen of them and I still didn't feel I was.

'Do you drink faster than your friends?' Yes. 'Do you drink every night of the week?' Yes. 'Is the availability of drink the first thing you look for at a function?' Yes. And so on. So what was the problem? I just thought I was a normal Irish person who liked his tipple.

My mother used to say that you were born an alcoholic in the same way you were born with blue eyes. She said a drink to an alcoholic was like a match to a flame, that a person could be an alcoholic even if he never tasted drink in his life. It was this kind of thinking that helped her understand my father more.

If I was an alcoholic I thought I was also a workaholic and a snookeraholic and a writeraholic and God knows how many other things besides. I preferred to think of myself as having an addictive personality and one of these addictions was drink. I also tended to prefer drinkers to non-drinkers as people. My father used to say he didn't trust teetotallers. Was this a convenient excuse for obstreperous behaviour?

After going on the dry I won a match and then lost one and was put off the team again. I went up to Joe and asked him why. 'You lost last week,' he said. 'I know,' I said, 'but you're allowed two defeats.' 'Yes,' he said, 'but Eddie is more reliable.' I said, 'Why didn't you say that first?'

I hated the kind of politics that went on. I knew Joe and Eddie were as thick as thieves in the pubs together. It was like a rehash of what had happened in the courier world: the close friends got the plum jobs.

The same week we were due to play the weakest team in the League, the only one worse than us. I didn't need to be a genius to figure out what was happening: Eddie wanted the game to make himself look good. A blind man could almost have beaten this side. They were the joke of the division and we always assumed the points were in the bag before we played them. It was like, 'Hey, we're playing these gobdaws next week, so that will bring us up to fifth position before Christmas.' Dave Allen could have counted on the fingers of one hand the number of times I got the call to play this side. I knew I'd never be picked before Eddie unless he'd had a quintuple bypass - or a frontal lobotomy.

The following Sunday Joe rang me up and said, 'I'm sorry about last week. You're in again. Mark won but he's busy at work. Are you all right for Tuesday?' I told him I was. When I looked up at the timetable it was the team heading the division. Once again I'd drawn the short straw. But it was pointless to protest.

When it wasn't happening for me on the big table I sold out to the little one and started going into pubs to play pool. My colleagues from the snooker team told me this would destroy my game, a comment I greeted with laughter. 'What game? I asked. I was delighted that I'd finally come to terms with my limitations in life, that I now realised I'd never be Jimmy White.

With pool there was the added incentive of being able to drink while I played because: Joe wasn't looking at me. And if you lost you weren't letting any side down - because you *were* the side. Winning or losing happened quickly and either eventuality was okay. If you won you stayed on the table and if you lost you went up to the blackboard and put your name down again. Neither did you have to talk about yourself because you were meeting different people every night. The conversations were generally about inconsequential things like the weather or the price of a pint or what was in the news that day. You were the same as everyone else in the pub, somebody killing time poking a stick at a white sphere.

I never saw myself as a winner in life but I always loved to compete. Playing for £1 to me meant as much as playing for £100. If someone hadn't £1 I'd play him for 50p. If he hadn't 50p I'd play him for 10p. There had to be something at stake even if it was only a matchstick. I'd have played a one-armed man sitting in a wheelchair if he put a bet on with me, or maybe I'd play him with one arm myself. If I was knocked off the table early in the night I'd gamble on other players to give myself a reason to stay in the pub.

I had a modest amount of success on the pool table. I learned early that it wasn't really about potting balls at all. What it was about was strategy, blocking up the pockets to make it easy for yourself to clean up if the chance came. One night I won so many games I managed to stay on the table from three o'clock in the afternoon until closing time, a record I could never equal afterwards. I don't know how many games I played that night but it felt good. I danced home on eggshells, greeting Mary at the door like an all-conquering hero.

Unfortunately she didn't share my euphoria. She said I was returning to the man I'd been before I married her. She hated the idea of lager louts spilling beer on me as I tried to play a game she regarded as little more than an excuse to pass the time on a wet day. Anytime we went to a pub for a drink she hoped there wouldn't be a pool table in it. If there wasn't I accepted it but if there was I was tempted. We came to an agreement that I'd limit myself to three games maximum but I could never hold myself to that. If I lost we just left but when I got on a roll I wanted to wait on. She'd be sitting there bored out of her tree as I begged her to wait on for another one, and another. Finally she'd say, 'This is insane. You're drunk. Let's go home.' I'd tell her that I was just after playing the game of my life and needed to stay on my lucky streak. She'd realise there was no way I was going to go with her so she'd just leave me to it. The irony was that often the idea of going to the pub in the first place would have been hers because she didn't like drinking at home. But I'd be the one that would end up spifflicated. It was like a reverse of the situation in the film *Days of Wine and Roses*.

When I got fed up of being a pub king I went back to Joe and asked him if I could have my place back on the team. He said I could on condition that I behaved myself but that I couldn't expect first shout. I'd never got that anyway so this was hardly a surprise. I was just glad to be back in the side.

The league matches were always up to two frames. If it went to one-all the tension became palpable. Hands shook and throats were cleared, the gentle kiss of the balls like a tap-drip in a church at midnight. The centre of my world was in those dirt-ravaged dives in the sticks playing people I didn't have two words to say to once the game was over. If it went to a tight third frame I willed myself to keep it together for just five or ten more minutes, to not do something stupid that would give the game away on a platter. If it came down to the black my hands sweated so much it was hard to even play the shot, never mind knock it in.

The ball could be hanging on the edge of the pocket begging to be potted and I'd miss it. 'Peter Shilts must be keeping goal in there,' your opponent would say, hugely relieved as it jangled on the edge of the pocket and ran safe. And so the tussle would continue, a war of attrition alternating with reckless abandonment as I sought to bring the night to some kind of conclusion. Sometimes I fluked the black, bowing my head in shame but secretly delighted as the other guy quietly cursed Lady Luck.

During an important match one year I fluked frame ball in the deciding frame and my opponent said, 'You must have been at Mass this morning.' '*At* it?' I replied, 'I said the fucking thing.'

We had these little jokes we trotted out with slight variations over the years, fancying ourselves as wits even if the lines were most likely borrowed from others. We used the same phrases over and over just as we played the same shots, our lives like carbon copies of soap opera characters in Yellow Pack emporiums. Afterwards there would be handshakes all around and nervous twitching as the dockets were signed.

If your opponent fluked a black, on the contrary, your heart would sink as he gave a mock-apology: 'Jaysus, mate, I'm sorry, you played great but, fuck it, that's life, you'll probably wipe the floor with me next week.' Either way you had to roll with the punches. There was no justice in the game, nobody to cry into your beer with you if it was two defeats on the trot and you were dropped from the squad the following Tuesday.

Some of the players I met in these matches had tables in their houses. They played on them all the time, especially if they were out of work. I had to grind out results with such players. That meant tying up the colours early like the old codgers used to do on me in The Cosmo. .Joe called it 'doing a Davis on them', referring to Steve Davis' proficiency at safety. I managed to beat one talented young player almost consistently with this strategy. I hated doing it but it was the only way past him. Eventually he refused to play me. 'You're so negative,' he said, 'You should be sponsored by Kodak'. (God forbid he should ever have been drawn against Cliff Thorburn).

A player from Crumlin asked me to throw a match one year. We were already doomed to the bottom of the table so the result wouldn't have affected us either way but I still baulked at it. He took out a wad of notes then, offering me a bribe. When I refused it he muttered some vague threat about this not being the end of the matter. I tried extra hard to win that night and fell over the line. (It was laughable really because there weren't even cash prizes for the League). The next I heard of my briber he was playing Gaelic football for Dublin. Was there corruption there too?

I had another problem with a player we called Macker. He'd been something of a teenage sensation, coming to the team trailing clouds of glory from the junior circuit. I never liked players with notions so I took care not to praise him when he was playing well. I knew it would make his head even bigger than it already was.

Macker had no car so it was left to me to ferry him to the venues. One night when I was in the middle of a match he nipped out for a pint. It was discourteous for teammates not to watch one another playing so I reminded him of this. 'Fuck courtesy,' he said. That was fine by me but when his own match started I went for a pint myself. He couldn't accept that I wouldn't want to watch his genius at work and refused to talk to me all the way home in the car. He even asked Joe if we could play on separate nights afterwards.

One night the schedule dictated that we play together. Being childish, both of us refused to watch one another's matches that night. When they were over I still thought he'd take the lift home with me. The fact that he didn't said something either about pride or stupidity. He lost that night as well, which lifted my spirits. It's a strange situation finding yourself rooting for the other side but I did on that occasion.

Some nights I felt I was only getting my place on the team because I had a car. Being a taxi-driver for the other three players guaranteed me that precious fourth slot. If I lost on these nights my agony was even greater than usual because all the other players would be in the car on the long journey back into town. 'There's always next week,' they'd say, or 'He was poxed' which only added insult to injury. I always preferred it when they said, 'You were brutal. Now let's talk about something else.' I hated the condescending humility, the falsely consoling, 'If you played the guy I did, you'd have put him away no bother.'

My philosophy of snooker was simple. Two people played a game and at the end of it one of them had more points on the scoreboard than the other. That person was the winner. Ergo, he was the better player. I didn't want to end up like Alex Higgins, blaming the girl in the flowery hat in the third row for the fact that my 37-ball plant didn't come off in the nineteenth frame.

I became captain of the team one year. The only reason was because nobody else wanted the job. It involved a lot of phone calls to people who didn't want to play. Sometimes I had to beg. My blood pressure went up that year. I dealt with players who acted like they were giving me the crown jewels by agreeing to accompany me across Dublin. Sometimes there was only me and one other player instead of three. That meant we forfeited one of our matches. The nadir was reached when we started forfeiting games as a result of not turning up for the *home* matches. This was like theatre of the absurd. The following year I let Joe take over again. I developed an increased reverence for him afterwards.

We had a bad team that year as well. I got a lot of matches because most of the other players went sick every other week. (Going sick meant staying home to watch Man. United play soccer).

In these situations the pressure was off because nothing was expected of you. You were being sent to a match because it was necessary to play it. If our club gave too many walkovers without due cause we knew we'd be turfed out of the league altogether. So you went to the venue, played your match, most probably lost, shook the hand of the other player afterwards, filled in the docket, got in your car and drove back to the club to deposit your cue until the next time. The person doing the late night shift would be reading a newspaper or a dog-eared book by someone like Stephen King or John Grisham and he'd casually look up from it and ask the inevitable question, 'How did it go?' The answer was almost always 'I came second'.

As I drove home I'd wonder what the point of it all was: a round trip of thirty or so miles to have your confidence shattered – probably by somebody who shouldn't even have been in your division.

I often played people who knocked in breaks of seventy and eighty-plus against me. I'd tell them afterwards that they should have been on TV. They'd say something like, 'Believe it or not, head, I've had fuck-all practice lately.' But you'd know by the way they said it that they had to be scraped off the table every night. 'I just hit some form,' they'd say. (And my granny was in the Merchant Navy).

It was always the same excuse: they just happened to hit a lucky streak. They really should have been cuter because no player ever needed an 80 break to beat me. Half of that would have been enough, or maybe even a quarter. But when there was an audience they couldn't resist showing what they could do. In lives punctuated by little except weekly trips to the dole office and nights in the pub it was the closest they'd come to smalltown glory.

Every time we came home from another bruising defeat we'd look for reasons, even if the reason was so obvious it was staring us in the face: we were a rubbish team. Instead of this we'd invent fall guys. I was one for a time, then Joe, then Darren. Or else Joe would pick a shot where it all went wrong, the turning point upon which the match supposedly hinged. He'd say things like, 'Why didn't you tickle up behind the green when you were fifteen points ahead. You were a madman to take on that stun shot, don't you realise that?' And I'd hang my head low and hope that he wouldn't be there for the following week's match so that I could at least die with dignity.

He always knew how to win matches – at least from his barstool where he pronounced his advice. He'd say things like, 'This fucker you're playing tonight is crap with the rest so leave the white as far away from the reds as you can. And don't talk to him between shots – it'll relax him too much.' It was like being told in teacher training not to smile at the pupils before Christmas.

One year we played a team of wheelchair victims. There were lots of unPC jokes about 'walkovers' but they took some points off us. As I watched them eyeing up the pots from their worm's eye vantage-point I was reminded of Alex Higgins hobbling round Goffs Sales Ring in his last hour of glory when he beat Stephen Hendry in an Irish Masters Final at a time when Hendry looked unassailable. The only thing you could say for sure about snooker was that there was nothing you could say for sure about snooker.

I never minded if I lost to a better player provided I wasn't bustled out of it. This was the term we used for players who did everything from stepping on your toes to spilling drink over you to disrupt your concentration. Neither did I mind losing if I played well. What hurt was being robbed of matches or making a cock-up at a crucial stage. These were the nights I came home in a temper and threw my cue at the wall, murmuring, 'Never again.' That night in bed I'd run every shot through my mind like a masochist, vaguely searching for the moment it all went wrong and vowing that I'd never make the same mistake again. (This usually turned out to be the case. The next night I'd make a different one).

The other worry I had was the old fear that my real identity would come out. That would have marked the end of my snooker life as well as of Peter Murphy. I came close to it one night when I was playing a match and two people I knew walked into the pub, one of them a journalist who knew me by my real name and the other a casual acquaintance from the snooker club who called me Peter. I tried to beat a hasty retreat but they were standing at the door as I tried to go out. 'See you, Peter,' said one of them. The other said, 'Goodnight Aubrey'. I thought my cover was blown, and maybe it was, but I never saw them together again. Nor did they ever refer to the incident when I saw them on their own so I could never be sure.

Another night Frankie said to me out of the blue, 'Who are you anyway?' He didn't elaborate. There could have been 101 ways he knew who I really was. I replied, 'I'm Walt Disney. What are you drinking?' As long as I wasn't directly confronted by somebody I was able to stave off situations but I was always worried that some night when I was driving the team to a match in Drimnagh or Stillorgan I'd have an accident and have to show my licence to a policeman. When he said my name, that would be it. Even without an accident I knew that if I was stopped I'd be in for a grilling because the courier van was only meant to carry two people. The other two were usually splayed out in the storage area.

Sometimes my writing and snooker lives collided. One night we were playing a match in Crumlin when I spotted Dickie Rock, the pop singer, on the next table. I was always on the look-out for people to interview for the publications I wrote for. If I met them informally in places like this and tried to set something up it meant I didn't have to go through agents or publicists. (I often found these middle men to be the ones with the egos and the difficult personalities, not the celebrities).

I waited until the end of the night before going over to him. My team-mates were in the car by then. I told him I'd like to interview him and he gave me his number. When I got back to the car Joe said, 'What were you talking to that fucking eejit for?' I said, 'I just wanted to tell him he was a lousy snooker player.' A few days later we sat talking in his house in Rathgar. The interview was published in the *Evening Herald*.

Something similar happened when I met the actor Donal McCann. I was in the Gravediggers pub in Glasnevin one night drowning my sorrows over yet another snooker defeat when he walked in. He was the worse for wear but in the mood for talking. I fell into conversation with him without telling him I was a journalist. After a while our conversation turned into an interview. I met him a number of times in the next few weeks and got to know him fairly well. He had a gruff manner and abused me when he was drunk (which was most of the time) but behind the tough shell he was a sensitive soul. On one of the occasions we met I noticed bruises on his face. When I asked him about them he said he'd fallen into his mantelpiece the night before after a night's boozing. (There was a lot I could identify with there).

The person I sent most of my articles to at this time was Damien Corless, the former editor of *In Dublin*. Damien never published anything I wrote, despite me sending about thirty articles to him during his tenure. In fact he didn't even acknowledge one of them. I thought this was unusual even by my own standards of one-way traffic. Years later when another *In Dublin* editor invited me to the Bleeding Horse pub on Camden Street for a few drinks, Damien joined us. 'I think you owe me an apology,' I said to him as he sat down. 'What for?' he said. 'For all the articles I sent you that you ignored,' I said.

He smiled at me. 'I knew you were a teacher in a secure job, Aubrey,' he said. 'Most of the people I published were on the breadline.' I was amused how he could pass it off like that. 'It wasn't the money,' I said, 'it was the rudeness of not getting back to me.' He had no answer to that. It was scant consolation to me for all those wasted time but at least I'd said my piece. At the end of the day he'd been consistent. I thought of David Niven's comment on Errol Flynn: 'You could always depend on Errol – he always let you down.' A subsequent editor of *In Dublin*, John Waters, published me quite frequently and had a much more pleasant manner. He was from Roscommon, my mother's county. I always felt a kinship for anyone west of the Shannon. It was a kind of brotherhood.

I also worked for the magazine *Books Ireland* over the years. I started writing for it back in the seventies when I was living in Iona Villas. Bernard Share was the editor then. He was also editing the Aer Lingus in-flight magazine *Cara* at that time. He'd arrive out to the house at cockcrow with a parcel of books under his arm. My mother would usually answer the door because I'd be in the land of nod. Often he'd be on his way out to the airport. One day he dropped in on his way to China. I thought that was a bit exotic.

Jeremy Addis took over the editorship after he left. Jeremy is English but he's been living in Ireland so long I often forget that minor detail. When I first started writing for him he used to send me huge hardback novels which would take me about a month to read. Nobody in Ireland can fill a Jiffy bag better than Jeremy Addis. He squeezes books into them so tightly I imagine Arnold Schwarzenegger would have trouble getting them out. I always recycle Jiffy bags except when they come from Jeremy. You have to cut his ones open brutally and then dispose of them. There should be some kind of award for this.

To give myself some light relief from the rigours of book reviewing, or even book writing, I also went through a phase of writing letters for a while. (I think I inherited this habit from my father). If Mayo lost a football match I'd write to the manager of the team telling him what the problems were, and even expecting a reply (which never came). I wrote to politicians telling them how to run the country and these too were ignored for some strange reason. I even wrote to Arsène Wenger, the manager of Arsenal, telling him I sympathised with him whenever Arsenal played Manchester United because the United players were always diving in the box.

After O.J.Simpson was acquitted I wrote to Marcia Clark, the lawyer who prosecuted him, to tell her where she went wrong. Mary and myself became so obsessed with this case we re-christened the living-room 'The O.J. Room' because we watched nothing else in there for the better part of a year.

The most famous person I wrote a letter to was Bill Clinton. I offered my sympathy to him at the height of the Monica Lewinsky affair when he was being witch-hunted by Kenneth Starr. I got a reply that seemed to be signed by the man himself but someone told me it was probably just a stamped signature. When he came to Eason's years later to sign his autobiography I queued up to see him with the letter in my pocket. For some strange reason, however, the security men wouldn't let me through. (It gets frustrating when people try to stop you seeing the President of America when you're carrying all-important missives to him).

After my letter-writing spree ended I went back to journalism. The fact that the *Evening Press* was gone could have hurt me more if it wasn't for three publications that took its place: *The Cork Examiner*, *The Irish Catholic* and *Senior Times*.

One of the most enjoyable phases of my writing was the time I spent with the *Cork Examiner.* When Sean Dunne became literary editor I used to send him in anything I had ready to hand and also phone him now and then for a chat.

I spent a lot of time in Cork in the early 1990s. Mary and myself used to swap houses with Audrey, who was married down there. The *Irish Catholic* was a more surprising outlet for me as I'd had many problems with the church over the years. I couldn't rightly explain it myself. Maybe I just wanted to be different. The church was an intimidating institution when I was growing up and I rebelled against it but after all the scandals emerged and it became roundly despised by most people in the country I found myself softening in my attitude to it. It was too easy to kick it while it was down. I felt a bit like

Brigitte Bardot when she said, 'I lived with my boyfriends at a time when it outraged France but now everyone is doing it so I want to get married.' Conformity was like the new rebellion.

I thought the paper could do with a film column so I suggested the idea to the then-editor David Quinn and he gave it the green light. This was before all the sex scandals in the church. Shortly afterwards Bishop Casey had to flee the country because of the child he fathered with Annie Murphy. It gave a whole new meaning to the expression 'It could happen to a bishop'. This was followed by a spate of paedophilia cases. The catechism had taught us that the Ten Commandments could be reduced to two. The church tended to misread that to mean the Sixth and the Ninth. How ironic that sex was now coming back to haunt it in its own backyard.

Mary put it well when she said, 'We were all shocked by Eamon Casey but now it looks as if he was the normal one.' No doubt the scandals affected the sales of the paper. People were much more inclined to buy titles with more glossy material. After *Playboy* went on public sale in Ireland I said to David Quinn, 'There was a time people used to hide their copy of *Playboy* inside the *Irish Catholic*. Now it's probably the other way round.'

The fact that I wrote for *Modern Woman* was also a surprise to people who knew me. It was edited by Margot Davis, a gracious lady who became a great friend, as did her sister Carmel and Tom Locklin, who also wrote for it. Margot lived in Navan but came up to Dublin every now and then. We spent most of our time gatecrashing parties and occasionally writing about them.

Margot asked me to do features on everything from child kidnapping to space travel. I'd get these late-night phone calls after an idea had just struck her and we'd talk about it, usually over a glass of wine. I often worked on these ideas through the night (helped by some more wine) and faxed them down to her at dawn the next day. I also met a lot of well-known people at functions with Margot. On one night alone I remember meeting Gerry Ryan, Ulick O'Connor, Linda Martin, John Lonergan, Jimmy Magee, Shay Healy and Anthony Clare. When *Modern Woman* closed down a number of years ago we were both devastated. It was like having a limb amputated.

The features I did for *Senior Times* were skimpier than the ones I did for *Modern Woman* but no less enjoyable on that account. The central focus of this publication was the elderly but it cast a wide net. Des Duggan, the publishing director, was helpful to me with articles and also with getting publicity for my books through the magazine. He became a good friend too. He was always telling me I needed to be more technological in my approach to writing. He threw up his hands in horror the day I told him I was still doing most of my work on an electronic typewriter rather than a computer.

Des was also unable to get his head around the fact that I was probably the last man in Ireland who didn't have a mobile phone. 'We're the new elite,' I informed him. He couldn't understand how I could survive without one. He did PR for the magazine and was forever calling people and being called by them. I rarely had a conversation with him when a call didn't come through for him on his mobile. It was like an extension of his arm.

The most unusual magazine I ever wrote for was a monthly entertainment glossy based in Dublin 4 which shall be nameless. I did general features on celebrities for this. Every few weeks the editor would ask me to profile some star of the stage or screen or maybe the sporting world. I enjoyed doing these because he usually gave me the cover and illustrated them nicely. The only problem was that I rarely got paid for them. I kept asking for my money and kept getting rebuffed.

One day I went up to him and said, 'Things have to change. I can't keep writing for you unless I get some remuneration.' He gave me a hard look. 'This magazine,' he said, 'is being run by a man heavily involved in the IRA. He prefers to keep his money for buying guns. If you ask to be paid again he'll probably break both your legs.'

I stopped asking after that.

Return

To take my mind off the rssures of writing, if not snooker, Mary and myself spent a lot of time travelling, especially after she left her job in the solicitor's firm. Most of our sumer trips were to Wales and England but at Easter and Halloween we usually went down to Ballina or Galway. I always felt a surge of elation when I crossed the Shannon, as if I was going home, and Mary felt the same. She always said she'd move back to Galway in the morning but I was more reticent about Ballina. I still liked going there but wondered sometimes if I was the same person who'd been whisked out of the town against his will all those years ago.

I always told people that if I hadn't been the youngest in the family I'd have stayed down there. I resented the fact that I never had the experience of having Norfolk to come back to like my older family members did. They had two lives going, even if only for a short while. That seemed to be the best way of finding out which one suited them best.

Any time we went to Galway the first few days were always spent with Mary telling me stories associated with the streets we rambled along. I usually repeated the pattern in Ballina.

In the mid-nineties we started to think seriously about moving west for good and on one trip we decided to scout locations for this possible move. We spent a few days in Galway looking at apartment blocks in Salthill and then decided to go to Ballina to sound out some auctioneers. A part of me also thought I'd like to live in Enniscrone and commute to Ballina, thereby having the best of both worlds. With this in mind we decided to go to Enniscrone first.

We were only in the town a few minutes when the idea of sending a day there, let alone our whole lives, seemed ludicrous. The sky was a dark grey and there wasn't a sinner on the streets. 'I've seen livelier looking graveyards,' Mary said to me and I had to agree.

We went into a pub but we were the only two people there so we didn't even finish our drinks. One of the tables had a tourist brochure and we read it with a mixture of amusement and shock. Enniscrone, we discovered, was now advertising itself as having 'Amenities'. The seaweed baths were also mentioned in the brochure and we were informed how many metres it was from the pub to the beach. All points of interest were tabulated. Everything but the Valley of Diamonds was described in painstaking detail. ' No doubt that day will come too,' I said nervously.

After we left the pub the streets were still deserted. How many days had I walked these same streets with a surge of excitement as I waited for the summer to begin? It was our own private haven then. A paradise eight miles from home. We felt we had a kind of ownership of it by coming here so much but now that ownership had a hollow meaning to me, or no meaning at all.

We decided to walk the beach. As we went across the bridge and down to the shore I told her about the games of hide-and-seek we played, how we had our own taxi driver to bring us there, how the days seemed endless as we postponed returning to the dull everydayness of Ballina. On the way back to the car I stood for a moment watching the sun sinking behind the dunes. As we enveloped ourselves in the silence I looked out over Bartra Bay and suddenly felt lonely – for all the people I knew who were dead and all the experiences I took for granted while they were happening, for the passing nature of all childish idiocies.

We decided to make for Ballina and on the way there I pointed out landmarks to Mary from my childhood. 'You should write a history of the town,' she said jokingly as I ranted on, 'It would be a lot more fun than listening to you talking about the Hibs, or Muredach's.' If only I could have been that learned, I thought, but it would have been impossible anyway. These places only meant something to me because of events I associated with them, not because of what they were.

As we got to the outskirts of the town she asked me if I was going to go into Norfolk but I couldn't really answer her. I'd only been in it a handful of times since we left he town and each time I went in it seemed to make me less comfortable than the time before.

'What about a drink first?' she suggested and I thought it sounded like a good idea. 'Let's go to some lively bar instead of the usual haunts,' she continued, and I thought that sounded good too. Suddenly I decided I wanted to kill the old me, the person who romanticised listening to my father in spit-on-the-floor places as I was sent out by my mother to collect him in the dim and distant past. If I was ever going to outgrow that past, what better time to start than now?.

After parking the car at the church we went to a pub in the centre of town. A bunch of people from Scotland were having a sing-along and we joined in. After a few minutes I felt we could have been in any town in Ireland. I wasn't sure if this made me feel happy or sad. I both wanted and didn't want to feel neutral.

Mary got talking to a soccer player from Dundee. After a few minutes he asked her out onto the floor and they did a jive. He moved her around much better than I could have. I was well aware I'd inherited two left feet from my father. When she sat down she was in a jolly mood. 'Let's not be too serious,' she said. 'The serious me is history,' I assured her. I meant it too. I decided to grab the moment. I had a whiskey and it went to my head. I asked her if she'd like to dance but she said no. She knew I'd make a fool of myself in front of the soccer contingent.

'Let's go before we get too drunk,' she said. I was glad she said 'we' instead of 'you'. Maybe I was less in the party mood than she was. The strange thing was that I never liked drinking too much in Ballina. I feared it would make me wallow in memories or self-pity. Neither did it fit. Coming back here I was trying to return to an identity I'd had before life gave me all my bad habits. Maybe it was a stupid excursion into the past, an adolescent attempt to return to a part of myself that probably never existed in the first place.

We decided we wouldn't go back to Enniscrone. Not just because we'd had drink taken but mainly because I didn't want to think too much. I wanted to spare her my midnight ruminations on the beach for once. 'Listening to other people's memories,' she said, 'is like listening to other people's dreams. You can never sound as interested as you're supposed to.' I knew what she meant.

We went up by where Aunt Nellie used to live on the Killala Road. She had died many years ago. Her house was knocked down and a petrol station put up in its place. I hadn't seen her much in her last years. Anytime I knocked on her door on visits to the town she was slow to answer. Her hearing was nearly gone. You had to ring her from the phone box outside Geraghty's when she didn't hear the knocking. She still had the same swagger about her but she became querulous in old age. She used to get annoyed if I went up to Tina's house before visiting her. They seemed to be the last two people I knew in the town. Now there were none.

We booked into a B&B behind the cathedral. I suggested it because it looked new. I felt I wouldn't be known there. It was run by a Dublin lady. That struck us both as being ironic. We felt we could now wear our Connacht colours without having to go into too much detail about who we were. I always hated the 'Oh so you're Hugh Dillon-Malone's son' speech I got from hoteliers over the years. It was usually followed by stories I'd heard a hundred times before. All this woman cared about was that we were quiet, that we wouldn't hare off tomorrow morning without paying the bill.

'You can go for a ramble round town if you like,' Mary said after we saw the room, 'I'm going to wash my hair.' 'What else is new?' I said. The only thing that would have prevented her washing it every day was a nuclear war. She probably knew if she came with me I'd bore her to tears giving her the history of every brick on the road, as if in revenge for her own Galway anecdotes.

'Maybe I'll go for a game of snooker,' I said. 'In that case I'll expect you back in about three weeks,' she said.

I stepped out onto the street and smelt the air. It was always clearer down here. I stood by the river watching a fisherman in wellingtons that went well above his knees. He was fishing from halfway across the river. I sat on a wall and listened to the church bell tolling with that doleful sound it always had, as if somebody had just died. I waited for it to stop and then walked over the bridge and up the town past where Wellworths used to be, and Queenan's shoe shop. I walked up King Street past Moylett's and the Oval bar and Gaughan's and the post office.

The Hibs was all boarded up. I'd passed it a number of times over the years since we left the town but never thought of going in. Maybe I would now.

I looked through the window but all I could see were cobwebs. When I stood on the sill I saw that the two snooker tables were gone. There was nothing in the room but the old card table and some builder's blocks. I recognised a 'Rules of the Game' placard that probably went back to the 19th century. On the card table there were some glasses and a mouldy-looking ashtray. I felt I was looking into the bowels of an old theatre.

When I pushed the door it opened. That surprised me. I walked inside and smelt the musty odour. As I sat at the card table a mouse ran across the floor and into a hole.

How many stories could these walls tell, I wondered. How many people had nurtured dreams like mine as they bent over the snooker table to line up their shots? I thought of the days I used to chase players around this room as we argued with one another about the score of a long-forgotten game, or swung our cues around like swords after coming out of some swashbuckling film in the Estoria.

The new generation wouldn't care about such things. A new hall had opened beside the Savoy. The tables were cleaner and there was no rough stuff tolerated. It had a salad bar. You could even bring your girlfriend in.

I stepped outside and pulled the door shut behind me. I looked across the road. Outside the post office a few old farmers were moaning about the weather, about the corruption of local politicians. I walked down King Street, passed shops with enamel signs I half-remembered from the old days, gave looks of uneasy recognition to faces behind counters that had formed an indelible part of my youth: a man with a shiny bald head in a jewellery shop, another man with glasses as thick as a Coca Cola bottle selling fishing tackle, a pub proprietor who looked as if he was growing out of his counter.

I looked at the faded names on shopfronts, the blacked-out display windows, the crooked pavements. None of the young people who passed me by knew who I was. Those I grew up with had left the town. I was relieved; I would have been uncomfortable trying to re-connect with them.

I bought the *Western People* and went into a cafe to read it. There were stories of drunken men kicking in doors after one too many or engaging in disputes about land and being confined to the peace afterwards, the kind of cases my father would have taken on. I remembered the days he defended people for begging at the Bishop's Palace, the pride he used to have if he got them off.

In the middle of the paper there was a photo of the new multiplex on Convent Hill, the set of cinemas that took the place of the Estoria It could show seven or eight films at once. The new generation would have their pick, unlike us.

I walked up Garden Street. Young people passed me by carrying mobile phones, dressed in Adidas tracksuits and Nike runners. They played Justin Timberlake and the like on their Walkmans. The only thing that made them different from Dublin children was their accents. It was refreshing to hear the brogue.

I felt the town had the aura of a child trying to grow up too fast, unaware of what it was, trying to conceal its insecurity under a kind of slickness that didn't suit it. The Celtic Tiger had brought the boom here as it did everywhere else but despite all the fancy goods shops and the designer gear, despite all the Spars and Centras and Xtravisions, I didn't think anything had really changed. We were still the pig in the poke, just a hop, skip and a jump away from the bog.

Hugo could never understand why I kept wanting to come back here. 'I found it a nightmare growing up,' he'd say. 'There was no culture, nobody to have an interesting conversation with.' I told him I thought it was no better or worse than any other town in Ireland. 'No matter where I grew up,' I said, 'I was going to have a sentimental connection to it. That's the kind of person I am. You were always more independent.' My nature was to look inwards and his to look out. That was all that needed to be said.

I turned into Arthur Street at Fahy's corner, went up by Syron's past the old laneway. Leonard's gate was still green. I remembered playing football against it, three to get in.

When I got closer to Norfolk I looked in at where the old school used to be. It was a car park now. The town hall had been converted into flats. Gildy Ahern's house was an ESB shop. The only thing I recognised was the set of petrol pumps outside Cottrell's house. The name had been changed to O'Reilly.

There was paint flaking off the walls on Norfolk. They were coloured an ugly purple. It was a community centre now so it was usually open in the day. Mary envied me that. 'You can go in anytime you want,' she said. He hadn't the same luxury with her Galway home, being too shy to ask the new owners if she could look around.

I scanned the notices on one of the windows: 'Slimming classes, Tuesdays.' 'Alcoholics Anonymous: First Friday of Every Month.' My father would have been amused.

I didn't know whether to go in or not. I usually didn't despite having passed the door maybe a dozen times in the past ten years. Sometimes I just walked in for a few minutes as a kind of duty. The first time I went back after 1969 I was shocked to see what they'd done to our old kitchen, to the back yard, to the bathroom that was half way up the stairs. It was like a different house.

The front door was like two half-doors now, almost like a saloon. I pushed it open and went inside. The hallway was more or less the same as it had always been. So were the rooms to the left and right downstairs.

I went into the sitting-room. There were easy chairs around the walls. I thought I recognised one of them from the pale wood and an orange cushion on it. Could it really have escaped Sean McDonnell's mallet?

The carpet was threadbare. The skirting boards hadn't been changed since our time. The floorboard to the left inside the door still creaked when you stood on it. I recognised a paint mark on the wall that I made one day behind where the piano used to be.

I remembered coming in here with Hugo as a child. He used to take books out of the sideboard and put them on the carpet with their spines sticking up in the air, creating the image of mountains. He moved my cowboy soldiers through the pretend valley between them. He used to make a clucking sound with his tongue for a horse.

Sometimes he made little movies for us as well, using shadows reflected onto one of my mother's sheets. He'd make shapes with his hands, using his thumb and forefinger to create the image of a gun or a rabbit. Other times he'd dress us all up in colourful costumes for the plays he directed, raiding every wardrobe in sight to get what he wanted. (That caused June and Ruth to go mad the next time they were looking for one of their missing garments). .

This was also the room where I used to play with a collection of matchboxes I had. Every time my father finished a box he gave it to me to keep. He smoked over a hundred cigarettes a day. That meant he went through a lot of them. When I had enough I used to stand them on their sides and put them in a weaving pattern. When you tipped one over, they all fell like dominoes.

Whenever my mother saw all the matchboxes she used to get worried about how much my father was smoking but he didn't actually smoke all the cigarettes he lit. Sometimes he might have two or three in separate rooms. He'd light one and forget about it and then light another one somewhere else.

He smoked a brand called Boston. They were a bit smaller than the usual cigarettes you saw. He must have started on the pipe when they went off the market. I remembered his fingers always being brown at the top from the tobacco, the lovely smell of nicotine that came off them when you were near him.

I pulled the curtains back to let the light in. A cloud of dust blew up from the carpet. It was nice sitting in the silence. Mary was right – I was lucky to be able to come in here. Why hadn't I done that more often? Maybe I was afraid of what I'd find. Or what I'd fail to find.

I looked out at the pale sky, at cars stopping and starting as they made way for one another along the narrow street. I used to look out at them when they sped up the road to Foxford and Swinford and wonder what towns lay elsewhere in Mayo, what they might look like.

Geography wasn't my strong point, as Jacko knew. The only town I was really familiar with was the old favourite of Enniscrone. How many summers had I cycled down to it, shouting at Deezer not to follow me, wondering if I'd go by the Quay Road or the main one, racing the other members of the family as we passed the familiar landmarks – Bunree, Skermore Castle, the old ship that lay marooned in the middle of the river since the war. I used to try and get there faster each time, measuring my speed against the time it took me the day or week before, trying to beat my own record to take my mind off the boring hills you had to climb before the first magic dunes came into view near Bartra.

Other memories flooded back: The games of soccer we played in Belleek with the Courells, the bottle of lemonade that was passed around at half-time with the cork made of paper stuck into the top of it, the day Dessie Callaghan took a penalty and kicked his boot into the goal instead of the ball. We called him UA. Why was that?

I remembered Hugo and Basil going down to Byron's for the latest records. Basil liked Cliff Richard but Hugo preferred Tommy Sands. One year I remember him coming home with Bob Dylan's 'John Wesley Harding' LP. I was fascinated by the sepia cover, the strange figures in their old world dress.

I listened to whatever records Hugo and Basil bought in those days, too young to have my own choices. Later would come Elvis Presley. I listened to him singing 'Such a Night' with Michael on an old record player Aunt Mary gave us. You got four songs of his on an EP. I used to think that stood for his name before someone told me it was Extended Play.

We got records from the jukebox in the Royal Café but the centres were missing because that was the only way they could play in a jukebox so we had to make our own centres, cutting out circles from matchboxes. (I had plenty of these).

Our radio was as big as a house. I loved all the lights on it when you turned off the main light in the room, the fluttery sound the dial made when you moved it through all the numbers. We listened to the Everly Brothers singing 'Cathy's Clown' on Radio Luxembourg on Sunday nights when we were supposed to be in bed, savouring the last precious moments before it was turned off. We went to bed singing 'Saturday night is my delight and so is Sunday morning, but Sunday night gives me a fright to think of school in the morning.'

I was back in that time now. I was still the child who played these games and listened to that music. Was that healthy? I didn't know.

On every trip home I seemed to be trying to burn something out of myself, some connectedness I didn't really want because it was too close for comfort. If I came back often enough, I thought, maybe

I could exorcise such a need and I wouldn't have the yearning anymore. I would be content in my new station, content to wear the dull suit of the present. I wouldn't fantasise about moving down here for keeps any more. I'd realise it was just the pipedream of a homesick child.

I went outside the house and sat on the window-sill. Once I could hardly reach it but now it was too low for me. A man passed by me with a bag of potatoes and tipped his hat. Some children were playing down the street outside a shop with 'Wholesale' written across three windows. Every morning of my youth I used to pass that on the way to school and wonder what it meant. 'Who' was written on one window, 'Les' on a second one and 'Ale' on the third. I never knew they were all part of one word.

I envied the children their gaiety. I wondered if they were happier than they realised. Maybe they wouldn't recognise real happiness until it was taken away from them, until they grew out of it, until it passed and they looked back on it as I was doing now, as old men and women, embittered and damaged. Or maybe just different.

The Estoria looked different as I walked up past it. There was nothing to suggest it had ever been a cinema now except the shape of the building. When I looked in the window I saw a poster with Myrna Loy's face on it, crumpled into a ball beside an old booth. The Savoy was gone too. The new multiplex generation wouldn't know about these places and wouldn't care either. Maybe they were better off.

A sign at the font and looked at the sign that said Teeling Street. It had been changed from Arthur Street in 1966, the fiftieth anniversary of 1916, but my father kept calling it Arthur Street and told the rest of us to do that as well.

I walked across the crazy footpath down Bury Street, past Benny Walkin's and the elaborate greenery of Tommy Burns' house. I turned left at King Street and went down past Clarke's shop where my father used to buy ice-cream, big jugs of it, lowering it like milk in one slug. But then he did everything to excess. Why should this have been different?

There were some stragglers at the bottom of the hill. They seemed to be talking about a football match. It was difficult to make out their words. One of them was drunk. He whistled at a pretty girl who passed by. She smiled at him, curtsying. One of them tipped his hat to me. I wasn't sure if he was being sarcastic or not.

Round the corner was the place where my father's old office had been before it caught fire. I only remembered it very vaguely. Tina told me the fire was reported in the *Western* at the time.

Would his life have gone differently if it hadn't burned down? Would it have increased his motivation to get out more, to drink less? I didn't know, none of us knew. Maybe things were always fated to happen the way they did.

The International Stores was gone too. That was where my father got all our Christmas presents. It had been replaced by any number of trendier shops. The parents of the town had many other places to get gifts from Santa Claus now. Or did children still believe in Santa Claus? Maybe they only believed in Benny Walkin, or whatever new Benny Walkin was supplying them now.

I stopped at Aubrey Burke's house, Number 2 Victoria Terrace. He owned the house next door as well. One year they knocked down the dividing wall and made the two houses into one.

His daughter was Mary Robinson. Who would have thought that she'd go on to become president of Ireland? I handed her a parcel one day at her house on the Sandford Road when I was working as a courier. I hadn't wanted to go at first in case she recognised me but then I thought: How could she? We didn't even know one another. She accepted the package graciously and looked at me as if she knew me but I didn't tell her I was from Ballina, that I was Hugh Dillon-Malone's son and that I was supposed to have been named after her father. What would have been the point?

My father had been impressed with Dr Bourke's pedigree. His wife was also a doctor and his brother Paget had been knighted by the Queen. Such things mattered to him. They didn't matter much to Mary Robinson, one of Ballina's few rebels. Was she its only one?

The bells of the cathedral tolled out. Why did they always depress me? It was something in the monotonous tone, the deadness of it. And that was always what religion meant to me growing up: a series of Good Fridays rather than Easter Sundays.

Somebody told me Paddy Murphy had paid for them. Mary and myself had met Paddy for a drink in the Downhill Hotel a few times in recent years but he was dead now too. Was there anybody left? I had only buildings and houses to connect me with this place.

I listened to the river gurgling, to the fishermen pulling in their nets. They slapped the wriggling salmon with batons and then threw them into the upturned row-boats on the bank. I watched them loading their catch into boxes, taking off their green wellingtons and putting the clasps on the end of their trousers as they sat up on their bicycles for the journey home.

Across from me the cathedral looked morose. I walked across the bridge and wondered whether to go in or not. Some children were chasing each other in the little graveyard opposite it.

When I stepped inside it was almost empty. Most churches usually were now unless there was some ceremony taking place. As I looked up at the walls I remembered Aunt Mary doing the Stations, the expression of awe that was always on her face, and also sadness. Were they somehow linked?

The night was coming on. The moon shone through the stained glass, spilling its light onto the floor. An old man in front of me coughed and then took out a handkerchief. I saw in a pew, looked up at the crumbling stucco of the pulpit, the statue of St. Francis perched behind it like an overseer.

I remembered how I used to sit in these same pews as a child looking at Audrey and Jacinta locked in prayer during the Mass. I never seemed to be able to share their involvement and wondered why. Maybe it was the nature of prayer itself that confused me: to me it had always seemed like little more than glorified begging. Even adoration had always seemed irrelevant to me. Why would a god need to be adored? Surely only insecure people needed that.

I was envious of their devotion to something this intangible when my own attention was usually more focussed on worldly things. It was as if I was always looking for something to break the spell, to pull the carpet from under the feet of the celebrant.

A memory came back to me of a day when I'd wandered into the church some years before during a wedding. The bride and groom were both getting on in years. The priest said to them in the middle of the ceremony, 'Wasn't it about time for ye?' The whole church seemed to collapse in laughter as he spoke and I was relieved that the atmosphere had relaxed.

Why did I object to anything sacred? I didn't really know. The closest I ever came to it myself was after confession on Saturday nights when I felt my soul was spring-cleaned, when the sins I was told would damn me to hell were airbrushed out of my life by the gentle whispers of the old man on the other side of the grill giving me my penance and asking me to say a Hail Mary for him.

As I got up to leave the old man left too. I thought I knew him but I wasn't sure. I made as if to speak to him but he didn't respond. We walked side by side to the door. As we got outside he walked the other way but kept looking over his shoulder at me. Could he have been a client of my father's? Maybe it didn't matter. I quickened my step to get away from him.

I decided to walk down to the college. The sun had sunk behind the bridge, the last fisherman was cycling down the Sligo Road towards Bunree. I looked up towards the B&B and wondered what Mary was doing. If she looked out the window she would probably have seen me. I thought of going up to ask her if she'd like to come down to the college with me but decided not to. What interest could she have in Muredach's? I hardly ever stopped talking about it to her. She had to be fed up of it to the back teeth.

It wasn't a boarding school anymore: that much I knew. Could anyone who taught me be there still? Would any of my classmates have become priests and ended up there? Hardly. (Unless they were masochists).

I walked up the curved driveway. The college still crowned the landscape like a mute colossus. How often had my stomach churned as I cycled up this same road, how often did I recite poems or prayers we were given to memorise the night before and would be asked to recite as soon as we got into the classroom?

When I got closer to the building it didn't look as imposing. The brickwork was cracked and some of the windows were broken. In a sense it just looked like a run-down tenement.

Could it still call up fear for its present pupils? I doubted that. There was a new arrogance abroad now. We were living, as people liked to remind us, in a post-Catholic Ireland.

In a few years I could see the college being torn down and sold. Would the church need the money to pay off a sexual debt? Such things would have been unthinkable when I was young. At that time only pupils committed sexual sins, not priests. Maybe a factory would go up in its place, maybe it would fall into the hands of some American millionaire looking for a tax break.

I decided to go inside, curious suddenly to see who would still be living within these ivy-clad walls. I knew most of the priests that taught me were dead. Others had retired to the surrounding parishes of Bohola and Attymass, to Bonniconlon and Knockmore. Was Jacko still alive? Maybe I was better off not knowing. If he was it would have been foolish to look for him. I hadn't stood up to him when it counted so what would it prove now to tell him what I thought of him? All it would prove was that I was still his prisoner, that I'd never outgrown a man who was now about to be put out on grass.

It felt strange walking down the corridors, an age-old kick of guilt making me expect a clip on the ear from some soutaned figure for being late for class or not having my copy with me. The very smell of the walls seemed to bring back this sense of expectation, this irrational fear of the next lash of Jacko's bamboo cane. Was he going to emerge from the shadows?

That was hardly likely. A deathly silence engulfed the place. All I could hear were my footsteps, the rusty squeak of any door I happened to open.

The benches where we'd scrawled our names were still there, sitting to attention as if waiting for new ghosts to inhabit them. They were all woodwormed now, the inkwells rusted. I searched in vain for my initials - AM or ADM carved into the surface with a penknife like a prisoner in a cell marking the days to his release. I thought I might find some message I would have written: 'AM, March 1966' or something like that. Kilroy Was Here. On my copybooks I used to write: Aubrey Malone Norfolk Arthur Street Ballina County Mayo Ireland The World The Universe The Solar System.

I sat on a bench for what seemed a long time. It could have been the very one I occupied when Butch Curry or Tag Loftus scratched words on a blackboard, summoning me up afterwards to repeat the lesson. I could sit forever now and not have to go to any blackboard or repeat any lesson: it was a pleasant sensation.

A cheer came from the field outside. When I looked out the window I saw a group of soccer players running up and down a pitch. They waved at me when they saw me and I waved back. They must have been wondering what kind of nutcase would sit in a classroom in the dark at nightfall. Maybe I was wondering the same thing myself.

When a whistle went for the end of whatever game they were playing I opened the window. They waved at me again, either in greeting or mockery.

I lowered myself down onto the grass. A cheer went up as they marched towards me. 'Can we help you?' said their trainer, a sandy-haired man in a tracksuit. He was decked out in red and white, the Muredach's colours. Behind him the players bickered, their voices raised over some trivial indiscretion. He smiled at me as an expletive rent the air, throwing his eyes to heaven in mock-frustration.

'You're out late,' he said, fixing me with a curious look. When I told him I was a past pupil he laughed. 'So am I!' he announced.

When I introduced myself he scratched his chin. 'Aubrey Malone,' he said, 'that definitely rings a bell. He snapped his fingers. 'Of course,' he said, 'I think I was in the class behind you.' 'That wasn't today or yesterday,' I said. 'It surely wasn't,' he agreed.

He dismissed the team and they went running towards the Rec. It must have been a changing-room now. I wondered if the old pushpenny table was still there.

'So what has you back here?' he asked me, 'Aren't you a city slicker now?' I told him I often came back on trips but kept a low profile. 'A wise man,' he said, 'This town is dangerous if it gets to know too much about you.' I might have been listening to my father.

As we continued talking it turned out he knew him. 'I believe he was quite a character,' he laughed, 'They still talk about him in the pubs.' There more than anywhere, I thought. He must have drunk a few of them dry.

He started to tell me about himself and I fell into his rhythm with some of my own anecdotes. We exchanged stories about canes being stolen, beatings administered for little or nothing, the petty mythologies of days most adults had forgotten about or pushed into some subconscious part of their brains. As I listened to him talking it seemed to me that it didn't matter what class one occupied or maybe even what year; the experiences would add up to the same thing in the end. All that differed was a person's reaction to them.

Out of the blue I asked him if he knew where Jacko was based now. 'Jacko,' he whispered, looking into the distance but showing no particular reaction to the name. 'He left the college a long time ago. I think he got a parish out in Lahardaun.' I nodded as if this was just some casual slice of news but I could feel my heart thumping.

I asked him if he knew exactly what part of Lahardaun. 'You sound very interested,' he pressed, 'Is there something I should know?' I made a gesture of cutting my throat.

'Ah,' he said, 'Of course. I heard he was a bit of a lad all right. Do you want to sort him out or what?' I paused. 'What's the penalty for murder in these parts?' I enquired. He laughed again and slapped me on the back. 'In that case you'll have to find him yourself,' he said. 'Good luck,' he offered finally, heading off towards the Rec.

I listened to the voices of the soccer-players echoing through the air as I walked back down the driveway. When I got back to the road the evening was coming on, the church spire throwing shadows across Ardnaree. As I made my way up the town I found myself suddenly feeling tense. I hadn't intended to seek Jacko out but now that I'd brought the subject up and got the tangible name of a place where he was living I felt somehow excited. Maybe this was the main reason behind my trip after all even if I didn't realise it.

When I got back to the B&B Mary was standing inside the door with her arms folded . 'When I said three weeks I didn't mean it literally,' she said tapping her foot, 'Where in the name of God were you?'

I told her I met Jimmy White in the Hibs and had been playing snooker with him since. She gave me a push. 'What was the final score?' she asked. I said, 'I beat him ten-nil, but then most people can nowadays.'

When I told her I had been down to Muredach's she groaned. 'Don't say you're still picking at that sore. I suppose you're going to tell me you beat Jacko up next.' I had to laugh at that. 'I found out where he's living,' I said.

'Don't tell me you're thinking of going to see him,' she said, suddenly sounding agitated. I'd borne a hole in her ear for many years about this man. 'The thought went through my mind,' I admitted.

I tried to watch television with her but I couldn't concentrate. It didn't take her long to twig this. She asked me if I'd like to go out for a walk or down to Cafolla for a meal. I said no, that I was feeling restless. 'You're not yourself,' she said. 'Is it your priestly friend that's bothering you?' It was pointless to pretend it wasn't. 'I think I need to see him,' I said. I expected her to get annoyed with me but she just said, 'I think you do too. I'll go with you if you like.'

'It's in the middle of nowhere,' I said, 'It'll be all hours before we get back.' 'Why don't we stay somewhere out there?' she suggested, 'Then we'd have a head start on the journey back. I haven't unpacked much of my stuff. We could go now if the landlady agrees.'

I thought that was a good idea. 'What will we pay her?' 'Whatever she asks for. She might let us off or charge the full whack, you never know.'

When we went down to her and told her something had come up she was very understanding. We gave her half the amount she would have charged for the night's stay and checked out there and then.

I started to feel excited again as we headed out for Lahardaun. I had a general idea about how to get to his house but no specific details. 'Are you sure you're doing the right thing?' Mary asked me as we got into the car, 'Will you be upset if it doesn't go well/' 'I'm expecting nothing so I won't be disappointed,' I assured her.

We drove in the dark on roads that were hardly familiar to me, listening to the sounds of cattle bleating and the occasional roar of a drinker coming home from some country pub. As we got close to Lahardaun we asked directions from some pedestrians and were told exactly where to go. As we approached the house I felt myself becoming tense again and took a deep breath as Mary thre her eyes to heaven..

His house was a modern bungalow with a trim lawn. There was a crucifix over the door so I knew I was at the right place. But now that I was here I started to wonder if it was a good idea after all.

'What's up with you?' Mary said, 'Don't say you've decided not to go in.' I told her I was trying to get my mind ready. She drummed her fingers on the dashboard in frustration. 'Stop making such a big deal about it,' she said, 'just go in. He's not going to bite your nose off.' 'No, I said, but I might bite his.'

She walked around to my side of the car and opened the door. 'Go on,' she said. 'You've talked about the poor man often enough. I don't want to spend the rest of my life listening to you yammering on about what you could have said to him if you met him. If you don't go in now you'll never forgive yourself.' I knew she was right but it was difficult for me. It was as if I was still the child of long ago who couldn't stand up to him regardless of what age he was.

She gave me a playful push and I got out. 'If I hear a shot I'll come in after you,' she said. I walked to the door feeling like someone going down the gangplank. I looked back at her once. She was making frantic gestures with her hands to get on with it. I stood in the doorway for a few moments and knocked. I could hear movement inside and then footsteps coming slowly towards the door.

When it opened, a face I didn't recognise looked quizzically at me. His hair, or what remained of it, was totally grey. His hands shook. He was dressed in a crumpled black suit. There was something cooking in a little kitchen behind him. 'What can I do for you?' he said in a thin voice. I asked him if I might come in. He said, 'Of course.'

He shook my hand and motioned me to a chair while he sat in one opposite. There was a Bible open on the table with an engraved bookmark on it. Everything in the room was spartan – the stone floor, the white walls, the bare wooden furniture. The only thing I recognised from the past was the electric globe he used to plug in to show us all the countries of the world for his geography class.

'I'm sorry to be calling so late,' I said, 'I'm an old pupil of yours.' He relaxed back into his chair. When I identified myself it didn't seem to mean anything to him. He changed the subject. 'Did you know my nephew is playing for Mayo now?' he said. I told him I did. The county had reached some All-Irelands in the past few years but failed to win any.

We talked about trivial things – the changes in the town, the Celtic Tiger, the slow pace of his life since he retired. He asked me if I'd like a cup of tea and I said I would but as he went to put on the kettle his hands shook so much I wasn't sure if he was going to be able to make it. I offered to help but he waved me away. 'It's the old Parkinson's,' he said. I asked him how long he'd had it. 'Nearly three years now,' he said. 'It's a curse but they have great pills to slow it down. The problem is trying to remember to take the blessed things.' He gave a rueful smile.

The kettle boiled and he poured the water into a cup for me. The saucer shook as he came over to me with it. As he reached for a biscuit for me I stood up from my chair. 'Do you remember beating me when I was a pupil of yours?' I said, the words coming out almost without me being aware of forming them.

He looked at me blankly. I gave him a gentle tap on the shoulder with my fist. 'Do you remember that?' I asked. He smiled and then shook his head amusedly. 'You used to use my shoulder for target practice,' I said. Again he appeared confused. I didn't know whether to pursue the subject or not. Neither did I know if he was pretending to have forgotten his reign of terror or if he genuinely had. Or had I exaggerated it wildly in my mind? Maybe he was no worse than any of them.

'I'm sorry,' he said eventually. 'You have the advantage of me.' As I looked at his shrivelled features I thought: Could this really have been the man who struck terror into my heart every day for four years? I remembered the line Burt Lancaster used in the film *Judgment at Nuremberg* to describe a Nazi war criminal: 'An old man now, crying into his Bible.' It made my anger abate.

The more we talked, the more his memory of who I was came back to him. He asked about Keith and Clive and other members of the family he either knew or taught. My father was also mentioned – perhaps inevitably. But I kept drawing the conversation back to myself. He said he couldn't remember having a set on me or treating me any differently to the other pupils. I still couldn't make up my mind if he was lying to me or not. Did it matter?

He asked me what job I was in and I told him I'd become a teacher too. The irony seemed rich. 'I remember you as a conscientious pupil,' he said, 'We never had any trouble in Muredach's with the Dillon-Malones.' No, I thought to myself, but the Dillon-Malones had a lot of trouble with you. At least this one did.

I listened to the ticking of a clock, the lowing of cattle outside. How ordinary his life was now, how peaceful. Was I going to disturb that? Would it be worth it for some petty vengeance?

We sat in silence and I wondered if I'd say anything more. I knew I had to get it out of my system but his confusion, or feigned confusion, made me feel faintly ridiculous, even cruel. But I couldn't leave the house without getting something out of him, some detail that might fill in the jigsaw for me.

'Do you not think you were a bit hard on us?' I said finally. He looked at me as if he was seeing me for the first time, or rather seeing the boy he used to know. I wasn't sure how many memories he'd blocked out, how many he'd share with me under my subdued taunting.

He put his head in his hands and sighed. There were rosary beads on his lap. He took his hands away from his head and put them around the beads. He cleared his throat and looked at me. 'There's something I have to tell you,' he said. 'I never wanted to be a teacher. I dreaded the idea of spending my life in St. Muredach's. My dream was to go on the Missions but Bishop Boyle wouldn't let me. I was shoved into a job I wasn't suited for. If I was tough it was because I was afraid of losing control. I never had confidence in myself. Maybe I swung the lead so nobody would suspect that.'

I had a tear in my eye, whether for myself or for him I didn't know. Could it all have been this simple? Were we all victims, him included? Maybe I could have saved myself three decades of hand-wringing. How many other agonies were the result of a bad memory? Or was he clever enough to have made all this up?

I found myself going over to him and giving him a hug. He grasped my arm and started to breathe deeply. He was wheezing, and maybe weeping. I wasn't sure. I felt awkward and disentangled myself from his grip. I told him I was sorry if I upset him.

He insisted on making another cup of tea. As he presented it to me he said, 'Sorry for boring you with my little outburst. I don't see many people now. When I do I talk too much.' I told him not to worry, that I was like that too. 'Do you like teaching?' he asked then. I told him I'd retired early, that my pupils had got the better of me. 'I believe they're very cheeky now,' he said.

There seemed to be nothing left to say. I thanked him for the tea again and got up to go. 'Maybe you'll call again sometime if you're passing,' he said and I promised I would. We stood awkwardly facing each other. He tried to say something but the words wouldn't come out. He was dribbling at the mouth. I reached into my pocket for a handkerchief for him but he waved it away. 'I was very immature when I entered the priesthood,' he said, 'I didn't know what

I was getting into. I'm still confused.' 'Join the club,' I said. He smiled and for the first time I saw the young priest's features reappearing. I'd been so busy fearing him I never realised what a handsome man he was.

We stood facing each other. There was nothing left to say. I listened to the clock ticking, the embers simmering. He asked me if I'd like another cup of tea but I said no, that if I had any more I'd turn into one. 'We can talk some more if you'd like,' he said but I shook my head. 'My wife is in the car,' I said. 'Ah!' he brightened, 'So you're married.' He seemed genuinely glad. 'She must be freezing out there. Would you not ask her to come in?' 'We have to be back in Dublin,' I lied. 'Of course,' he said, 'but I meant it when I said I'd like you to call again. It gets lonely out here in the sticks.'

He shook my hand firmly. 'Make sure you shout for Mayo in the next All-Ireland,' he said. 'I always do,' I assured him. It hadn't done me much good so far. The last time they won it I wasn't even born.

As he made his way to the door to open it for me he stopped suddenly. 'I'm slow on the uptake,' he said, 'and I apologise for any problems I may have caused you or for not remembering you earlier.' By now I was almost feeling embarrassed by his capitulation to me. I eased myself towards the door and told him to forget about it, that it was all in the past now. I said I'd drop in on him the next time I was down west but inside myself I knew I wouldn't. There would be no point.

As I went out the door he seemed lost. He looked towards the car and gave a half-wave at Mary. He smiled gently at me before closing the door. As he did so I almost felt like crying.

Mary was practically blue with the cold when I got back to the car. 'I didn't know whether to get out when he waved to me,' she said, 'Should I have?' I told her it didn't matter. 'That was some marathon,' she said, 'I was about to send in a search party for you. What happened? You seemed very cuddly together. Am I invited to the wedding? Should I buy a hat?' I knew she was trying to relax me. I must have looked tense. 'He's lonely,' I said. 'He wanted to talk.'

She wanted to know if I said all the things I'd wanted to say to him. 'Most of them,' I said, 'It wasn't like I expected.' She waited for me to say more but I didn't feel like talking. 'Well at least you didn't come to blows,' she said. When I didn't answer her she added, 'Or did you?' I found myself laughing in relief and she laughed too. 'He's not the worst,' I said. 'We sorted out a few things.' 'But you're not going to tell me what they are.' 'Not yet. I just want to relax now. I feel a bit strange, burned out.'

It was true. The last few years seemed to have taken it out of me. I felt I had no resilience left. I was capable of blowing up over the least thing and yet another part of me was removed from everything, as if it was all happening to somebody else. I knew I needed to forget myself, to forget everything that happened so I could focus on the future.

I gunned the engine. 'There was nothing major,' I said, 'but I think I know him better now.' 'And yourself?' she said, 'Do you know yourself better too?' 'Hardly. That would be asking too much.'

'As you came out of the house,' she said, 'the pair of you seemed to be very touchy-feely. I thought I was seeing things. Has the old devil reformed or what?' 'Maybe,' I said, 'or maybe I have.' She groaned. 'But you have no news for me. Have I waited an hour for that? Maybe it was too much to expect a Dillon-Malone to ever come to a straightforward conclusion.' 'Maybe,' I said, 'This Dillon-Malone anyway.'

She continued to press me for details but I didn't say anything. Maybe there was nothing *to* say. I wanted to feel purged but all I felt was flat. It was as if I'd been blowing something out of proportion my whole life. I knew I should be able to move on now, as the expression went, but I wasn't sure I could. I'd been worrying the wound too long for that.

I stopped the car suddenly. 'We're supposed to be looking for another B&B,' I said. We looked out the window at the infinity of fields. She said she doubted we'd find anything in the area. There weren't even any signposts. I didn't know if I wanted to drive straight to Dublin or not.

'How would you feel about going back to Ballina?' I asked her. She laughed. 'I can't believe you said that,' she said, 'It defeats the whole plan.' 'I know it does,' I said, 'but when you think about it what are we in such a hurry to get back for?' She threw up her hands in frustration. 'I'll never understand you,' she snapped, 'go wherever you want. At this stage I couldn't care less if we end up in Honolulu.'

I felt sorry for her. She was like my mother, sensible and mature, and I was like my father, confused and childish. I never knew what I wanted.

I turned the car around and went back the way we came. As we passed Jacko's house I beeped the horn for fun and she laughed. 'That's a start,' she said.

Now that we were going back to Ballina, all the tension seemed to go out of me. It was as I needed to grab onto a sliver of something I was leaving even in the very act of leaving it. I wallowed in the quietness of the night, the serene countryside, the fields of cows. As we got to the edge of town I surveyed the old landmarks as if I was seeing them for the first time.

The quietness disappeared as we reached the town. It was like going from a hermetically sealed room to the middle of a football match. Mary jumped up in her seat. 'There's something going on,' she said, 'look at all the people.'

They were spilling out of doors and bars, a lot of them looking drunk. The market square was full of stands. As we went to drive down Garden Street we were stopped by a Garda. He pointed to a detour sign so we had to turn the car round. 'Another U-turn,' Mary said, 'This is getting to be a habit.'

I stopped the car. People in weird costumes were parading up and down in droves, some of them chanting in rhythm as they pounded on drums with wooden spoons. I asked a passer-by what was happening. He took a Walkman out of his ear and said, 'Did you not know the festival was on?' He was a stranger but he spoke to me as if he knew me. Maybe that was the thing I always loved most about the town, the instant familiarity.

We parked the car and walked towards King Street. Our path was blocked by throngs of people chattering. The ones in modern clothing looked like the oddities as a pageant of medieval jousters weaved past us. I looked at the mass of them swaying back and forth rehearsing dance moves. I thought I'd never seen as many people in one place, not even in America. It looked like the whole population of Mayo had come to the town for this one night.

On the bridge there were travellers selling cowboy hats with flashing lights on top of them. I bought one, and also a pair of psychedelic sunglasses. 'If you put those on I'm going back to the car,' Mary warned me. Just then a belly-dancer from Brazil passed us by, dressed in a leopard-skin bikini. She had little objects strapped around her ankles that jingled as she danced. I felt like pinching myself to make sure I was really in my home town. The only processions I'd ever witnessed in my youth were religious ones where we all kept our heads down and prayed.

The parade proper didn't start until well after nine o'clock but there were still dozens of children present. The streets were lit up as brightly as if it was mid-day. We got a viewing place on Garden Street behind a barrier. There were a horde of dancers coming towards us with painted faces. They swirled back and forth to the sound of jungle music being beaten out on little drums by men and women whose expressions remained impassive. Some of the dancers resembled whirling dervishes. Others looked as if they were just happy to be dressed up, making the occasional movement as they waved to relatives in the crowd. Some people drank beer as they looked out of upstairs windows in the surrounding buildings, having their own makeshift party indoors.

Every few minutes the parade moved on and a new act made its way into the vacant spot. Dancers were followed by fire-eaters and acrobats. A twenty-foot high man on stilts shook hands with us with artificial limbs that clicked open and shut by means of hidden switches. There was also a horde of strange modes of transport on display – boats shaped like little arks which were carried along on wheels, three-wheeled motorcycles and five-wheeled bicycles.

Children watched open-mouthed, locked between wonder and confusion, unsure whether to laugh or scream.

The crowd started to thin out when the last man on stilts passed by. I told Mary I'd never seen anything like it in my life and she said she hadn't either. We started to walk back towards the car when suddenly someone shouted, 'Fireworks!' I looked across the bridge and the sky lit up with a multi-coloured array of sparks like an electric flower opening in outer space.

For the next half hour I stood entranced as crackers exploded over the Moy. Many of them were sent up parallel with the spire of the church as if they were exploding that too. It seemed like a symbol to me, the replacement of one world with another. Would it be for better or worse? Who knew? 'Paganism has come to Ballina!' Mary shouted out. I told her she'd have got six of the best if she'd said that in Muredach's – or even the Convent of Mercy.

Both of us were lost in the frenzy of activity. Beside us a young man jumped on top of the bonnet of a moving car, refusing to allow it across the bridge. Two members of the gardai leapt on him within moments and carted him off. Somehow that little incident seemed to break the spell of the night. The fireworks were still going on but people started to disperse. 'Maybe we should go,' Mary said, 'we have a long drive to Dublin. I'd love to stay another night but it's too late to book in anywhere else now.'

I watched a straggler in a tattered clown's outfit making his way towards Ardnaree looking like something out of a Fellini film as he carried a flowing wig in his hands. I felt surreal, as if I was a part of a dream that had just ended. But I wasn't able to wake up.

'Let's go back to Enniscrone and wait until it gets bright before we drive home,' I said suddenly. Mary screwed up her eyes at the suggestion. 'I should have known I was marrying a madman,' she said. But I felt I'd have killed both of us if I attempted the long drive east now. Maybe she knew that too. 'Why not,' she said, 'Let the good times roll.'

My head was dizzy with a kind of weird excitement as we drove to Enniscrone. We went by the Quay Road, hugging the river as the last arrows of light disappeared from the sky. The clouds looked like so many ships on a celestial ocean as the moon crept in behind them. As we passed the old Protestant church at the top of the hill a fox crossed our path, slinking along the edge of the road before disappearing through a crevice in a wall. These were the sights I missed in Dublin, sights I wasn't even aware of missing until I saw them here.

The dunes came into view and I got the rush of expectation I used to get as a child when we crested the last hill on our bikes, or in Pat Hughes' car. I freewheeled down the last stretch from the Y-fork where the Main Road met the Quay Road, dragging the journey out. When we got to the beach I parked the car beside the caravan site opposite the little bridge. I took a can of beer from the boot of the car and we walked towards the sea.

We sat on the sand watching the waves as I sipped the beer. I'd left my overcoat in the car, which caused Mary to look at me helplessly. 'You do realise you're going to catch your death of cold, don't you?' she said. She threw a scarf at me and I wrapped it around my neck.

The waves pounded, sloshing into the stones on the shoreline and then sucking themselves back. It was the same motion but I couldn't help watching it, over and over again. I could see Mary starting to nod off and I felt my eyes going too. I closed them and lay back on the sand. I could hear a wind getting up, the occasional wheeze of a car leaving the town or coming into it.

The next thing I knew it was morning. I had a sleeping bag over me and the beer can was still in my hand. Mary was gone. I stood up and looked around me. In the distance I saw the car. As I walked towards it she got out and waved. I felt groggy and unreal. 'I slept in the car,' she said, 'You're lucky we had the sleeping bag or you'd have got pneumonia.'

The sea seemed to be miles away. A raw dawn bit through me. The day was overcast, the houses of Enniscrone barely visible in the distance. We walked across the bridge towards the tennis courts, the amusement arcades, the place where the cinema used to be. The town looked like a sleeping giant, its silence broken only by the screeching of gulls, the occasional tinkle of a milk-bottle on a doorstep. As I looked out at the sea a kind of sadness overwhelmed me, the kind of sadness I used to feel on this same beach years ago for no reason. Was it to do with the huge emptiness of it all or maybe something inside myself? I never knew.

But then, equally mysteriously, it disappeared. The day started to settle into itself and I felt a weight lifting. We walked up the steps towards the street and then down the hill past the shops in a circle, the massive beach stretching out before us like a newborn child. As we made our way to the car it seemed as if the past had drifted away from me to some unknown place and for once I didn't care. There was a kind of safety in my distance from it, my indifference.

Mary asked me if I was all right and I said I was. She told me I looked different and I said I felt different too. I couldn't explain why and neither did I want to. All I knew was that I felt cleansed of something, secure in my neutral abandonment as we walked back to the car.

We drove all the way back to Dublin in silence.

Sedentary

My life returned to familiar routines once we got back to Dublin. I thought the trip to Ballina might have sorted something but as soon as I got home I was back to my old self, for better and worse. I still moaned and groaned about nothing and still chased butterflies.

I continued to write but in a slapdash manner without rhyme or reason. The typesetter I'd been using for twenty years retired without warning, leaving me high and dry. I tried to get my articles put onto floppy discs but nobody would do it for me, telling me floppies went out with the Indians. I approached publishers with book ideas but I was informed they were either untimely or misconceived. The reason didn't matter; a lie worked as well as the truth when someone wanted to get rid of you. In a panic I started recycling old articles but they were thrown back in my face.

My doctor told me my cholesterol was high and that I needed to change my diet and slow down the pace of my life. Mary put me on low-fat foods but I had a sweet tooth and often broke out. She said that was stupid but I had to have some fun. 'If I knew I was going to live this long,' I said, 'I'd have taken better care of myself.' She didn't laugh, having heard all of my old jokes a million times by now.

I immersed myself in boring routines as if to mirror the bland diet. In the mornings I sat in the front room and watched children going to school, dragging their feet behind them as the days took shape. After they were gone it was quiet except for the birds helping themselves to any scraps of food they dropped. Now and then an old man or woman would trudge by on the way to Mass and wave to me.

I tried to rouse myself to some activity but rarely succeeded. I flicked through books I'd read so often I could almost quote them word for word, uninterested in finding anything new. I made a tame effort to read *The Outsider* in the original but didn't get beyond the first sentence, 'Mama meurt aujourdhui' – the one that had affected Hugo so much.

I bit my nails until they bled and then plastered them so I wouldn't bleed more. I cruised the malls of Coolock and Donaghmede looking for something to distract myself among the hordes of people. I drove to indeterminate locations – Howth, Sutton, anywhere to get my mind off myself – parking the car in outlying areas as I looked out at the horizon, nurturing vague dreams of travel I knew I'd never realise.

Mary was working as a kindergarten teacher now. She enjoyed it so much she regretted not having left the solicitor's office twenty years before. I collected her most days from work and we went for lunch or maybe a walk on the beach. In the evenings we watched videos and played music.

I dropped out of the snooker team and tried to drink less, living a life that was neither ecstatic nor tortuous but at least stable. In the summers we still went to England or Wales on the ferry, booking into self-catering accommodation and touring the local beauty spots for a week or two. Back home I busied myself with jobs around the house, trying to make my immediate environment better rather than always looking over the rainbow for a non-existent one.

We got the kitchen extended and the garage converted into an extra sitting-room. I felt myself settling into middle age like an old shoe. I wondered if I'd be joining Neighbourhood Watch some day soon, or the local Active Retirement Association. Mary said it was preferable to her than the old me chasing my tail but I didn't like it. It was as if the grass was growing under my feet. I felt I was living a pale imitation of life rather than the real thing. 'It's called getting old,' Hugo told me. 'It happens to the best of us – if we're lucky.'

I fell back into my old habit of watching television nonstop. We got a digibox and there were about fifty channels on it. I button-hopped till I was blue in the face watching tripe. I found an American station with a series of Reality shows where they brought on people to talk about unique exeriences they'd had. Some of the contestants they came up with were, to say the least, unique: 'I was kidnapped by aliens'. 'I'd love to make love to a penguin.' 'My mother is really a telephone box.'

Other stations offered me high-tech stereos, tantric sex and helicopters at bargain prices. (Just what I always wanted – a helicopter you could park in your back garden). I searched in vain for a station that might have the secret of eternal life on offer. I'd have been quite happy to pay for it with my Visa card.

It also had six movie channels. There was a time when the only film I knew by heart was *Shane* but now I was also able to lip-sync the dialogue of such modern-day masterpieces as *Police Academy* and *National Lampoon's Holiday Vacation*.

I watched the same bulletins coming up on Sky News a hundred times a day, the remote control becoming like something I hit almost without realising it. The Biography Channel, the History Channel, National Geographic, At Home and Abroad. It was like the Bruce Springsteen song '57 Channels (And Nothin' On)' come home to roost. I got so worked up over *Who Wants to Be a Millionaire* sometimes it was as if I was the contestant trying to decide whether he'd phone a friend or do a half and half.

Every other night there seemed to be a game show that was organised on the basis of the gradual elimination of the contestants. Many of these shows focussed on music. People like Simon Cowell and Louis Walsh became tin gods. It was as if they held the future of civilisation in their hands by giving some teenage wannabe the thumbs up - or down. I awaited the day a disappointed hopeful would do themselves in because they got booted off *The X Factor* prematurely.

There were programmes on the radio that had quizzes with questions like, 'Which of the following is a famous Irish footballer, David Beckham or Roy Keane?' A holiday in the Algarve went to the winner. Other quizzes focussed on mystery sounds. You heard a guzzling noise and rang in your suggestion. Was it a sink? Atoilet flushing? A waterfall? Sometimes these ran for weeks as dozens of people sat by their radios racking their brains as if their lives depended on the answer.

Other programmes spent hours every morning analysing the traffic situation. A man called Conor Faughnan became a celebrity because he had ideas about how you could get to work faster in the morning. Was this the end of civilisation as we knew it? There was a time such slots would have been filled up by discussions on the meaning of life. Now we were listening to road rage incidents on the M50 for our kicks.

I became addicted to the *Big Brother* show that was on Channel 4 and E4 for three months every summer. This was a bit different from studying the literary nuances of Ernest Hemingway for my M.A in UCD. How could I get so worked up about a dozen nobodies parading themselves round a house in Elstree Studios in various stages of undress and getting panic attacks about things like whether their last set of chick peas were undercooked? As well as watching the show I found myself scanning the tabloid newspapers for gossip about the contestants' private lives. If we were on holiday and the hotel didn't get Channel 4 I'd frantically scour internet cafés to find out who was the latest evictee.

The year Brian Dowling won it for Ireland I stood in Eason's queuing up to meet him as he signed the book Channel 4 put out on the series each year. I had to pinch myself to make sure I was really there, waiting to meet a man who was famous for nothing more than inhabiting a house in South London with a bunch of other nobodies. Had my life descended to this?

Somebody said it was like *Lord of the Flies*, where people in confined spaces basically reverted back to their animal natures. It also reminded me of my teaching days, with children ranting on interminably about some trivial object like a lost pen or a missing sandwich. Were adults any different?

At my lowest point I was reduced to watching the housemates sleeping, thanks to some state-of the-art laser cameras that worked in the dark. If they got up to go to the toilet in the middle of the night it was like a major event. I said to Hugo, 'I've finally found a group of people whose lives are even more boring than mine.' He laughed, but the sad thing was that I meant it. Maybe that was the attraction. Finding someone you could look down on made you feel not so bad about the fact that your own life was at Ground Zero.

'Why don't you go more places with Mary?' he said, 'You have nothing tying you down.' I knew I should have but I felt I'd done so much travelling in the past there was nothing left to see. Television had made the world into a village. Nobody needed a passport anymore. All you had to do was watch travel programmes all day long. Sometimes they seemed better than the real thing. I thought of the film *If It's Tuesday, This Must Be Belgium*. Then I went back to watching *Big Brother*.

In theory I could have upped sticks and gone anywhere because I had no ties. Most of the people in the family had children except me. Children would have been nice, and Mary said I would have made a good father, but I wasn't sure. I was too enclosed in my own space. If I saw a child in the house I'd probably have been like the poet W.B. Yeats, who was supposed to have said once about his daughter, 'What's she doing here? Who is she?' Whenever anyone asked me if we had any children - they usually made it sound more like an accusation - I gave them the old Brendan Behan line, 'Only one, me.' (Mary said I acted that way often enough).

In some ways I saw my books as my children. Many of them were stillborn, others were aborted and others still became victims of *coitus interruptus* (or even *publisher interruptus*). But some of them were unleashed on the public and I lived to tell the tale. Neither did books have to be babysat, a big advantage when your *au pair* was unavailable. And you didn't have to get up in the middle of the night to change them. Well not much anyway.

Mary wrote a book as well, a fantasy novel, but she didn't have as much hunger as me to get on a shelf and didn't bother much with sending it out to publishers. She was much more interested in socialising and spent many nights out with her friends and family. Meanwhile I kept in intermittent touch with my own brothers and sisters. We met up in the way most families do – at births, weddings and funerals. We promised to build on such rendezvous but generally we just slunk away to our respective caves afterwards. A part of me wanted to return to the enchanted realm of childhood but a part of me feared that too, as if it was a dangerous indulgence. I resisted the feelings these family meetings called up. Sometimes I behaved badly at them as a reaction. With drink on board I became the self-appointed grouch of the family, someone quick to take offence.

Hugo also distanced himself from family gatherings, believing them to be incestuous. I said to him one night, 'Why don't you keep in touch with the family more?' He replied, 'I do, I'm with them every night – Kathleen, Lorna and Patrick.' (Lorna and Patrick were his children). He thought it was unhealthy that everyone in the family knew everyone else's business. 'If someone sneezes,' he said, 'it's out on the tom-toms and the next thing you know you're getting a phone call from America about it. I find myself suffocated with all that.'

His theory was that it all went back to Ballina. The reason our upbringing was sheltered, he said, was because our father had an inferiority complex about not being able to support us properly because of the drink. He turned this into a superiority complex by telling us we were too good to pal around with anyone and my mother went along with it, or maybe she was just too shy to push us out the door. The result was that none of us ever really went anywhere.

Another theory was that we immersed ourselves in each other's company to cushion ourselves against the cruel world outside our doors. This would hardly have been the case in Ballina but it could have been applied to Dublin as the violence increased each passing year with the upsurge of the drug culture. Sometimes it seemed as if the heroin dealers were running the country, like Chicago under Al Capone. 'The good old days,' in Mary's view, 'was when people just robbed your handbag. Now they'll attack you even if you're not carrying one.'

Every day when I turned on the news there seemed to be a report of a stabbing or a body found in some canal. Crime writers gave the drug barons cuddly names and then complained that we were becoming desensitised to crime. But surely the conferring of such names, like something from a Martin Scorsese movie, was precisely the cause of desensitisation. 'Dublin is getting like New York,' Keith said, but I hadn't ever remembered New York being this bad. We were a long way from De Valera's comely maidens dancing at the crossroads.

Rudi Giuliani cleaned up New York with a policy of zero tolerance. Could that ever come in to Ireland? I doubted it because it flew in the face of the liberal agenda. My father thought a benign dictatorship was the ideal political regime. 'Whatever you might think of Genghis Khan,' somebody said to me one night, 'in his country, little old ladies had no reservations about going out on the streets after dark.' It was a point worth considering. Maybe we could have done with the old demagogue in dear dirty Dublin.

The fear factor was gone from the world. I remembered my father saying to me about capital punishment, 'That little piece of rope dangling in the air kept a lot of us alive.' In today's world people like O. J. Simpson walked free even though 99% of the population thought he was guilty. On the odd occasion that someone was put away, the prisons seemed like hotel rooms with plasma TV screens and all the comforts of home.

Whenever I expressed these notions to Hugo he said, 'You're turning into a right-winger.' I'd hit back with something like, 'And you're just a wet liberal.' One night on a radio programme I heard a man quoting some advice a barrister had given him before testifying in court: 'If the law suits you, quote it. If it doesn't, ignore it. And if you don't know whether it suits you or not, jump up and down in front of the judge to confuse him.'

One year a young girl was raped and murdered outside a disco in Ballina. For me this was like the end of an era. A snake had entered my lost paradise. The murder made headline news for a while in the *Western* but then it became just another story, being replaced with items about water charges and political stories.

If a murder had taken place when I was living in Ballina it would have been the scandal of the century. In his whole life my father never had a murder case. Mostly the people he was called on to defend were just drunks arrested for disturbing the peace after having had one too many.

Suicide also became rampant in our brave new Ireland. A journalist wrote in a newspaper: 'Between the time I write this column and the time you read it, a man, woman or child will have shot, drowned or hanged themselves in this country. More male teenagers killed themselves in one year at the start of the new millennium than in the decade beforehand.'

Almost every day I picked up the paper there was some scandal about clerical paedophilia as well. It gave a whole new meaning to the phrase 'Suffer the little children to come unto me'. When I was growing up we crossed the street when we saw a priest approaching because of awe, or fear. Now people were crossing the streets out of revulsion. A lot of priests were afraid to smile at children in public in case they were tagged as paedophiles. We'd gone from one extreme to another, from being a priest-ridden society to a priest-hating one. Possibly for that very reason.

Vocations were also drying up, either because of these scandals or a general erosion of faith in the country. People started saying that in the next generation we'd mostly have black priests ministering to us. It was ironic. When I was young we sent out Irish priests to 'convert' the pagans. Clive was one such. Now it looked like they'd have to come back to re-evangelise us. The comedian Ardal O'Hanlon had a joke about it: 'I remember giving money to the Black Babies as a kid but I never thought they'd come over and thank me personally.'

Was the wealth of the Celtic Tiger responsible for our new paganism? I watched a person getting an epileptic fit one day in Spring Garden Street and everyone just walked by. There was a time that would only have happened in America.

Somebody said the country was like a poor person who'd just won the lottery and didn't know how to handle the money because it came too suddenly. On the surface we were a thriving society but all the so-called developments were only cosmetic. We got places faster on the Luas and the Dart but where were we going? We had

NCT tests to make our cars safer but road fatalities were at an epidemic level. We had brown and black bins to compartmentalise our rubbish but we were still a nation of litter louts. In a nutshell, we were going nowhere fast.

That was my general speech at our family reunions. Hugo would usually give me a round of applause after it. 'You should run for politics,' he advised me. Mary added, 'Or maybe the Vatican.'

As if to protect himself from our troubled society, Keith retired early from his accounting job in Unidare. They were bringing in computers and he couldn't abide that. He got a 'golden handshake' from his boss and thought he might use the money to buy a hotel in Cork. Jacqueline had a background in catering and David was studying to be a chef.

He dropped that idea because it was too risky. Instead he started work on a book about the movies. He certainly had enough raw material. There were about a thousand videos in his house. He talked of it as his life's dream.

His book focussed mainly on the forties. That was the decade where his love of the cinema was forged. He didn't really want to know much about what happened afterwards. He condescended to watch *The Deer Hunter* when I dragged him to it one night but he left you in no doubt that Robert De Niro or Meryl Streep couldn't really cut it with icons like Humphrey Bogart or Lauren Bacall. I didn't argue with him.

He was so engrained in the forties he wouldn't even watch *Shane* now. 'Ladd's golden age had passed him by before that,' he proclaimed one night, to my horror. This was the film I'd grown up identifying with all the magic of childhood. I remembered the excitement I felt when it was reissued in the 1970s. I went to see it all over Dublin. Hugo even brought his Fuji camera into a cinema and filmed the saloon scene at the end. Then it came out on video and suddenly it didn't seem that precious any more. Like everything else it was too available.

If you went around to Keith for a visit an old movie would inevitably be shown at some stage of the evening. Watching it for him was research. Or rather re-watching it. He'd seen most of them dozens of times. Jacqueline told me he often put on a film during the day that he was going to watch again with company that night. It was as if he was vetting it for suitability. But we were all glad he'd found some dream to carry him into his retirement.

Hugo also retired early from his job like myself and Keith. He loved teaching much more than I did and was a million times better at dealing with the children but he took on too much and ran his health down. When Kathleen told him he should call it quits she expected an argument but he knew he was burning the candle at both ends. Maybe he realised he'd smoked too many cheroots and eaten too many cream buns all those nights he'd stayed up till dawn running old Marlon Brando movies and writing poems and songs. Like me he was a nocturnal animal and something of an insomniac – not an ideal characteristic for someone who had to be in peak condition for forty pupils every morning.

It broke his heart to leave teaching. It was much easier for me to cast aside my last stick of chalk. I had nothing to lose so I wasn't as worried about how I'd fill up my days. Hugo was such a live wire every minute was like an hour to him if he wasn't active. I told him he should go into acting full-time but he said he wouldn't have the discipline for that. It was the same with his writing. He just liked to flush it out and then get on to something else, like a Renaissance man.

Maybe what he liked to do best was talk. Like my father he boasted about being able to clear a bar when he was in full flow. Nobody else got a word in edgeways. One year he got a book slot on the afternoon programme *Seoige* on RTE and thrived on it. You could always be assured of an original viewpoint about a book when Hugo got his hands on it, though sometimes I thought even the people who wrote the books he was talking about would have been confused by his angles. I used to tease him by saying he should ring them up and tell them what they meant.

If work was the big problem of most of the family in our early years, retirement became a different kind of challenge as time went on. I was reminded of the plight of George Best, who said he drank so much after he retired from football because he needed another high to replace the thrill he'd always got from scoring goals. Hugo preferred talking to drinking but it seemed to me as if the same thing was going on. We all needed our highs.

Life looked like a glorified form of *Groundhog Day* for me a lot of the time. Getting motivated became a struggle. I enjoyed the old things less and was loath to experiment with the new. Sometimes it seemed as if we lived in the main narrative of our lives in out early years and after that there were just subplots. We became more obsessive about fewer things, always looking for the pearl in the oyster and usually being frustrated. Like Sisyphus we kept rolling that boulder up the hill. 'Aren't you lucky to be able to work from home,' Basil said to me, but a part of me missed the challenge of the outdoors.

As my life became more sedentary I developed a bad back from sitting around too much. After a while I had to have all the furniture in the house adjusted to stop it getting worse. Some days I was so bad with sciatica I couldn't even tie my shoelaces. I went to every osteopath I could find for treatment but none of them did much good. When I asked one of them what my problem was he said, 'Probably the fact your ancestors came down from the trees.' The gist of his point was that apes didn't suffer from spinal problems. Oh to be an ape.

A kinesiologist from Ashbourne threw me up on his kitchen table one night and manipulated my vertebrae while his wife sat peeling potatoes in the corner. He was brilliant if you didn't mind the pig smells coming in the window. (He was also a farmer.) He gave me great relief but unfortunately it didn't last. A few days after visiting him I was walking around like Frankenstein. Would I ever play snooker again? Would Mary have to tie for shoelaces for the rest of my life?

I became more and more of a recluse, more and more Mr Suburbia as my life shrunk to the dimensions of the house. We got builders in to do jobs but they usually let us down. One year we got an infestation of rats from a hole being left on the kitchen floor. Another year a builder snapped a cable and knocked the power off while we were away. The ice from the fridge spilled out and flooded the kitchen. There was always something. I'd lose my temper as Mary tried to keep a lid on things. She'd try to calm me down, saying 'Don't worry, we'll get someone else to solve the problem.' It made me even angrier that she took things so placidly.

It was an endless cycle. I needed to wind down and she needed to wind up. I said to her, 'I wish you'd at least pretend you're annoyed with these people for my sake. It'll cool me down to know that you realise what I'm going through.' She said she couldn't do that because she hated falling out with people. She did her best to act annoyed but it didn't work. I always came across as the hothead in the family and the builders played on that.

In frustration I took on some jobs myself. I usually went at them like a bull in a china shop. Mary would prepare a room for painting but I tended to shoot first and ask questions afterwards. I wrecked my back hanging out of windows trying to get to awkward areas instead of looking for a ladder. I stood on the bonnet of the car in the driveway one day to paint an upstairs window and she groaned as she watched me. She thought it would have made as much sense to just throw the can of paint at the wall than what I was doing and christened me 'Slob It On Milosevic'.

My bad back cost me my place on the snooker team when I made one last bid to return to it. I played a few games for Joe but was hammered in each one. Some nights I found it difficult even to hold the cue. I felt like Paul Newman in *The Hustler* after he had his thumbs broken.

I had more time for writing now but I couldn't think of anything to write about because I wasn't having any interesting experiences in my life. Editors asked me to interview people now and again but I didn't get the cream of the crop. Instead I was delegated to the also-rans, the off-Broadway people. Trying to think up questions for someone who was almost famous, or famous last year, bored me. I tried to make these people believe I thought they were interesting but they knew I didn't and weren't very good at hiding that fact. Henry Kissinger once said that being famous meant you could bore people and make them think it was their fault. But it worked the other way too. If you were interesting but unknown, nobody cared.

I lost interest in even writing about these people, never mind interviewing them. Jiffy bags were left on the doorstep with review books inside them but I ignored them. It was hard to muster up energy to be interested in other people's lives when my own was a shambles. Mary told me I needed to get out more to lift my spirits. 'I'm not a people person,' I informed her, 'You're lucky you have that gift.' She said I had the wrong attitude, that I had a lot of things to be thankful for in life. 'Name one,' I challenged.

She continued to enjoy the children in the crèche and came home with funny stories about them most days. I told her I loved children once too - before they started to make my life hell. I doubted that would ever happen to her. Obviously all my speeches about them eventually driving teachers off their trolley had no effect on her whatsoever.

I had repeatedly warned her not to be a teacher but she hadn't listened to me. 'I never wanted to be a secretary either,' she told me, 'In fact I never wanted to be anything. If I was allowed to do nothing all my life I'd have jumped at it.' Like Hugo her main interest was people. She formed friendships at the drop of a hat. People tended to confide in her when they hardly knew her and she returned such bonding in kind. Sometimes that worked against her. One year she applied to join the Samaritans but they said it mightn't have been wise for her to do that, that she might have become too involved with the callers. (Should that have been a problem? I didn't think so).

She was the complete opposite of me, hardly able to go outside the door without running into somebody she knew, either from teaching or the people who lived on the street. She was also still working for the Vincent de Paul and that meant even more contacts. 'Living with you is like living with Mother Teresa,' I told her. 'And living with you is like living with the man on the moon,' she countered.

I turned into a couch potato, developing a beer belly to go with my bad back. 'We'll have to shoot you,' Mary said as she watched my waistline expanding daily, 'You look like you're going to have triplets.' I made promises to go to gyms but they went the way of most of my promises in life. I had a treadmill in the garage but it was more a piece of furniture now than anything else, or something to hang wet shirts on. There were cobwebs growing out of it from lack of use. Somewhere along the line I seemed to have convinced myself that if looked at it long enough I'd lose weight. People who came to the house saw it and went, 'I see you're into fitness.' The reality was that the only time I went near it was to move it from one side of the room to the other. I had an exercise bike as well which served the same purpose - or lack of purpose.

Mary kept telling me I needed something to stimulate my mind. 'If the journalism isn't working out,' she suggested, 'why don't you go back to the stories you used to write when we got to know each other first?' To pacify her I dug them out of the attic again and tried to re-work them but I was a different person now to the one who'd written them. Reading through them I felt like a schizophrenic. I couldn't believe all the angst that was in them. No wonder David Marcus told me there was less to them than met the eye.

I told Mary I must have been one seriously fucked-up dude when I wrote them. 'You mean you're not one now?' she said. Encouragingly.

After abandoning the stories I went back to the old chestnut of journalism. I got the odd crumb tossed at me from editors I knew but usually under sufferance. Maybe I was losing whatever small talent I ever had, or strangling it out of existence to try and make myself into something I wasn't.

'You're too impatient,' Keith said when I went into one of my familiar moans, 'Look how many articles you've had printed in the past.' He reminded me of my mother. She was always telling me to see the glass half full. I was far too greedy for that kind of serenity. If I didn't have something published every week I panicked.

Keith was cut from a different cloth than me. He was wetnursing his book into birth like a prize petunia while I wanted to be the fastest gun on the draw, with all the compromises that brought with it. I'd been spoiled with too much early exposure and fell into bad habits as a result. I reminded myself of someone who had a hit movie in their twenties and spent the rest of their life trying to reprise that buzz. I thought of something John Travolta said once: 'I was 24 when I first heard the words, "Your career is over." At 25 I was making comebacks.'

Would I make a comeback at 50? Or even later? Sometimes I told myself success was all about image, about what people *thought* you were. The world was full of bad writers who were on the bestseller lists because they sucked up to editors. Some of them couldn't write 'Fuck' on a dusty venetian blind to save their lives.

It wasn't the tale, it was the teller. My father used to say, 'Many great men lived before Agamemnon but died for the want of a poet to sing their praises.' In other words nothing succeeded like success. Hugo said to me, 'I'd be happy if I had a quarter of your books out.' He might have been but I wasn't. How could you compare people? There were dozens of other things in his life besides writing books.

I told myself once that I'd retire from writing when my tally of published books equalled my age. I was 50 when I made that promise to myself but by the age of 55 I had over 60 books out.

Afterwards I told myself I'd retire when the tally reached 74, the number of my house. If I got that far maybe I might revise it again and go for 100. Who ever retired from writing anyway? It wasn't like any other job.

Writers were always postponing stopping for any number of reasons, most of them ridiculous. I told myself I'd keep at it not because I thought I was any good but because it was an incurable disease. I didn't look on my greed as a negative quality. I needed something to get me up in the morning. When you were used to applause, the silence after it was a million times more deafening.

Family Fortunes

When I got into my mid-fifties I started to bond more with the family and let sleeping dogs lie as regards old war wounds. 'None of us are going to be around forever,' Basil said to me one day on the phone, afterwards going into a list of people he'd called from the past who were located everywhere from Coventry to China. Two of his engineering friends had also died within a short succession of each other and these tragedies had also affected his attitude. 'When you get to my age,' he said, 'you find yourself going to more funerals than weddings.'

Maybe that was why the family seemed to get closer as the years went on despite the fact that so many of us were recluses. Hugo still thought being too closely knit was a hazard but he started to mellow too, reserving his hostility for distant figures like politicians that he would probably never meet. He called out to Keith to watch films more often than in the past and also brought June out with him quite a lot in his car.

June and Audrey were on the phone to each other all the time too, and there were emails every other day from the States as well as letters and cards. In the old days we'd only hear from them at birthdays or Christmas but now there was communication almost on a daily basis. Clive even phoned now and again. That would have been unheard of a few years before. The world seemed to be becoming a smaller place. Or were we all just cosying up together as we'd always done, as a comfort blanket of camaraderie against the tempests outside?

We started visiting each other's houses more and get-togethers were organised like in the old days in Iona Villas or Norfolk. I tried to enter into the spirit of these but I was usually too taken up with my own thoughts to give myself fully to them. Eventually it would come to a part of the night where somebody would ask me how I was and I wouldn't know how to answer them. Maybe that was because I felt everyone in the family talked too much - and as my mother once put it, 'Aubrey only speaks when he had something to say.' I preferred when we had sing-songs or people did party pieces. These seemed to offer me some security against personal communication.

Keith only came down to us rarely but when he did he acted out scenes from films like *Gone with the Wind* and *Double Indemnity*, putting on the voices of the stars to perfection. Hugo did the same for more modern stars like Clint Eastwood or Jack Nicholson. If Basil was home he'd recite the courtroom speech Burt Lancaster did in *Judgment at Nuremberg*. He also learned off some of my father's recitations, or he might sing a raunchy rugby song he used to do with the engineers all those years ago in Earlsfort Terrace. June knew all the songs from films like *Oklahoma* and *Carousel* and sang them beautifully. Audrey and Jacinta usually did a duet of the Hayley Mills song 'Castaway' from the film of that name.

If I was asked to sing a song I'd usually do Kris Kristofferson's 'Sunday Morning Coming Down', accompanying myself on Hugo's guitar with the only three chords I knew. (I could never play the guitar properly because the strings hurt my fingers too much). Or I might croon Dean Martin's 'Little Old Wine Drinker Me'. The fact that both songs were about drunks seemed curiously appropriate.

Most of us became nostalgic on these nights, especially if we were drinking. 'Wouldn't it be great if we were all back in Norfolk?' June would say, reminding me of the way the characters reminisced about their past in Chekhov's *Three Sisters*.

Jacinta and Audrey liked to tell stories about growing up in Ballina. Names of people I only half knew would be trotted out: Fonshey Padden, Noreen Cox, Martha Ginty. Basil would talk about Pascal Gallagher, the boy who used to eat worms on Arthur Street. Keith re-enacted Doc Loftus belting him on the back of the neck when he was president of Muredach's. Audrey told us how a teacher called Miss Halvey made her mouth go dry every day in the Convent of Mercy when she called on her to say something. We were all scarred in one way or another – and all addicted to recounting the source of the scars.

I wondered what we were trying to recapture. Was it a non-existent past? So many clones of our better selves? The farther we got away from our memories the more desperate we were to retrieve them. Ballina became the elephant in the room, the real absence, the ghost in the machine.

The members of the family who went to America were as sentimental about Ireland as those of us who lived in Dublin were for Ballina. Jacinta romanticised the old bog road, Basil the harp on the head of a pint of Guinness. I always thought it was the same thing that was going on. Some of us replaced a small town with a big one and some of us a small country with a larger one. But we were all yearning for what we'd left behind, even if it was our own decision.

Basil was on the phone all the time from New York, as excited as ever about anything that was happening in his life. He was in a new firm now, Arcom Electronics, and travelling as much as ever. He seemed to need 25 hours in the day to fulfil his obligations. He worked like a dog in the office and then came home to chip away at all the books he was writing. One of them was about James Joyce, a big obsession of his. Another one attempted to align the Ming dynasty to American popular culture. He became so immersed in the writing he seemed to forget books actually had to be published.

'That's your department,' he said to me when I nagged him about the pragmatic side of the industry. He seemed to regard it as some kind of optional extra to the writing. Keith also had that attitude. The pair of them spoke of publishers as people who could break them rather than make them. They reminded me of the poet Li Po who used to destroy his poems after writing them so nobody would ever see them. I knew I could never be that pure.

Keith's book grew like a leviathan. He was always collecting anecdotes and quotes but seemed oblivious to the fact that these things had to be cleared for copyright. He went to second hand shops all over Dublin and brought home barrel-loads of books with him for his research. When he filled every available spot in his library for them, Jacqueline had to store the rest in the attic. Mary said a book about Keith himself would have been more interesting than any book a person could ever write about movies, including Keith. At times I thought he was afraid to finish it, as if there'd be nothing left for him then. I thought of Truman Capote's comment: 'Ending a book is like taking your child out to the back garden and shooting it.'

I kept pushing him to put the finishing touches to it but he always postponed that, coming up with some new idea just when he seemed ready to have it typed up. Mary told me not to nag him, that he had his own way of doing things, but I had to. 'If you're going to get rich on this book,' I said to him, 'It would be best to have it published while you're still alive.'

Every few weeks we'd get summoned up to his house to view the latest additions to it. He had it divided into twelve different folders. These were so elaborate they reminded me of The Book of Kells. There were reproductions of movie posters on every other page, reminding me of the ones I used to see on the stairs of the Estoria. He also showed us letters he was receiving from obscure film agencies about even more obscure screenwriters.

The evening usually ended by us all watching one of his videos. I found this difficult because we had different tastes. I made a bargain with him: If I watched one of his Cagney movies he had to watch one of my Robert de Niro ones. I said to him, 'You show me yours and I'll show you mine.' It worked up to a point. The main problem is that he demanded a churchlike silence during his ones, and you also had to watch every minute of them. If you went to the toilet he pressed 'Pause' on the remote until you came back. It got to the stage that I needed to tank up on drink to get through these nights. One night I threw up all over his carpet after downing half a bottle of whiskey during a showing of *Raging Bull*, which I thought was the greatest film ever made. (He didn't agree).

Clive was typing parts of the manuscript up for Keith in Zambia. He came home at two-year intervals and stayed with him. Every night they watched two videos from Keith's collection. It was like what we called the 'small' picture and the 'big' picture in the Estoria. Sometimes they'd even get in a third during the day: 'The matinee'.

Now and again Mary and myself joined them. We almost expected to have our tickets checked at the door by an attendant, and ice cream served at the interval. We called the house 'Ardmore Studios'. (That was where the Irish film industry had its headquarters. Keith's address, appropriately, was Ardmore Drive). My heart went out to Jacqueline having to put up with this every night. She'd have been much happier watching *Emmerdale* on her little portable upstairs. As Keith sat entranced watching Cagney and Bogart it seemed nothing at all had changed since the Ballina days. He was just bigger now, with longer trousers.

The bubble was burst for all of us in 2003 when Audrey and Jacinta both lost their husbands within a short period of each other. The coincidence was uncanny. Audrey had gone over to Florida to see Dan, Jacinta's husband, after he became was seriously ill but a few months later her own husband Bobby was gone too.

Bobby was as affectionate as Dan and equally boyish in his way. He was an accountant by trade but much more lively than most of the ones I knew in UCD. He loved hearing eccentric stories about the family and his eyes lit up when Audrey told them, even the same ones over and over again. 'All he ever wanted was the *Irish Times* and his remote,' Audrey said after he died. Armed with that paper he could sit watching car racing on the television for hours, unwinding from all his pen-pushing.

Dan was a simple soul simple too, uninterested in all the waffle the D-Ms went on with, analysing everything out of existence. 'Why couldn't I have realised that?' she said after he died, but she knew there was no point in beating herself up, that we were all who we were. 'I know Dan loved me and his life just ran its course,' she said simply. Audrey felt the same. 'Bobby went home,' was the way she put it.

Jacinta often commented on how similar all the men in her life were. Dan and my father she saw as children at heart and so was Donie. All three of them liked their drink too much as well. Was there something in Irish women that made them look for their father in every man they met?

I remembered how funny Dan was. He picked me up at the airport in Washington when I went there in 1973. He'd just bought a new car and drove all the way to his apartment with his right foot up on the windscreen to show it off. 'Do y'all still drive that stick-shift rubbish back in Ireland?' he asked me. When he came to visit us the following year, he got diarrhoea and blamed my mother. 'She never takes the goddamn soap off the dishes when she washes them,' he complained. My mother could only laugh at this. Nobody could get annoyed with Dan. Behind all the bravado he was a pussycat.

Audrey and Jacinta had a lot of teary phone calls to one another into the small hours in the months following the two tragedies. Jacinta talked about leaving Florida and coming back to Ireland to live. If she did she'd probably have moved to Cork to be near

Audrey. Seeing them together I thought of them going up Convent Hill in their gabardine coats or reading the *Bunty* comics together after school.

'I can't bear the thought of living alone,' Audrey said after Bobby's funeral. All her life she'd been surrounded by people and she thought she needed to continue that. My thinking ran the other way. For me a good day was one where I didn't see anyone.

I asked her if she'd consider going back nursing to get her mind off Bobby but she said it was too early to consider anything like that. 'If I could only have him back,' she said, 'even for a day.' For the next few months she could hardly go out of the house. A friend of hers told her it would take her at least five years to get over it, that it would affect everything she did. Jacinta agreed. She said to me on the phone one night, 'When one thing changes, everything changes,', a sentence that became one of her catchphrases.

On another call she said, 'The older we get, the more of ourselves we become,' and this also became a catchphrase. 'In that case,' I said, 'there's no hope for me at all.' She wasn't sure if I was joking or not and neither was I.

Dan's death made her uneasy in Florida and for a while she considered moving elsewhere. She got to hate everything about it, even the climate. She found it hard to get a breath in the muggy heat and for a while thought she might go up to New York to live. She would have been near Basil there. Another possibility was moving to North Carolina where her son Darren was studying law.

She put her house up for sale one year but took it off again when the market collapsed. It was also too much trouble having it in peak condition to show potential buyers what with her swimming pool and all. Everything seemed like too much hard work but she still promised herself she'd get out some day. .

She never felt rooted in Florida and a lot of that was due to Dan's job as a nursing home administrator. 'Whenever we felt settled in a place,' she said, 'he moved.' Every time a promotion came up he had to go with it – from Tampa to Tallahassee and finally Ocala. Now that he was gone it seemed crazy to stay on but two of her children were still there. If they moved away maybe she would too. 'Your children can leave you,' she said, 'but you can never leave your children.' She was starting to sound like my mother.

I phoned Ruth every now and then and she gave me about a hundred messages to relay to the rest of the family. She was hugely interested in everyone's life but afraid to come home for fear she'd be too heartbroken having to face going back to New Jersey afterwards. Everytime she talked like that I thought of Ruth from the Bible: 'Sick for home, she stood amid the alien corn.' The only time she came back to Ireland since she left in 1973 was when my mother was dying. Despite this she kept in touch with everything that was happening. We used to joke that when we wanted some news about the family in Dublin we'd ring Ruth to America to get an update. She seemed to know more about us than we knew about ourselves. I'd say to Mary, 'I wonder how Keith is?' and she'd say, 'Why don't you ask Ruth?' (Keith only lived up the road from us and Ruth was over 3000 miles away).

'Is there any chance of us seeing you before the end of the next millennium?' I asked her on one phone call. The subject was now a joke between us after twenty years of postponements. 'Why don't you come out here?' she countered, 'It's easier for you'. But I told her that wasn't possible, that I got vertigo licking air mail stamps, never mind sitting on a plane.

I hadn't been in the States since the eighties. In fact I'd hardly been on a plane since then. I took a trip with Mary to Jersey one year with a small airline and it nearly finished me. Not even triple vodkas stopped me thinking we were going down for keeps on that vomit bucket. After 9/11 I was even worse. Now terrorism was added to my problems along with vertigo and claustrophobia. I went everywhere by sea afterwards. Ruth's husband John teased me one night with the suggestion, 'Why don't you get the boat to New York?' I told him I'd think about it. (Even al-Qaeda would have found it difficult to hijack a ferry).

Ruth was like me in that she didn't go out much but she still liked collecting things. She was like many of the family in that. She also spent a lot of time bulk-buying items in the local supermarket. She was hoping she could give them as presents to her friends and any members of the family who visited but nobody ever seemed to want them. As the years went on the number of items grew. 'When is Ruth going to declutter?' we all kept asking. 'I collect things to stop me thinking about Ireland,' she said, 'they're my substitutes.'

Like Keith and myself she kept a lot of her things in boxes in her attic. She got into a panic one year when she heard what she called 'a creature' moving around up there among the boxes. My imagination went into overdrive when I heard this but it was never identified. She also told me she saw a snake outside the kitchen once, and there were bears in the woods a few hundred yards from where they lived. John sent me an email attachment one day that showed one of the bears climbing a tree in their back garden. Another time a bat got into their attic. That would have freaked me out completely but neither of them seemed to mind it at all.

We got our own attic converted in 2006, turning it into a leisure room. I brought all my CDs up there and played the same ones nonstop, usually Elvis and Bob Dylan. I tried to get Mary to come up with me but she found the staircase too rickety.

Hugo gave us a painting for one of the walls. Kathleen had a hut built for him at the bottom of his garden after he retired and he spent hours there every day dusting up his canvases. He wrote poetry as well and continued to act in plays in local dramatic societies. 'You're doing a lot more than me with your retirement,' I said to him. 'Maybe,' he said, 'but I have the same restlessness as you do.' It seemed to be a family disease.

One year Hugo featured in an RTE documentary about his life. The theme of the programme was the importance of realising our most treasured ambitions before it's too late. Hugo said his main one was to be a stand-up comic so that became the idea behind the programme. He did some dummy-runs in a pub called The Comedy Cellar and then he was set up at a huge venue in Cork to appear with another comedian called Karl Spain. He drew a lot of laughs when he took the stage but he found the whole experience anti-climactic. For him it epitomised the truth of the old saying 'Be careful what you dream for.'

Another thing he started doing at this time was reading people's palms to tell them what was in store for them. He tried to read mine a few times but I told him I wasn't into that. 'I find it difficult enough to deal with the present,' I said, 'I'm not really interested in the future.' (Though I wouldn't have minded if he could have given me next week's lottery numbers)..

He was spending much more time in Achill now, climbing mountains by day and doing Elvis impersonations in the pubs at night. 'There are a hundred different sides to me,' he said often, but I felt there were many more than that.

Needless to say he was also writing a book – another family disease. It was about his problems with All Hallows. It had closed down as a seminary now and this he partly attributed to his own departure. Hugo liked to relate external events to himself and I was a bit like that too. (Mary said I'd have made a link between myself and World War 2 if I'd been born a few years earlier).

Another thing Hugo started doing around this time was predicting the weather. He carried a red plastic bag around with him sometimes and said that when he held it tight he knew if it was going to rain or not. It was as if he was turning into Elvis. (I remembered reading somewhere that Elvis thought he could make it rain if he looked at the clouds long enough).

I felt I could influence things too. One day I wanted Jimmy White to win a snooker match against Stephen Hendry and I kept looking at the score on teletext trying to force it to change in his favour and eventually it did. When I told Hugo this he said, 'Why do you not believe me when you're at it yourself?' I couldn't answer that one.

Hugo liked snooker almost as much as me but he was more in to Alex Higgins than Jimmy White. I remember the night Higgins came back from 7-nil down against Steve Davis in the Coral UK to pip him 16-15 in the decider. All during the match Hugo was on his knees screaming at the television set, 'Let the spirit flow! Let the spirit flow!'

It seemed to work too. Another time he dreamt Germany got into the final of the World Cup in soccer and they did.

The pair of us met up for a drink every now and then and no sooner would he have sat down than he went full tilt into his pet obsessions: Picasso, Maria Callas, The Waterboys. If we were talking about politics he'd bring up Mikhail Gorbachev and Lech Walesa. His sporting idols were Martina Navratilova and the Real Madrid footballer Cristiano Ronaldo. He was always excited about something. I thought of the times when he'd come home from the Estoria in the sixties and tell us the whole story of the film he'd just seen, taking longer to tell it maybe than the film itself had been. He still did that now. It was just that people like Robert de Niro had replaced people like Robert Mitchum.

He usually got upset if the talk turned to politics. Charlie Haughey and George Bush were two particular pet hates. He got agitated in the same way my father used to when he talked about people he disapproved of. The more he raised his voice, the more stressed Kathleen would become listening to him.

'Hugo is the one I worry about most,' my mother used to say to me. She thought he inherited my father's nerves. Maybe we all had in some way. The lucky ones were the ones who took after my mother. We could all have done with a few of her genes but I don't think many of us got them. I know I certainly didn't.

Sometimes I wondered how different my life would have been if I took after my mother rather than my father. I often went up to the attic and scoured old albums I had for photographs of the pair of them. Because of the fact that my father was almost fifty when I was born I'd never known him in his prime. Maybe that's why I was so interested in photographs of him from that time, and also photos of my mother. I found myself trying to build up tapestries of their lives by linking the photos together. I also used to wonder how differently my life have gone different if I'd been born first, or in the middle. They said the oldest children in families tended to lead and the youngest to follow. It seemed to apply to me but often I didn't know what I was following.

Other photographs in the albums I looked at created different tapestries for me. There was one of my father looking like a dandy in his Trinity days, another one of myself in a cowboy suit as Clive lifted me up in his arms on one of his rare visits home. I also had one of Keith and Clive standing beside one another at their graduation from UCD. I hadn't remembered going to Dublin for this but I was in it too. Was that the year I climbed Nelson's Pillar? The year I saw the Cosmo for the first time?

Looking at old photographs always made me think my life was lived by somebody else rather than myself. Did we really become more of who we were when we got older, as Jacinta said?

Sometimes I thought I was two people. My past seemed to have happened so long ago it was as if a different person had lived it and maybe I was now trying to reclaim it for myself with all these old albums and curiosities. I also kept old letters they'd both sent me from the past, and even diaries and newspaper clippings.

What was it about my family and clutter? We must have all inherited it from my father. He found it difficult to dispense with anything, even yesterday's newspaper. It was like a disease of nostalgia. Apart from Ruth and myself, June had it as well. Even Jacinta, three thousand miles from Ballina, had mementoes of childhood in her home which she guarded like the Crown Jewels. Maybe we were all terrified to let go of the past.

Keith's clutter came from his movie memorabilia. As well as his collection of movies he now had a stack of books that must have been the size of a provincial library but his book was still no nearer to completion. 'I can't get the illustrations I want for it,' he complained to me every time I saw him. He was still gathering data without seeking permission and still investigating the lives of people nobody had ever heard of who wrote scripts for films maybe a half dozen people in the country might have seen. I had a list of publishers as long as your arm that I wanted him to approach with his project but he always seemed bored when I brought that thorny subject up.

As time went on he seemed to care less and less about the book being published. He just wanted to finish it before he died. It was like Christopher Wren with St. Paul's: 'If you want to see my epitaph, look around you.' He told me I should understand obsessions because of the way I went on about Ballina. He was right but it was hard to see these things in yourself. 'I'm doing it for Jacqueline,' he promised, 'I want to have something to leave to her.'

Jacqueline had her own problems by now. One day when she was shopping in Artane Castle with Clive she collapsed into his arms and had to be brought to hospital in an ambulance. It turned out she had a huge tumour on her back. It was benign but very painful. She had an MRI scan and then they operated to remove it. Afterwards she was in a nursing home for months. 'At least you're getting a break from Keith's videos,' we joked. When she came home she had to walk with a crutch. It broke her heart not to be able to do her gardening.

Clive told Keith he'd have to realise she wasn't the woman she used to be, that he'd have to learn to do more things for himself from now on. The next month a carer was delegated to the house and she proved to be a great help to both of them. She kept the house spick and span and also did some shopping. She did her best to prise Keith away from the television but he wouldn't budge. There always seemed to be some black and white oldie he needed to watch on Channel 4 even if the sun was splitting the stones outside.

'You must have seen every film that was ever made by now,' I said to him one day. 'I have,' he replied, 'but sometimes I like to get better prints of them.' There was no way you could win a point with him.

I told him it was time to stop watching them and start writing about them instead. He disagreed. 'You have to write a book in your head before you put it on the page,' he claimed. He spent most of the time he wasn't watching films taking files out of cabinets and putting them into other ones, getting all his ducks in a row like the accountant he was. His organisation was impeccable but I wondered if the whole enterprise wasn't some kind of guilt trip for taking premature retirement. He'd worked long and hard in Unidare but his puritan side wouldn't allow him to sit out the 'golden years' without some work ethic.

I wondered how many people would want to read a book about forties movies? I saw it all as therapy for him, a cathartic filling in of the days that allowed him to re-visit his past with a purpose. 'Maybe it isn't so much the movies you love as the past,' I suggested to him one day, 'You're trying to re-live the Ballina days from the Estoria.' He dismissed the accusation out of hand and I felt guilty afterwards for making it.

'What about copyright?' I asked him repeatedly. 'What about it?' he'd reply with a cavalier disregard. He firmly believed that if he found a rare photograph of a screenwriter somewhere, that very discovery entitled him to use it in his book.

He had me searching for photos as well. Sometimes he asked me to get a book for him from England that I thought he wanted to read. As soon as I gave it to him he'd tear out a photograph and give it straight back to me. 'That's a screenwriter,' he'd say, 'The photo has him talking to a famous director. That means it's doubly precious to me. Readers of my book will look at the director and then get interested in the screenwriter.' But what if they weren't interested in either of them?

After Clive went back to Zambia he started sending drafts of the book out to him to be typed on his computer. He even gave him instructions about typesetting. 'That should be the final step,' I said, 'You haven't even found a publisher and yet you're getting Clive to process the material as if it's ready for the bookshelves.'

I could never understand why he was fast-tracking the whole process when he hadn't even submitted a sample chapter to anyone. Was he afraid they'd say no? Sometimes I thought he'd be in a state even if he managed to get some publisher interested in his book. He'd have been far too shy to do interviews or promotion. But if he published it privately he'd still be in breach of copyright for the quotes and illustrations he was planning to use.

'Sometimes publishers make an example of people like you to scare off bigger fish,' I warned him, 'If they come after you they could take your house. You'd be out on the street with your precious masterpiece. How do you think Jacqueline would like that?'

He looked hurt when I said that. 'Why are you coming down on me so heavy when you've got so much stuff out yourself? Are you jealous of me? That would be very sad.' There was no way of telling him I was trying to protect him. He was in his own cocoon. Just as the movies insulated him from a cruel world, so did his book.

He also had Basil co-opted into helping him with his research. Because Basil was based in New York he was close to some of the major bookshops and he could also order material from the internet. He posted some books to Keith and brought others with him on his visits.

Basil made as many trips home as he could, tying them in with business conferences he had to attend in London and Europe. (He called them 'boondoggles'). He met a lot of famous people at these conferences and, being Basil, often had his photograph taken with them. 'It's a pity Keith won't write about living screenwriters,' I said, 'You could furnish him with the whole illustrated section for his book.' By now Basil had also embarked on another book. This one was about celebrities . 'You're just like Keith,' I said to him, 'The pair of you will have thousands of pages written but none of them will go anywhere.' He just laughed when I said that so I knew I might as well have been talking to the wall.

Mary and myself often met him at the airport when he got to Dublin and June and Keith usually turned up as well. As he came through the Arrivals area he'd already have his arms out. He'd nearly knock you over with his hug. He always had a story to tell about someone he met on the flight. He was so enthusiastic it was hard to keep up with him. After he got back to the house he'd ring all the engineers he knew from his year in UCD and arrange to meet them for 'a pint or ten' in the Old Stand pub in Exchequer Street. Sometimes he asked the rest of us to tag along for moral support. When we got there he'd hold forth with some anecdote or bring the room to a standstill doing one of my father's recitations like *Babette* or *The Green Eye of the Little Yellow God*.

As Basil got older he talked about religion a lot. So did the rest of the family. It seemed to be buried deep in all of us, even myself. Ruth had often brought the subject up on phone calls but with the rest of us it seemed to have been kept under wraps until we reached a certain age. Now suddenly we were all starting to indulge in heavy discussions. Maybe it was the influence of my mother. She had religion in every pore of her being even though she wore it lightly.

Keith and Hugo also became more religious as age gained on them. Were we all starting to get intimations of mortality? Were we starting to invest in a spiritual form of fire insurance?

Something that usually reminded people of religion was failing health. We were starting to show 'twinges in the hinges' in that regard. Conversations that once revolved around football games and Hollywood stars now started to contain terms like carpel tunnel, mitral valve, prostate.

Keith had an underactive thyroid. Ruth was getting trouble with her eyes. Hugo had given up cigarettes but was going through Nicorettes as if they were going out of fashion. June had a problem with her feet and was going to a chiropractor for it. One day she told me she was going to 'Chiro' and I thought she meant the city of Cairo in Africa.(I was stunned at this because she was such a homebody).

Keith was still leery of doctors and often refused to take the medication he was prescribed for his thyroid. 'I think they're a bunch of chancers,' he said, 'We're all like guinea pigs in their hands. Well they won't get this one.' When he wasn't reading film books his head was buried in dusty medical journals that had folk remedies for diseases I couldn't even pronounce (and which he certainly wasn't suffering from). I got the impression he'd be disappointed if the hospital cured his problem: it might interfere with his cynicism.

I made this point to Ruth one night on a phone call and she started crying, for Keith and for everyone else on the planet. 'Isn't life very hard?' she said then, 'isn't life very hard?' It wasn't as if she was saying it in a self-pitying way. She meant it philosophically. It made me think of the Hemingway quote about life breaking us all, 'and afterwards many are strong at the broken places.'

Was I? Was Ruth? We were all mollycoddled by my mother but that made it harder when you tried to break out of the womb. Ballina was like a cotton wool ball enfolding us all. It meant that as adults we would probably suffer twice as much as everyone else in the world. Yes, life was hard, and harder still for being so joyful in youth. Maybe Jacko did me a favour by cutting through all that in Muredach's. He was like a preparation for life for me, a harbinger of an uncertain future.

'We're all getting on, aren't we?' Ruth said on another call. 'When Mum and Dad died it was a different generation but now people from our own one are going and it makes you think.' I told her most of the phone numbers in my little red book were medical ones now instead of social contacts. She laughed but I hadn't meant it as a joke. The deaths of Dan and Bobby had marked all of us. We could take nothing for granted any more. It was as if every new day was a bonus.

'The moving finger writes,' my father used to say, 'and having writ moves on, nor all thy piety nor wit shall lure it back to cancel half a line, nor all thy tears wash out a word of it.'

When Keith hit seventy he started telling us he was on borrowed time. He resembled my father when he talked about having bypassed 'the Biblical span'. I told him Dad had broken all the laws of nature and still lived to a ripe old age.

He didn't want to hear that, or anything else that might put a bright gloss on his days. He was good-humoured generally but he didn't like you telling him he looked well. 'It's how you feel that counts,' he'd say, another old line of my father's. He spent so much time checking every little change in his health there didn't seem much danger of an unknown illness sneaking up on him. Despite his age, and a tendency to exaggerate his maladies, there were days he could have passed for fifty instead of seventy.

With all his vitamins and dietary supplements, sometimes I thought he'd see the lot of us down.

Where We Are Now

The Celtic Tiger capsized some years ago and everyone took a hit, especially the poor. Shortly before it expired Tony Gregory died of cancer. I had always seen him as Ireland's most honest politician so it didn't look like a good omen for the future.

Corruption was exposed in the banks and the whole country seemed to come to a standstill almost overnight. Fianna Fail was blamed for most of our problems but they were happening overseas as well so it wasn't that simple.

At the time of the financial crash Ireland was being governed by a pantomime leader called Brian Cowen, a man who fell into the trap of arguing with his accusers instead of just accepting that he'd come into power at a time when the house of cards built by his party was about to crumble. His predecessor Bertie Ahern had got out just in time but still left a tarnished legacy. Enda Kenny eventually became Taoiseach but he must have been wiping his hands in glee that he wasn't elected earlier because he would probably have been blamed for the recession if it happened on his watch. .

The banks were eventually bailed out by the International Monetary Fund, thereby plunging the country into in what was almost certainly going to be decades of austerity. People lost their jobs left and right and the houses of those who'd never done anything wrong except trust their mortgage providers were forced to hand over the keys to the very banks that had caused them their problems in the first place.

The businessman Patrick Rocca was the first high profile casualty of the recession that I can remember. He shot himself amidst mounting debts one morning outside his house and everyone was shocked, especially his wife who didn't seem to know just how much he'd been affected by the slump. His funeral service was held in St. Mochta's Church in Porterstown where I used to take the children from the school I taught in to prepare them for First Communion and that seemed to make the tragedy even more graphic for me.

Afterwards more people started to come out of the closet with their problems. Before long we witnessed an almost daily unfolding of distress. The jobless became the homeless and the homeless either became depressed or suicidal or both. The newspapers were so full of tragedy it was difficult to give the proper degree of sympathy to any situation no matter how bad it was. Barack Obama seemed to be ushering in a new dawn in the States but that was three thousand miles away and he didn't have Ireland in his sights, unlike his predecessor Bill Clinton.

I found myself watching old movies to immerse myself in a bubble of comfort in these dim times. Sometimes I thought Keith had the right idea after all with his escapist videos. As T.S. Eliot had once said, 'The human kind cannot bear too much reality.' Keith had always realised that and now I was starting to see his point. I used to give out to him in the old days when he talked about the Dream Factory, preferring to trawl the underbelly of Hollywood Babylon, but that underbelly was too close for comfort now, it was everywhere around me, and I sought solace in his forties musicals and screwball comedies, bathing myself in their soft-centred hues to blot out the gloom.

Unemployment, meanwhile, grew to epic proportions. So much so that people took to laughing about it as if to blot out its enormity. One day somebody told me a joke about a man who fell into the Liffey. After he fell in, another man jumped in after him. The drowning man called out, 'I don't know how I'm going to repay you for rescuing me,' and the other man said, 'I'm not trying to rescue you, I just want to know where you used to work.'

Young people looked at our dole queues with disbelief but the older members of the country, myself included, weren't too surprised. We had, after all, been through the hungry fifties and the almost-as-hungry eighties. We knew what begging for jobs was like. The difference now, though, was that many of the unemployed were from the well-heeled set. I heard of one PhD graduate who became a night watchman at a tobacco plant and was delighted to be there. (I could imagine people like that burning Glenn's DOGS to keep warm).

Another difference was that there was nowhere to go to escape unemployment now because it was worldwide. That's why I felt sorry for the opprobrium heaped on Cowen. It could so easily have been Kenny who was in the wrong place at the wrong time. Under Bertie Ahern we were too flushed with the age of plenty to vote yes to the Lisbon Treaty. Now it looked like we were going to crawl to the polls for the sequel to endorse it unequivocally, desperate for whatever scraps Europe threw at us to take out of the mire.

When I walked through Temple Bar now I found the shops almost all half empty. For once people weren't bumping into each other on the pedestrianised streets. When you got served in the cafés and bars you heard the voices of Irish waitresses and barmen again after a decade of foreign caterers. In a way I found this strangely reassuring. It was as if we were finally getting our country back, miserable and all as it was.

My writing went on in fits and starts. I published the odd book (sometimes very odd) and wrote film reviews for people who were good enough to keep me on their payrolls even when others with more qualifications might have been deemed better suited to the jobs. At previews of movies I was sent to I rarely recognised the other critics there. They all seemed to be under twenty now, wearing Levi's and scruffy jumpers and talking about 'film' as if it began with

Quentin Tarantino. Some of them had biros that glowed in the dark so they could write their reactions as they watched the films. I felt a bit like Finn McCool, a man out of his time.

I pitched some book ideas to editors but they were usually greeted with a frosty response. They wanted material submitted through agents, and digitally, but my Russian agent had died in 2000 and writing on a computer seemed to dry up any ideas I had so I fell down on both counts there. I used a computer now and then but usually with reluctance, preferring the physicality of sticking a sheet of paper into a typewriter . That always made me feel good, as did banging my fingers on the typewriter keys like a woodpecker with my two index fingers in the same way my father had.

Under pressure from another agent I managed to get an email address one year but shortly after it was set up in my name it was hacked into by a woman called Anna Malone from Tucson who had a daughter called Aubrey whose Facebook account she was trying to get into before 'accidentally' hacking into my account. I felt this was God's way of telling me to dispense with technology so I went back to sending messages to people using my battered old Canon typewriter.

Shortly afterwards a British publisher asked me to do a series of humorous quotation anthologies. By now I had almost 300 quotation books in my library so it was simply a matter of sifting through them and combining them with other quotes I'd amassed over the years. I could have done these books in my sleep but after they came out people looked at me differently. I was expected to entertain them with pearls of wit at every passing turn.

Why was it that we were defined by what we wrote? When I was a young man nobody expressed the vaguest interest in my views but as soon as I became a writer they were queuing up to listen to me. When I started writing funny books they decided I was Bobo the Clown and went into hysterics when I told the most banal jokes. I realised what Groucho Marx meant when he said he didn't enjoy going to parties because people were always putting him on the spot to entertain them. Like the rest of us, he needed a night off every now and then.

I remembered the old days in Ballina when members of the family would be having these high level discussions and I'd come up with some one-liner that undercut the whole conversation. Maybe I was still that upstart in their eyes, that joker in the pack. I wanted to be taken seriously but I cut off my own chances by trivialising everything.

One day I rang Jason O'Toole, the editor of Maverick House Publishing, to ask him if he'd be interested in looking at a book I'd written on Hollywood. 'No good, Aubrey,' he said, 'Why don't you do a crime one? That's where it's at now.'

After I put down the phone I looked up the Maverick catalogue. I found it frightening to see the number of books they had on the subject. Crime had become a genre all to itself in our island of Saints and Scholars. In the bookshops you found it in the Real Life section, not the Fiction one. People like Paul Williams of the *Sunday World* were as busy as the chicklit writers who seemed to define the previous era. In bookshops there was blood and guts on one side and sex and Sangria on the other. When a drug baron was shot in the head down the road from where I lived, the man in the local hardware shop said to me, 'It's getting closer.' His words chilled me.

Apart from the crime, the country was broke. In one survey I read it claimed that one in three people were just a pay cheque away from homelessness. The sound of keys being dropped into auctioneer's letterboxes became commonplace. The health service was also in tatters. The average waiting time in A&E units was about ten hours. The Minister for Health became The Minister for Trolleys.

I felt like emigrating but where was there to go? Somebody told me that Poland had signs up in their shops saying 'No Irish Need Apply'. Was this because we'd given them such dire wages when they were here? Or because we killed so many of them?

I went on the familiar tack of blaming Fianna Fail for all our problem but Mary was having none of it. 'Why do they always get it in the neck?' she said, 'It's a worldwide recession. Have people forgotten that?' People called for corrupt bank officials to serve custodial sentences but we all knew white collar men hardly ever went to jail. Nick Leeson had to bankrupt a bank to be put behind bars.

'We'd only have given him some community service here,' a friend said to me. It was a joke but I saw his point. I couldn't remember a rich man going to jail since O. J. Simpson. They'd finally nailed Simpson but the circumstances smacked of absurdity. It was as if he arranged a ridiculous robbery so he could be caught, as if he couldn't live with the guilt of being free. (I was going to write to Marcia Clark again and tell her O.J. had now prosecuted himself... and won).

I tried to make the best of my wounded city, sleepwalking through my days like a demented dinosaur. On many mornings I could hardly muster the energy to get out of bed. I put the radio on at full volume to try and get my brain cells moving. Sometimes I put on the television as well, the twin cacophonies duelling it out as I sat at my typewriter not so much with writer's block as writer's apathy. Some days the only person I spoke to until Mary came home from work was the postman. 'Thank you, okay I'll sign for that,' I'd say to him as he delivered a book I ordered. Then it was back to more stasis.

I went on a binge of buying foreign DVDs off the internet for a while and nearly bankrupted myself. There was no logic to it; it was merely to stave off the boredom. I started off with French ones and then graduated to Spain, Germany, Italy, Poland, Norway, Iceland...anywhere would do. It was some obscure desire to escape the commercialism of Hollywood. They all built up in the post office and then one day the postman arrived with a bag as big as himself. He said to me, 'Would you please throw that fucking computer out?' I was probably giving him more work than all the other houses put together.

In the middle of my spending spree someone tried to hack into my Visa card but they couldn't buy anything because it was maxed out. Sometimes it was an advantage to be skint.

Two magazines I wrote for went to the wall around the same time and that was another punch in the gut. Had I the inverted Midas touch? Mary told me everyone was suffering. She was right of course but I still didn't like anyone interfering with my pessimism.

I drank to drown my sorrows, or at least to teach them how to swim. I wasn't trying to get drunk anymore, just to pass the time. Health freaks asked me if I was getting my five a day but the only thing I did in fives was bottles of beer. To anyone who would listen I related my favourite joke: 'An Irish coffee is the healthiest drink anyone can take because it contains the four best life-saving ingredients – alcohol, coffee, sugar and cream'.

Night life continued to become more dangerous. Once or twice I thought I heard the sound of bullets in the street where I lived; time was it would only have been a tyre blowing out. One night two drug addicts were killed in a shoot-out around the corner and another one at a garage. Another evening when I was doing some photocopying in the local Spar, a young man in a tracksuit jumped across the counter and helped himself to whatever was in the till. After he ran out the proprietor told me I could continue my photocopying. It was as if we were all suffering from scandal fatigue.

To pass the time I found myself doing ridiculous things – re-arranging furniture, tidying the clothes in my wardrobe (what few I possessed, as Mary kept reminding me), going through old writings that went all the way back to the Iona Villas days. I was reminded of my father at the end of his days when he'd empty a shelf of books and then put it back almost exactly the same way the day after. It was a bit like Beckett, but maybe it was necessary therapy.

My mother used to say, 'Everyone's life is trivial,' and I agreed with her. Most people denied this, feeling an undeserved sense of importance about themselves. But how could you be doing important things every day? Or even every year?

I went on occasional trips to Ballina but the older I got the more tense the town made me feel. Maybe the visit with Jacko had opened up a Pandora's Box for me. I walked past Norfolk one day and was almost afraid to go in for fear of what memories it might call up. When I walked down by the college I seemed to miss its power. I also missed the power of the church. It was as if the richness of memory was in some way intertwined with the fear. If you got rid of one you got rid of the other as well.

Walking down past the Valley of Diamonds in Enniscrone I felt independent of this too. It became just seashells and stones, a forgettable hammock of sand squashed in between Bartra and Skermore. I felt my midnight walks alongside its shadows would hold few charms for me any more. But I also felt that going back to these places over and over again only made it more apparent that I'd never fully outgrow them. I would always be secondguessing myself.

Towards the end of 2010 the Belvedere Past Pupils Union wrote to me to say they were having their fortieth anniversary and would I like to attend. I wasn't so much touched as horrified. Could it really have been four decades since I spent that miserable year in North Great Denmark Street trying to be a Dubliner? Suddenly I felt ancient. Being the youngest of the family I always had the idea that I would be forever framed in some kind of bubble like Peter Pan. Even when I saw my hair going grey – or worse, disappearing – this feeling persisted. But being informed that you did your Leaving Cert forty years ago was a reality check. It stopped me in my tracks.

I was now nearing sixty and the prospect of that milestone gave me pause. How could you be sixty when you still felt sixteen inside? Maybe that was another reason I liked to watch the old movies: they were my version of Dorian Gray's picture in the attic. For ninety minutes on a given night I trod in the footsteps of the forever young and felt I was their age again. I was ready for my close-ups, Mr DeMille.

Life outside Ardmore Studios, meanwhile, continued to go downhill. Everywhere you looked there were horror stories. People being turfed out of their homes, people being killed, people losing jobs and marriages they thought were for life. Mary told me I should stop watching news programmes. She buried herself instead in Jeremy Kyle, Judge Judy, Steve Wilkos. She told me I reminded her of Peter Finch in the film where he said he was mad as hell and couldn't take it anymore. I told her I saw that character as an optimist.

The hospitals continued to go downhill. They didn't seem to be places you went to if you wanted to be cured anymore but rather to get MRSA or vomiting bugs. The A&E departments were still thronged as well. I read about a man who got a trolley one day but vacated it for a few moments to go to the toilet. When he came back it was gone. Maybe that was a job somebody could apply for: Trolley Guardian. It might be one of the last few in the country.

I told Mary I felt like one of the new poor. She thought that might be better than being one of the new rich. In the first category at least you knew where you stood. .

And yet big money still seemed to be available in some circles. A newspaper cartoon covering Mary Harney's exit from office suggested that she was leaving 'to spend more time with her pension.' It reminded me of what the Canadian writer Mordecai Richler heard someone saying about Jimmy White after he lost a match at Goffs: 'Everybody feels sorry for Jimmy fucking White but he owns property worth more than a million quid in London.'

I thought of doing a different kind of cartoon that might reflect the situation in Ireland. Or rather two cartoons. The first would be set in 1991 and have a hoodie on O'Connell Bridge beseeching alms from a man in a pin-striped suit. The second would be set in 2011. This time the man in the pin-striped suit would be sitting on the bridge with a Styrofoam cup, looking for money from the hoodie. Maybe it would typify Ireland's enforced form of socialism - a shifting of roles that would have a refreshing sense of justice about it.

There were no jobs in the country so everyone started doing courses to pass the time. I said to Mary, 'We'll get to the stage where the only job left in the country will be Course Giver.' But there would be no jobs at the end of the courses.

The number of homeless people rose by the hour. One of these days, I told Mary, they'd outnumber the housed of our society. Could we not put them all into the ghost estates that were proliferating around the country, the ones the bankrupt builders couldn't afford to finish? 'That sounds too sensible for this country,' she said.

House prices came down but nobody could benefit because nobody had any money to buy them any more. 'Affordable Housing' had become Fianna Fáil's holy grail shortly before they were booted out of office but it was really a white elephant. People's dream now was to hold on to what they had rather than seek fresh pastures. One of the websites dealing with property was called DAFT and I thought to myself: There's something appropriate about that name.

In a way I was relieved the country was on its uppers. During the boom years people seemed to think there was something wrong if they didn't own three apartments in the Algarve or jet off to New York every other weekend to buy handbags at two grand a pop. Now they hardly owned the clothes on their back. They went around the place saying, 'I'm in negative equity,' as if it was something trendy. Suddenly you were nothing if you weren't in negative equity. It was like the new posh.

Nobody seemed to be able to talk about anything anymore except money. The economist David McWilliams even developed a kind of fame because he found a funny way to talk about it. Eddie Hobbs had done the same thing before him and Vincent Browne after him. Browne got a show on TV3 talking about just that subject for five nights every week. Would Angela Merkel give us a reduction on the debt? Who cared. The difference would probably go into the politicians' pockets anyway.

In time money became the new sex. It even became sexier than sex because nobody had any. A popular belief was that the slump would return Ireland back to its 'spiritual' values but I doubted this. We were told often that people were praying more now that Ireland was broke, but I suspected that what they were praying for was, yes, more money.

It was affecting the publishing trade as well. Everyone suddenly started talking about ebooks and Kindle as retail outlets closed down. Was this my future, to be read only off a computer screen or on someone's iPhone?

I wrote a biography of Jimmy White but the publisher went bankrupt and somehow this seemed appropriate to me. I only played snooker rarely now and seemed to lose interest in Jimmy now that I'd said everything I wanted to say about him in the book. When he came to my local club in Harmonstown for an exhibition match it was like the mountain coming to Muhammad but I couldn't really get excited. I thought of all the years I nearly killed myself driving down to Kildare to see him. Now he was around the corner and I was hardly bothered to see him.

He took on nine local players and wiped them off the table. There was even a chance I could have played him myself. Mary said, 'Maybe we'll invite him back for a cup of tea afterwards.' She'd had such stress with me over the years when I'd be up to ninety if he was losing a match. That was all gone now but in a way I missed the old madness.

Alex Higgins died of malnutrition in 2010. Maybe the surprise was that he'd lasted so long. I passed him once on Henry Street and he looked like skin and bone; it was as if a ghost had just slid by.

The death of the broadcaster Gerry Ryan soon afterwards was more of a shock. The year I left teaching to become a courier I listened to him non-stop in my Fiat Uno as he droned on forever about everything and nothing. The national outpouring of grief over his passing was immense and unexpected. It was as if a head of state had died. The man we loved to hate was now being touted as a treasure. One writer called it our Lady Di moment as he watched crowds lining the streets to mourn him.

But then the results of his autopsy were released and they showed there was cocaine in his system. Suddenly the hero became the villain. Ireland, once again, built up a man to tear him down. I'd met him once when I was on a night out with Margot Davis and told him he'd have made a better fist of *The Late Late* Show than Pat Kenny. He gave me a funny look when I said that, not quite trusting my praise. Maybe he remembered a scathing article I'd written years ago in the *Evening Press* about his show *Secrets*. Or maybe the flattery was tainted by his friendship with Kenny.

It's possible he died watching himself on television. On the night he had his heart attack RTE was airing an interview he had done with Heather Mills. There was something scary about that thought. It reminded me of the fact that I was watching a film called *The Omen* when my father died.

As if in tandem with his untimely death, the national gloom deepened. A poll was held to find out if the Irish people would prefer Enda Kenny to Brian Cowen as Taoiseach. The answer that came back was that we wanted neither. Maybe, I thought, if I ran myself I might land the job. Things were that bad. The old joke was recycled: 'Would the last person to leave the country please turn out the lights.' Shortly afterwards I saw a piece of graffiti scrawled on a wall in Ballymun in a spidery black marker. It said 'Fuck Life'. I thought that pretty much covered everything.

Micheal Martin challenged the leadership of Brian Cowen in early 2011 but Cowen held him off just as Enda Kenny had held off a similar challenge from Richard Bruton not long before in a proposed Fine Gael heave. A few days later a number of Fianna Fáil ministers jumped ship, including the beleaguered Mary Harney. None of these individuals were going out on grass without a hefty stipend. Cowen tried a hasty re-shuffle and the Green Party exploded. It was a bit like watching Zig and Zag. We had a rudderless government, a lame duck Taoiseach and now even his own troops were walking out on him. It looked a bit reminiscent of the last days of Hitler in the bunker.

Cowen stepped down only after his own party turned against him. He had refused to go when the recession hit and again when the banks scandal unfolded but when members of his cabinet started to worry about their own seats the writing was on the wall. His apologists said he put the country first but he hardly did that.

Around the same time the Minister for Education approved an initiative that allowed schools to take on teachers who were on the dole. There was only one problem: they weren't going to pay them anything. Bad and all as things were in my time, at least I didn't have to work for nothing. The 'National Tramp' moniker now took on a more sinister resonance. The President of the Students Union put it in a nutshell: 'When I talk to my friends it's a case of 'What country are you moving to?' rather than 'Which school do you hope to work in?'

Fine Gael destroyed Fianna Fáil in the general election as expected, the people engaging in a revenge vote against the party that had been in power when the country went bankrupt. I was glad for Enda Kenny, a decent skin who hailed from my home county, even if he didn't have a great personality. Maybe the only way he could have become Taoiseach, I thought, was if Fianna Fáil slipped up. I said to Mary that it was a bit like Jimmy White winning a match against Steve Davis only because Davis took his foot off the pedal. 'Do you have to relate *everything* to snooker?' she replied.

She was one of the few people in the country to feel sorry for Fianna Fáil. Her parents had been ardent Fianna Fáilers all their lives and some of that had rubbed off on her. It was now nearly a century since the 1916 uprising. Would De Valera have turned in his grave? Would Mary's parents? Fianna Fáil would be a minority party in Ireland from now on and maybe that would be no bad thing. I didn't think Fine Gael could get us out of the mess we were in unless they bombed the IMF people into oblivion. I had a fantasy of seeing Merkel and Nikolas Sarkosy on a balloon bound for Armageddon.

Mary told me not to get worked up about things I could do nothing about. She was right but I couldn't take her advice any more than my father could take my mother's. 'Men are from Mars,' I said to her, 'and women are from Venus.' 'It's a pity some more of you wouldn't stay up there,' she replied.

My life took on a simple pattern. I made decisions not to make decisions. Every now and then I'd get a book out and go on a holiday somewhere to reward myself but apart from that I just vegetated. I didn't have a plan in life. Just getting through the day was enough. Mary told me I needed to get out more but I knew I'd only end up getting into arguments if I did that.

After she left for work I tried to set routines for myself to eat up the hours. Some days things happened too fast and on others there was nothing at all. I never seemed to be able to get the mix right. I might spend hours waiting to meet someone in town and town and then be late for the appointment. There was no logic to it.

I put on the radio at full blast to try and wake my mind up, turning it off again when I felt the adrenalin flowing. I mainly listened to country music on a station called Sunrise. There was very little talking on it and I liked that. It was more like a juke-box than anything else. The songs were generally banal but they relaxed me. The same ones were played over and over until I almost knew them by heart. I felt like Jim Carrey in that film where his life is part of a film but he doesn't know it. Now and then a presenter would come on and do a few interviews and then there were more songs again.

The main presenter was a woman called Lynsey Dolan. No matter what time of the day or night you turned on the radio she seemed to be on it. I wondered if she ever went home. I tried to picture what she looked like but then one night she appeared on television and the mystique was gone.

As the economy continued to go downhill my own bank account did too. I rang the bank and asked them for an increase on an overdraft I had so they said they'd send me out some forms. When I got them I thought I'd need a degree in engineering to understand them. They wanted to know how I planned to pay it back, when I planned to pay it back, what my earnings were, how much I paid for the phone, the electricity, the television, my car and innumerable other things – including my mother's maiden name. I said to Mary, 'It's a wonder they're not looking for my inside leg measurement.' She said, 'Don't speak too soon.'

When the tsunami hit Japan in 2011 it put things in more perspective for me. The news reports described it as Biblical and it was. The cheeriness of the survivors made it all seem unreal. They smiled even as they were being tested for radioactivity. One piece of footage showed a car on top of a roof, the way you sometimes saw them in garages. But this was no stunt, just the result of a raging sea. The speed was given as sixty miles per hour but at times it looked sluggish. It was all the more ominous for that.

Osama bin Laden was assassinated coming up to the tenth anniversary of 9/11 and that gave me something else to think about. Liberals wrung their hands at the fact that he was shot in cold blood while other people high-fived each other at the removal of the world's most dangerous man. All I could think about was what al-Qaeda was going to do to get revenge.

I sought refuge from such worrying thoughts the way I always did, by focussing on trivia. The Eurovision Song Contest was in the offing and it grabbed much more headlines than anything to do with tsunamis or global terrorists. Clearly, someone was getting their priorities right.

For Eurovision 2011 we chose Jedward, the Lucan twins whose hairstyles seemed to be going on for careers of their own. They seemed a minor improvement on Dustin the Turkey, a previous entrant, even if they didn't seem to be able to say anything more than 'Oh my God' ten times a minute as they finished each other's sentences. The world was going to pieces all around us but we still managed to get excited about a song that didn't seem to have any discernible lyrics. It was called 'Lipstick'.

Did Ireland need 'Lipstick'? Yes it did. Even if we didn't have food to put in our mouths we needed to put 'Lipstick' on. Maybe even moreso now. It was our 'Let them eat cake' moment. When you were in the last ditch, as Beckett said, the only thing left was to sing – even if you hadn't a note, like Jedward. (To compensate, they were millionaires with the other kinds of notes, the ones that folded).

In the end they came a respectable eighth. This was bottom of the bill, our fate in recent years. We seemed to win when the economy was buoyant and finish way down the line when it was bad. Maybe if things picked up a bit financially we could wheel Johnny Logan out of retirement on his Zimmer frame and he could do it for us again with something like 'What's Another Decade'.

In the meantime we had to watch Azerbaijan scoop the victory this time. The song wasn't great but it gave most of us a new word to try and pronounce, or spell. It also sent us scurrying to our atlases to find out where the hell it was. By now I'd stopped listening to the songs because most of them were so dire. I thought of it as the 'Eurovision Voting Contest'. It was much more fun watching all the Eastern bloc countries voting for each other, just as we once did in the West. Revenge was sweet. And Jedward were going to go from strength to strength anyway, God help us.

Ireland had visits from both Queen Elizabeth and Barack Obama in the same month. Security was unprecedented for both of them because of the threats of the Real IRA and al-Qaeda. Why did Obama visit us just after he'd authorised a bullet to be put into the head of Osama bin Laden? (Their names were uncannily similar). And why did Queen Elizabeth ignore us during all the years of the boom and chose now to visit us when the cost of protecting her was going to cripple the country even more?

I couldn't get interested in a woman who'd spent the last six decades of her life drinking tea and walking her corgis; a woman whose only claim to fame in life was an accident of birth. In the newspapers they talked of the necessity of Ireland 'moving on' from its dark past with England but I didn't really understand what that expression meant in the circumstances.

Usually people were only expected to 'move on' when the wrongdoing was mutual, not something caused by 700 years of colonial occupation. Sky News talked about the 'troubled' history between the two countries. It was a very soft phrase. The fact was that our 'trouble' was caused by another country coming into ours. Brendan Behan believed England always fought their wars in other people's countries. That seemed to hold true right up to Tony Blair hanging on to George Bush's coat-tails as he invaded Afghanistan and Iraq.

After the Queen left, Obama arrived. If a Martian landed on earth and saw the teeming hordes greeting both dignitaries he'd never have realised the country was bankrupt. But then that was Ireland. We were always good at whistling in the graveyard. (Maybe that was why we were always in the graveyard).

Unlike the Queen, Obama had the personal touch. In Moneygall, where his ancestors came from, he had a pint of Guinness in a local tavern and made a joke about the fact that it tasted much better than the last time he'd sampled it, on the way to Afghanistan. 'You guys must keep all the best stuff for yourselves,' he chided.

He claimed to have come to Ireland to look for the missing apostrophe in his surname. 'Welcome home,' the papers beamed. We always grabbed on to anyone with the slightest bit of the shamrock in them even if it was 160 years old.

After he went back to Washington the economy continued to deteriorate and in no time at all people were calling for Enda Kenny's head on a plate, telling us that fine Gael were 'even worse than the old shower' with their proposed new house taxes and water charges.

The years rolled on and we became accustomed to austerity like a used second suit. Everyone started to feel the pinch, even Pope Benedict, the first pontiff to leave office in 600 years.' If the pontiff can't hack it,' Mary said to me, 'what chance is there for the rest of us?'

The two of us decided to go down to Galway for a break to get away from it all. Now that I'd got Ballina out of my system it seemed to be the most obvious place to go. The original plan was to take the train but considering we usually packed enough luggage for a lifetime on these trips it made more sense to throw everything into the back of the car. In the old days I used to enjoy driving through the little towns you passed on the journey west but now with the motorways that was all gone. I hated the M50 as much as I hated most things about modern Ireland.

We stayed at Jury's Hotel at the end of the main street. That meant we were in the middle of a hive of activity as soon as we stepped out the door. That was one of the things I loved about Galway, the constant hurly-burly. It was like having a Mardi Gras all the year round.

'I'd be in heaven if we lived here,' Mary said, clapping her hands in tune with a busker we passed. She started to reminisce about Salthill when she was growing up, about the colourful characters who lived near her. She had a dozen stories for every street we walked down and told them as if they happened yesterday. My memory of Ballina was never quite as photographic, or maybe I wasn't trying hard enough. Maybe I felt that the more pictures I painted the harder it would be to lose them if they couldn't be matched by my other life in Dublin.

The day before we came back we were walking through Salthill when we saw a dog moving dangerously through the traffic. We brought him to the side of the road and tethered him to a railing, using a reed from a ditch. He had a lead round his neck with two phone numbers on it and Mary rang them both. A man's voice answered the first number but it was only an answering machine. A woman answered the second one. We told her about the dog and she said she'd drive up to collect him. We gave her directions.

A few minutes later a car pulled up beside us. When the driver got out it turned out to be one of my favourite musicians, the accordionist Sharon Shannon. I couldn't believe what I was seeing. She was the owner of the dog. I thought the chances of this had to be about one in a million.

Mary started chatting to her. It turned out she'd been living just two doors up from Mary's family home until recently. I could hardly speak from surprise. I muttered something about how her dog was nearly knocked down. 'He's a clever dog,' she said, 'He isn't afraid walking around here because he knows the cars go slow near the prom.' I had to laugh. It was so much like Sharon Shannon to say something like that, as if a dog could think. The comment made me nostalgic for a simpler time but shortly afterwards we heard Sharon's partner had died of a heart attack so even this magic little universe had become sullied.

When we got back to Dublin I was disoriented. I always seemed to be like that after these trips away. There was a heap of letters on the floor but I didn't feel like opening them. A few people left messages on the answering machine as well but I didn't want to hear them. I sat in a chair and fell asleep, exhausted for reasons I couldn't understand.

In the next few days I forgot jobs I was supposed to do or mixed them up with other ones I'd already done. I picked up the phone to dial a number and then forgot who I wanted to call. When I boiled a kettle for a cup of tea I had to stand beside it or I'd forget I'd put it on. It was as if I was suffering from ADHD.

Hugo phoned and suggested meeting up. There was a call from Keith too, something about a new chapter in his book that Clive was typing up. He wanted to check the date of birth of some obscure screenwriter.

Jacinta and Basil became very close in America and Audrey and June in Ireland. Many of their children had left home now so they had more time for one another. Audrey's children were leaving too, for far-flung places like Qatar and Australia. June's daughter had moved to London to join a headhunting firm.

The family seemed to be returning to itself whether it liked it or not. During a trip to Washington D.C., Jacinta felt weak for no reason and an ambulance was called to have her checked out in hospital. Basil sat up all night beside her bed. 'Why do people have to get sick to get close?' he asked. They ran a lot of blood tests on her but could find nothing wrong. Shortly afterwards Basil got a scare when his doctor told him he had an irregular heartbeat. I thought both of them were suffering from burn-out. Maybe we all were. The fact that Basil was on fifteen cups of coffee a day didn't help. It was the trademark executive diet, a formula for an ulcer if nothing worse. He said he was going to cut down...to fourteen cups of coffee a day.

Hugo called over occasionally and talked about the big subjects: life, love and the whole damn thing. He didn't like idle chit-chat, the bullshit the rest of us traded daily on emails and on the phone, but I told him I didn't have the stomach for abstract discussions any more, that my life had become earthier. 'You were always the existentialist of the family,' he said and I wasn't sure if he meant it as a compliment or an insult.

Keith stayed reclusive but Mary and myself brought Jacqueline shopping most Fridays and as we waited for her to get ready he talked the hind legs off us about the old movies. No matter what one you mentioned to him he'd give you chapter and verse about its cast list and plot with his elephantine memory. After Jacqueline and Mary went into the shopping centre I sat in my car listening to the news, the daily inventory of murder and misery we were all still immune to.

I took refuge in the attic, playing my Bob Dylan tapes at ear-splitting levels as the world went crazy around me. He was seventy now but still refused to lie down, grinding out the old standards in every corner of the globe as he spat in the face of age. 'Take me disappearing down the foggy ruins of time,' he sang in that wizened voice that made you think he was going to croak at any minute but each time I heard it I found myself shivering with the old excitement.

On a Canadian website I discovered a man who had bootleg copies of every concert he'd done since the sixties. I bought about fifty of them and spent the next few weeks listening to him singing the same songs fifty different ways. How did he make them sound different? Probably because he had to, because the gnawing boredom of life that got to us all eventually must have plagued this man more than the rest of us. .

I put the volume up to full tilt and blasted my eardrums. They were amateur bootlegs so they picked up sounds from the people at the concerts as well. Sometimes these people's voices even drowned out Dylan with their chattering and in a way it made the whole thing more authentic, as if you were at the concert yourself, in the middle of all that din. In a subsequent order I even managed to get the concert Dylan did in Earl's Court on June 30th 1981, the one I'd been prohibited from going to by the headmaster of the school I was teaching in at the time. Listening to it now gave me an added buzz. It was like a revenge of sorts on the constraints of my past.

When he came to the O2 arena in Dublin I couldn't get tickets so I asked my friend Michael, my friend from the Hibs, if he could help out. He was running a record shop in the centre of Ballina now and often joined myself and Mary for a drink when we went back on visits. It was strange to be ringing Ballina for something like this but he got me the tickets so it was worth it. 'At last the old dump did something useful for me,' I joked to Mary. A few days later I picked up the *Western People* and was amused to see they were talking about having a Dylan week in the new arts centre. In my day it would more likely have been a Seán Ó Riada one.

On my last visit to Ballina I had a strange experience. I was passing by Norfolk with Mary and wondering whether I'd go in or not when I spotted a poster of someone who looked familiar. When I walked in the door I saw it was of Gerry Cowley, my friend from Muredach's who'd been in America at the same time as me in 1972 when we tried to get to San Francisco to see Elvis. He was now a well-known doctor and politician. Some years back he'd been Mayoman of the Year as a result of his work helping the elderly and returned emigrants.

I wondered why he would put a poster of himself in our old home but a few minutes later the penny dropped: it was there because he was having a meeting with one of his constituents upstairs. Our house had now become his base.

We walked up the stairs and got to the landing. I heard voices coming from the front room on the right, my parent's old bedroom. I knocked on the door and a voice said 'Come in'. When I walked in I saw Gerry sitting at a table talking to a farmer. He recognised me immediately and stood up. 'I don't believe it,' he said, 'How many years has it been?' It must have been 25 at least. The last time I saw him was in Claremont Court after my mother died.

He knew Mary too and greeted her warmly. He said he'd nearly finished his meeting. We arranged to meet for coffee at the Ridge Pool, a hotel down by the Moy. I said to Mary, 'This is one of the strangest experiences of my life.' The wheel had come full circle.

We walked down to the Ridge Pool and sat sipping coffee and soon afterwards he joined us. He looked tired but he'd hardly aged at all. I wondered if he remembered the old days as vividly as I did.

His subsequent reminiscences assured me he did. We talked about the times we used to go down to the local golf club and crawl through the barbed wire after all the officials were gone home so we could have a game. We had only one club each. Gerry would stand at one end of the course and whack the ball at me and I'd stand at the other end and whack it back at him. I think we were using putters for this exercise. It was hardly The Masters at Atlanta.

'Little did I know then,' I said to him, 'that I was playing with a future Mayoman of the Year.' Gerry had been a wild child and went on to become a student radical when he was studying Medicine at UCG. I remember him walking all the way from Galway to Dublin once with a group of other students, carrying a coffin with the word 'Democracy' written on it. Of course he was still a radical in politics. The only difference was that he'd formalised it now.

His mobile phone rang constantly as we talked so he kept having to get up from the table to answer it. I could hear him trying to console people about their predicament as he walked up and down by the river. How was it, I wondered, that our lives had gone so differently? He was like Ballina's answer to Nelson Mandela while I was writing adolescent joke books for a living.

I said as much to him when he came back but he didn't agree. 'Don't run yourself down,' he said, 'We all do what we can in life in our own way. You do it through your writing.' This was generous of him but when I examined my conscience I didn't believe I wrote to help others; I did it to help myself.

I remembered the day Butch Curry, our English teacher, gave out to Gerry for spending too much time with the girls from the convent when he should have been attending to his studies. Another day Fr. Curry asked everyone in the class what they wanted to do after they left Muredach's. When Gerry said he wanted to be a doctor there was laughter all round the room because he was such a harum-scarum. Little did we know then that a few decades down the road he'd become a household name.

He asked me if I'd like to go back to Ballina to live but I couldn't give him an answer any more than I could give one to Mary or anyone else in the family who'd put the same question to me over the years.

Does it matter whether I go back there or not? Have I exaggerated its importance for me over the years? Is it possible that if I hadn't been taken out of the town when I was that I would probably have lived as boring a life there as most of the people in any small town in any county in Ireland?

I think about these things sometimes when I'm on visits there. I walk by Ardnaree or Bohernasup or drive down to Belleek where we used to play soccer and I sit among the trees on the hill and feel myself suffused with an almost religious sense of calm. I pass the old landmarks that once meant so much to me – the font at the top of Arthur Street, the mosaics of St. Patrick's Well, the Humbert Monument that my father told me P. J. Malone unveiled with Maud Gonne MacBride. Sometimes I feel I'm actually back in the past rather than just remembering it. In my mind's eye I see somebody in a red and white jersey scoring a goal and I feel like cheering, as if the apex of human achievement is in that image.

Now and then when I sit in my father's old office in Norfolk I even get the crazy idea that I'd like to buy the house itself back from whatever governmental agency owns it now. Could I return to the little boy who buried his father's keys in the backyard all those years ago? Who knows. Too much has happened since then. Maybe I can love the town better from a distance, as my father used to say about his relationship to Aunt Nellie.

Ballina made me what I am, for better or worse. I was born under a wandering star. I was always restless growing up and a lot of that came from dissatisfaction with my circumstances. When people say they were born on the wrong side of the tracks they usually mean they want to be more middle class but what I really wanted was to be *less* middle class.

Maybe I got my wish because of my father's drinking, which pulled the family down, but that's beside the point. A crumbling mansion is still a mansion and that's the part of my past that bothers me, the sense of decayed grandeur. I didn't want that and I didn't want the double-barrelled name I was saddled with either.

These things were only baggage for me. A bigger problem was the shadow my father cast over me, almost as large as his own father's over him. Mine is friendlier but no less cumbersome on that account. I try to console myself by telling myself that most children of larger-than-life parents carry some degree of confusion within them but that's really Job's comfort. I envy parents who are so easy-going they manage to grow up with their children. My father never grew up and maybe I didn't either. But there are worse things you can be in life than a permanent child.

Where does that leave me now? I'm not sure I know. Whenever I think I've got an insight into how I feel about myself or someone around me something happens to blow my theory out of the water. As a result I've tried to stop having opinions about things. My father used to say that no matter how many educated discussions people have about a subject, more often than not they leave a room with the opinion they came in with. That's usually been my experience too. It may sound cynical but cynicism is often a protection against disappointment.

Writing is less important to me now than it used to be. I work on books still but only as a sideline. I wouldn't want 'Writer' on my passport as a job description. That would be far too limiting. 'Liver' is better. When you look at things from the outside you lose them. It's like when they say a photograph 'captures' a scene. Why would anyone want a scene captured?

I realise now that there are no answers to life's problems, only attitudes to them. We can contemplate the big questions but we can't do anything more about them than a child crying in the wilderness. So meanwhile we plod on, moment by inconsequential moment, until one day we reach a catharsis that explains everything that went before in a blinding light of revelation.

Or maybe we don't. I can live with that possibility too.